RESEARCH AND

INNOVATION

IN THE MODERN

CORPORATION

Related Works by Edwin Mansfield
THE ECONOMICS OF TECHNOLOGICAL CHANGE
INDUSTRIAL RESEARCH AND TECHNOLOGICAL INNOVATION
DEFENSE, SCIENCE, AND PUBLIC POLICY

EDWIN MANSFIELD
Wharton School, University of Pennsylvania

JOHN RAPOPORT
Mount Holyoke College

JEROME SCHNEE
Columbia University

SAMUEL WAGNER
Temple University

MICHAEL HAMBURGER
Federal Reserve Bank of New York

Research and Innovation in the Modern Corporation

W · W · NORTON & COMPANY · INC · NEW YORK

Contents

PREFACE

For the past fifteen years, a number of economists have been engaged in an intensive effort to expand our knowledge of the way in which new processes and products are invented, commercialized, and accepted. Technological change has become a very fashionable area for economic research. This emphasis, after many years of comparative neglect, is both welcome and needed. Few observers of the modern economy would deny that technological change is one of the most important factors—if not the most important—influencing the shape and evolution of our society.

This book reports the findings of a number of related studies carried out under my direction, and with my participation, over the past five years —studies supported principally by grants I received from the National Science Foundation and the Ford Foundation. I am extremely grateful to these organizations for their generous support. John Rapoport, Jerome Schnee, and Samuel Wagner were graduate students at the University of Pennsylvania during 1967 and 1968. Their excellent work on these studies constituted their doctoral dissertations, which I had the pleasure of directing. Chapter 2 is the work of Wagner and myself, together with Michael Hamburger, who worked on this project while he was an Assistant Professor at the University of Pennsylvania. Chapter 3 was done by Wagner and myself. Chapters 4 and 8 were done by Schnee, and Chapters 6 and 7 were done by Rapoport. Chapter 5 was done by Schnee, Wagner, and myself, and I did Chapters 1, 9, and 10, as well as the conversion and adaptation of the parts into a book. The responsibility for the topics we explored and the approaches we used is, of course, mine.

I am indebted to the many firms who contributed information and expertise. Close working relationships were established with some of these firms—for example, the ethical drug firm discussed in Chapters 4 and 5. I appreciate very much the fact that the top research executives of this firm, and other firms, spent a considerable amount of time helping us to obtain data, and reading and commenting on our findings. As will be evident from the book, the results are based on data obtained from hundreds of firms, without whose cooperation the work could not have been carried out. Also, I am grateful to William Comanor, of Stanford University, Thomas Marschak, of the University of California at Berkeley, and Richard Nelson, of Yale University, for their comments on the manuscript, which have proved extremely useful.

Finally, this book is the latest in a series of volumes summarizing the results of a continuing set of studies of the economics of technological change that I have been carrying out. Previous books in this series are *The Economics of Technological Change* (W. W. Norton, 1968) and *Industrial Research and Technological Innovation* (W. W. Norton, for the Cowles Foundation for Research in Economics at Yale University, 1968). The present book extends and builds on the results of these previous works, and presents, as well, findings regarding areas untouched by the earlier books.

EDWIN MANSFIELD

Philadelphia
January 1971

RESEARCH AND

INNOVATION

IN THE MODERN

CORPORATION

1 INTRODUCTION

1. Technology in the Modern Economy

The modern economy is influenced in countless ways by the advance of science and technology. New industries are born as a consequence of the mating of new technologies with new or existing consumer demand. Industries, old or new, shift their location and change their characteristics—and the nature of their work force—in response to technological change. The mechanism and style of management also change as new technology filters into the boardroom as well as the shop floor. The burgeoning literature devoted to pointing out the effects of technological change documents all this in detail—sometimes complete with color photographs and ringing phrases—in publications ranging from learned journals to Sunday supplements. Every schoolboy takes it for granted that technological advance is an enormously potent force that helps to shape the contours of the economy.

The purpose of this chapter is to provide some basic information that is needed to place the studies discussed in subsequent chapters in their proper context. We begin by trying to indicate what we mean by terms like *technological change* and *research and development*. These terms are difficult to define in a neat and simple way, as we shall see in subsequent sections. Then we look at the extent to which our society invests in research and development, the returns from such an investment, and the uncertainties involved. Next, we discuss the processes of *invention, innovation,* and *diffusion,* and describe the effects of industrial organization and the role of the government in promoting technological change. Needless to say, our discussion of these many topics must be brief and rather superficial, but it is sufficient for present purposes. (A much more detailed treatment is available elsewhere.[1]) Finally, having taken up these preliminary matters, we discuss the general objectives of the studies contained in subsequent chapters of this book.

---

1. See Edwin Mansfield, *The Economics of Technological Change* (New York: W. W. Norton, 1968).

2. Technology, Research, and Development

Technology is society's pool of knowledge regarding the industrial arts. It is made up of knowledge used by industry, agriculture, government, and the professions concerning physical and social phenomena, knowledge concerning the application of basic principles and theories to work in these fields, and knowledge of the rules of thumb and lore of craftsmen and practitioners. Typically, technological change—the advance of technology— takes the form of a capability to produce a wholly new product, a new process of making an existing product, or new ways to organize or manage industrial establishments. It is necessary to recognize at the outset that technological change is not the same as scientific advance. Pure science is aimed at understanding, whereas technology is aimed at use. The distinction between science and technology is imprecise, but important.

Changes in technology often occur as a consequence of inventions that depend on no new scientific principles. Until the middle of the nineteenth century, there was only a rather loose connection between science and technology. For example, the inventions that laid the groundwork for the industrial revolution owed little to pure science. During the latter part of the nineteenth century, science and technology began to come closer together, particularly with respect to the chemical and electrical industries. Toward the end of the century, commercial research laboratories began to appear on the industrial scene, some of the early laboratories being established by Thomas A. Edison (in 1876), Arthur D. Little (1886), Eastman Kodak (1893), B. F. Goodrich (1895), General Electric (1900), Du Pont (1902), and the Bell Telephone System (1907). During the twentieth century, expenditures to promote the advance of technology grew at a rapid rate, as we shall see in section 3.

An important characteristic of the modern corporation is that it not only is influenced by technological change, but itself invests considerable resources in an effort to influence the rate and direction of that change. Although some firms have long maintained this type of pursuit, the frequency and extent of such investment has increased markedly in recent years. The firm's undertakings of this sort are called research and development. Included in research and development are activities of three broad types. First, there is basic research, which is devoted entirely to the creation of new knowledge. For example, the mathematician who tries to prove a certain theorem, without any particular application in mind, is performing basic research. Firms carry out some basic research, but as would be expected, it accounts for a relatively small proportion of their R and D work. Second, there is applied research, which is expected to have a specific practical payoff. For example, projects might be carried out to determine whether lasers might be useful for a certain purpose or whether a new type of material might be superior to an old material in a particular product. The distinction between applied and basic research is unclear at best. The distinction is based on the aim of the work, basic research being carried out to obtain new knowledge for its own sake, applied research being carried out to promote specific practical and commercial aims.[2]

Finally, there is development, which attempts to reduce research findings to practice. Relatively minor development projects try to bring about slight modifications of existing products or processes. Major development projects try to bring into being entirely new types of products and processes. By the time a project reaches development, much of the uncertainty concerning its technical feasibility has been eliminated, but there often is considerable uncertainty concerning development cost, development time, and the profitability of the result. The tasks that are carried out in development depend, of course, on the nature and purpose of the development project. Frequently, prototypes must be designed and constructed, or pilot plants must be built. The distinction between research and development often is not clear-cut. The distinction between them relates primarily to the orientation of the work, the degree and type of uncertainty, and the length of time work can be expected to go on without any practical payoff. Research is oriented toward the pursuit of new knowledge, whereas development is oriented toward the capacity to produce a particular product. Research generally entails more uncertainty of outcome, and requires more time for completion, than development. Although research and development are not the same, they do tend to shade into one another.

3. Expenditures on Research and Development

One of the most noteworthy features of the post-World War II economy has been the rapid growth of expenditures on research and development. Between 1953 and 1970, total R and D expenditures in the United States increased at an average annual rate of about 10 percent per year. In 1953, total R and D spending in the United States was about $5 billion; in 1970, it was about $27 billion. Expressed as a percentage of gross national product, R and D expenditures in the United States were 1.4 percent of the gross national product in 1953, and 2.7 percent in 1970. Table 1.1

2. The definitions of research (basic and applied) and development put forth in this section are those of the National Science Foundation. They are the standard definitions in official use today. For a discussion of them, see *Methodology of Statistics on Research and Development* (National Science Foundation, 1959).

Note that one important problem in making the distinction between basic and applied research is that the company (or government agency) paying for the research may have a specific application in mind whereas the researcher may be interested strictly in the advance of science. Of course, there are many other problems as well.

TABLE 1.1
Total Expenditures on R and D
United States, 1953–1970

YEAR	TOTAL R AND D EXPENDITURES	YEAR	TOTAL R AND D EXPENDITURES
	(millions of dollars)		*(millions of dollars)*
1953	5,207	1962	15,665
1954	5,738	1963	17,371
1955	6,279	1964	19,215
1956	8,483	1965	20,449
1957	9,912	1966	22,285
1958	10,870	1967	23,680
1959	12,540	1968[a]	25,330
1960	13,730	1969[b]	26,250
1961	14,552	1970[b]	27,250

Source: National Patterns of R and D Resources (National Science Foundation, 1969).
[a] Preliminary.   [b] Estimated.

shows the very impressive increase in R and D expenditures during 1953–1970. Inspection of the figures shows that, as would be expected, the rate of growth of R and D expenditures has been declining in recent years. The very high growth rates experienced during the mid-fifties and early sixties were obviously unsustainable over the long run. In addition, there has been some lessening of public enthusiasm concerning science and technology, as we shall see in section 9.

Much of the research and development performed by one sector of the economy is financed by another sector. Table 1.2 shows that in 1970 industry performed about 70 percent of the R and D carried out in the United States, but that the federal government financed about 55 percent of the R and D carried out. The federal government is an important source of funds for researchers in universities and other nonprofit institutions as well as for researchers in industry. A few major industries perform most of the research and development in the United States. In 1967, five industries —aircraft and missiles, electrical equipment and communication, chemicals and allied products (including drugs), machinery, and motor vehicles (and other transportation equipment)—were responsible for over 80 percent of all R and D spending by industry.

According to figures published by the National Science Foundation, the two leading performers of basic research were the chemical industry (including drugs) and the electrical-equipment industry; the two leading performers of applied research were the aircraft and missiles industry and

TABLE 1.2

Transfer of Funds Used for
Performance of R and D, 1970[a]

PERFORMERS OF R AND D

SOURCES OF FUNDS	GOVERNMENT	INDUSTRY	UNIVERSITIES	OTHER NONPROFIT INSTITUTIONS	TOTAL
	(millions of dollars)				
Government	3,780	8,512	2,630	634	15,556
Industry	2	10,738	60	85	10,885
Universities	1	—	570	—	571
Other nonprofit institutions	2	—	140	231	373
Total	*3,785*	*19,250*	*3,400*	*950*	*27,385*

Source: *National Patterns of R and D Resources* (National Science Foundation, 1969).
[a] These figures are estimates. The total differs slightly from that given in Table 1.1.

the chemical industry (including drugs); and the two leading performers of development were the aircraft and missiles industry and the electrical-equipment industry. To a considerable extent, the reason some of these industries undertake so much R and D is that they are performing this work for the federal government. In 1967, the federal government financed about 80 percent of the R and D in the aircraft industry and about 60 percent of the R and D in the electrical-equipment industry. The situation in all industries in 1967 is shown in Table 1.3.

The bulk of the money spent on R and D goes for development, not research. Basic research is relatively most important in the chemical (including drugs) and petroleum industries, but in no case does it take more than 15 percent of an industry's total R and D expenditures. Development accounts for a particularly large proportion of the total in the machinery, electrical-equipment, and aircraft and missiles industries. Surveys of business plans for new plant and equipment provide additional data regarding the character of the R and D being carried out by industry. For example, one survey in the early sixties found that about 47 percent of the responding firms said that their main purpose was to develop new products, 40 percent said that their main purpose was to improve existing products, and 13 percent said that their main purpose was to develop new processes.[3] However, lest there be misunderstanding, it is important to recognize that one industry's products may be part of another industry's processes.

3. McGraw-Hill, *Business Plans for Expenditures on Plant and Equipment,* annual.

TABLE **1.3**

Performance of R and D and Federal Funds
for R and D, by Industry, 1967

INDUSTRY	R AND D PERFORMANCE	FEDERAL FUNDS FOR R AND D
	(millions of dollars)	
Food	168	1
Textiles and apparel	52	n.a.
Lumber	14	—
Paper	94	n.a.
Chemicals and allied products (including drugs)	1,565	212
Petroleum	469	38
Rubber	195	30
Stone, clay, and glass	152	7
Primary metals	245	8
Fabricated metal products	165	12
Machinery	1,478	393
Electrical equipment and communication	3,806	2,240
Motor vehicles and other transportation equipment	1,377	389
Aircraft and missiles	5,568	4,510
Instruments	464	147

Source: Research and Development in Industry, 1967 (National Science Foundation, 1969).
n.a. Not available.

4. *The Firm's Choice of a Research and Development Program*

In many respects, some of the most difficult problems faced by a firm are in the area of research and development. For example, how much should a firm spend on research and development? This question is extremely difficult to answer because it is so difficult to predict the returns from many R and D projects. In practice, firms often tend in the short run to maintain a fairly constant ratio between R and D expenditures and sales. In the longer run, firms obviously change their desired ratio of R and D expenditures to sales, such changes occurring in response to changes in the perceived profitability of research and development and changes in the profitability of the firm. Also, there is a tendency to follow the leader, with the result that an increase or decrease in R and D expenditures by certain firms may influence others to act in the same way.

Another important question is: How do firms decide which R and D projects to accept and which to reject? As we shall see in Chapter 3, many firms seem to use simple modifications of capital-budgeting criteria—like the pay-out period and the rate of return—to help determine the selection of projects, particularly development projects. As a project moves from research toward the market, it is subjected to more intensive scrutiny from both a technical and an economic angle. When projects are in the exploratory-research phase, the screening of proposals may be relatively quick and informal, since the costs at this stage are relatively small and it is difficult to predict the outcome of such work. However, as projects enter development, where costs and predictability are greater, a much more detailed economic evaluation of proposals is generally carried out.[4]

To repeat, it is extremely difficult to estimate the returns from research and development. For some years, the McGraw-Hill Economics Department gathered data from firms regarding the *expected* profitability of their R and D programs. Table 1.4 shows for each industry the distribution of firms in 1961, classified by their expected pay-out period for research and

TABLE 1.4
Expected Average Pay-out Periods from
R and D Expenditures, 1961

	PAY-OUT PERIOD		
INDUSTRY	3 YEARS OR LESS	4 TO 5 YEARS	6 YEARS OR MORE
	(percent of companies answering)		
Iron and steel	38	50	12
Nonferrous metals	64	18	18
Machinery	51	39	10
Electrical machinery	61	32	7
Autos, trucks, and parts	54	40	6
Transportation equipment	43	44	13
Fabricated metals and instruments	77	14	9
Chemicals	33	41	26
Paper and pulp	50	32	18
Rubber	38	38	24
Stone, clay, and glass	38	46	16
Petroleum and coal	17	33	50
Food	54	43	3
Textiles	76	24	0
Miscellaneous	71	25	4
All manufacturing	55	34	11

Source: McGraw-Hill, *Business Plans for Expenditures on Plant and Equipment,* annual.

4. For more discussion of the topics of this section, see Edwin Mansfield, *Industrial Research and Technological Innovation,* (New York: W. W. Norton for the Cowles Foundation for Research in Economics at Yale University, 1968).

development. The pay-out period is, of course, a very crude measure of profitability, but it is all that is available on a widespread basis. The McGraw-Hill surveys indicate that about 90 percent of the firms expected their R and D outlays to pay off in five years or less. Since it usually takes considerably longer than this before a radically new process or product even hits the market, the emphasis on short pay-out periods seems to indicate that most R and D in these firms is geared toward improvements or minor changes in existing products. More will be said on this score in subsequent chapters.

For a small group of firms and industries, some very tentative and experimental estimates have been made of the marginal rate of return from R and D expenditures. If the production function is Cobb-Douglas, if total R and D expenditures, as well as labor and capital, are inputs, and if R and D expenditures have grown exponentially, one can obtain relatively simple expressions for the marginal rate of return from research and development. Using these results, estimates of the marginal rates of return have been made for ten major chemical and petroleum firms, and lower bounds for the marginal rates of return have been estimated for ten manufacturing industries. For reasons discussed in detail elsewhere, these estimates are merely experimental and should be viewed with great caution.[5]

In addition, studies have been made of the relationship between a firm's R and D expenditures and its output of significant inventions, these studies being limited to the major firms in the chemical, petroleum, and steel industries. When the size of the firm is held constant, the number of significant inventions carried out seems to be highly correlated with the size of its R and D expenditures. Thus, although the output from an individual R and D project is obviously very uncertain, there appears to be a close relationship over the long run between the amount the firm spends on R and D and the total number of important inventions it produces.

The evidence from these studies also suggests that in the chemical industry, increases in R and D expenditures in the relevant range (when the size of the firm is held constant) result in more than proportional increases in inventive output. But in the petroleum and steel industries, there is no real indication of either economies or diseconomies of scale within the relevant range. Thus, except for chemicals, the results do not indicate any marked advantage of very large-scale research activities over medium-sized and large ones. Finally, when a firm's expenditures on R and D are held constant, increases in the size of the firm seem to be associated in most of these industries with decreases in inventive output. Thus, the evidence suggests that the productivity of an R and D effort of a given magnitude is lower in the largest firms than in the medium-sized and large ones.[6]

5. *Ibid.*, Chap. 4.
6. *Ibid.*, Chap. 2.

5. Uncertainty and Learning in Research and Development

Research and development is marked by considerable uncertainty, particularly when projects are aimed at reasonably large technological advances. A long string of failures may occur before any kind of success is achieved. However, the extent of the uncertainty depends on how ambitious a firm's R and D program is. If a firm is content with very limited advances in technology, the risks are, of course, much smaller than if it attempts to go far beyond the current state of the art. The total risks involved in R and D —the combination of *both* technical and commercial risks, in the language of Chapters 2 and 3—tend to be relatively high.

A survey of 120 large companies doing a substantial amount of R and D indicates that, in half of these firms, at least 60 percent of the R and D projects never resulted in a commercially used product or process. (The smallest failure rate for any of the firms surveyed was 50 percent.) Moreover, even when a project resulted in a product or process that was used commercially, the profitability of its use was likely to be quite unpredictable. As would be expected, most research projects tend to be scrapped before the development stage. For example, one study of twenty large firms reported that less than 2 percent of the proposals initially made were forwarded for development.[7]

It is also important to note that *research and development is an activity which is aimed at reducing uncertainty.* That is, R and D is aimed at learning. For example, suppose that a firm which is trying to fabricate a part can use one of two alloys, and that it is impossible to employ standard sources to determine their characteristics. If the firm were forced to make a choice immediately, it would probably choose alloy A because it believes that there is better than a 50-50 chance that alloy A is stronger than alloy B. But there is a good chance that this decision would turn out to be wrong. Thus, the firm may do some research and development to reduce its uncertainty concerning the relative strength of the two alloys: it will attempt to learn more about the strengths of these alloys.

The process of uncertainty reduction lies at the heart of the development task. When a firm carries out a development project, it must answer at least four questions: What will be the approximate performance attributes for each of the components or subsystems comprising the desired system? How interrelated should the components be? How should the project's resources be distributed among various kinds of uncertainty-reducing activities—construction of mathematical models, review by spe-

7. Booz, Allen, and Hamilton, *Management of New Products* (New York, 1960). Note, however, that the percentage of projects that never result in a commercially used process or product may be quite different than the percentage of R and D funds spent on such abortive projects. See Chaps. 2 and 3.

cialists, testing of physical models, testing of prototypes, testing of production items, and so forth? How many parallel approaches should be taken in the development of each component? All of these questions, with the possible exception of the first, are concerned at least in part with the reduction of uncertainty.

Many R and D projects use parallel approaches to help cope with uncertainty. For example, in the development of the atomic bomb, there were several methods of making fissionable materials, and no consensus existed among scientists as to which of these alternatives was most promising. To make sure that the best one was not discarded, all methods were pursued in parallel. The wisdom of this decision was indicated by the fact that the method that was first to produce appreciable quantities of fissionable material was one that had been considered relatively unpromising early in the development program. Contrary to popular belief, conducting parallel efforts may produce results more quickly and more cheaply than attempting in advance to choose the optimal approach and concentrating all one's efforts on pursuing it. Based on reasonable assumptions and definitions, analysis suggests that the cheaper it is to run each approach and the greater the prospective amount of learning, the more likely it is that parallel approaches will prove economical.[8]

Finally, it is important to recognize that the effectiveness of a firm's R and D department depends heavily on its relations with other parts of the firm. Whether the output of the R and D department is used is often dependent on the marketing people. It is easy to cite cases where good ideas emerging from R and D were blocked by marketing people who failed to grasp their significance. It is also easy to cite cases where scientists had little or no appreciation of the styling, pricing, and distribution problems faced by a marketing manager. Relations with the production department are also very important. The production people must produce the new item emerging from the R and D department. Often there are considerable problems in translating jobs to be done from the language and methods appropriate to R and D engineers into terms that are useful to draftsmen, production engineers, production supervisors, and ultimately, operatives.

6. Invention, Innovation, and Diffusion[9]

Invention has been defined in many ways. According to one definition, an invention is a prescription for a new product or process that was not

8. For further discussion of parallel approaches, see Thomas Marschak, Thomas Glennan, and Robert Summers, *Strategy for R and D* (New York: Springer-Verlag, 1967); and R. Nelson, "Uncertainty, Learning, and the Economics of Parallel Research and Development Efforts" (*Review of Economics and Statistics,* 1961).

9. This section (as well as parts of others in this chapter) is based largely on sections of Mansfield, *The Economics of Technological Change, op. cit.* (or the abridged version).

obvious to one skilled in the relevant art at the time the idea was generated. Other definitions add the requirement that the product or process must be useful as well as novel. Inventions can occur in many ways, chance often playing an important role, and they can result from the efforts of independent inventors as well as corporate research laboratories. In organized R and D activity, inventions can occur in either the research or the development phase of the work, although the central ideas often come from research, and inventions in patentable form often arise in the course of development. Invention is inherently a very difficult process to analyze, map out, organize, and direct. Contrary to the popular impression, this process often moves from the observation of a phenomenon to an exploration for a use for it, not from a clearly defined goal to the discovery of technical means to achieve this goal. The process takes unexpected twists and turns, need and technique interact with one another, and it is not always apparent ahead of time from which disciplines or technologies answers will come. For example, a process for drawing brass rods arose from an adaptation of candle-making technology. Moreover, the attempt to solve one problem may result in an answer to quite a different problem.[10]

An invention, when applied for the first time, is called an innovation. Traditionally, economists have stressed the distinction between an invention and an innovation on the ground that an invention has little or no economic significance until it is applied. This distinction becomes somewhat blurred in cases like Du Pont's nylon, where the inventor and the innovator are the same firm. In these circumstances, which are quite common, the final stages of development may entail at least a partial commitment to a market test. However, in another important class of cases, the inventor is not in a position to—and does not want to—apply his invention, because his business is invention, not production, or because he is a supplier, not a user, of the equipment embodying the innovation, or for some other reason. In these cases, the distinction remains relatively clear-cut.

Regardless of whether the break between invention and innovation is clean, innovation is a key stage in the process leading to the full evaluation and utilization of an invention. The innovator—the firm that is first to apply the invention—must be willing to take the risks involved in introducing a new and untried process, good, or service. In many cases, these risks are high. Although R and D can provide a great deal of information concerning the technical characteristics and the cost of production of the invention— and market research can provide considerable information regarding the demand for it—many areas of uncertainty can be resolved only by actual production and marketing of the invention. By obtaining needed information regarding the actual performance of the invention, the innovator plays a vital social role.

10. D. Schon, *Technology and Change* (Delacorte Press, 1967), Chap. 1.

Once the invention is introduced for the first time, the diffusion process begins. How rapidly an innovation spreads is obviously of great importance; for example, in the case of a process innovation, it determines how rapidly productivity increases in response to the new process. In a free-enterprise economy, firms and consumers are free to use new technology as slowly or as rapidly as they please, subject, of course, to all the constraints imposed by the marketplace. Diffusion, like the earlier stages in the creation and assimilation of new methods and products, is essentially a learning process. However, instead of being confined to a research laboratory or to a few firms, the learning takes place among a considerable number of users and producers.

When the innovation first appears, potential users are uncertain of its nature and effectiveness, and they tend to view its purchase as an experiment. Sometimes considerable additional research and development is required before the innovation is successful; sometimes, despite attempts at redesign and improvement, the innovation never is a success. Information regarding the existence, characteristics, and availability of the innovation is disseminated by the producers through advertisements and salesmen; information regarding the reaction of users to the innovation tends to be disseminated informally and through the trade press. Learning takes place among the producers of the innovation, as well as the users. Early versions of an innovation often have serious technological problems, and it takes time to work out these bugs. During the early stages of the diffusion process, the improvements in the new process or product may be almost as important as the new idea itself. Moreover, when a new product's design is stabilized, costs of production generally fall in accord with the so-called "learning curve." That is, unit costs of production decrease as the producers gain experience and learn by doing. For example, in the case of aircraft production during World War II, there is some evidence that average labor requirements tended to be reduced by about 20 percent for each doubling of cumulated output.[11]

7. Technological Change, Size of Firm, and Market Structure

Economists have long been concerned with the effects of market structure on the rate at which an industry develops and adopts new processes and products. According to John Kenneth Galbraith, and others, the "modern industry of a few large firms [is] an almost perfect instrument for inducing technical change."[12] According to other observers, an industry

11. W. Hirsch, "Firm Progress Ratios," *Econometrica* (April 1956).
12. John Kenneth Galbraith, *American Capitalism* (Boston: Houghton Mifflin, 1952), p. 91.

composed of a larger number of smaller firms is generally more progressive than an industry dominated by a few giant firms. The available evidence is certainly too limited to permit us to come to final conclusions on this score. However, enough is known to cast considerable doubt on Galbraith's assertion.

With regard to expenditures on research and development, the indications are that there is usually no tendency for the ratio of R and D expenditures to sales to be higher among the giants than among their somewhat smaller competitors. Moreover, as noted in section 4, what little data we have does not indicate that the inventive output per dollar of R and D is higher among the giants than among their somewhat smaller competitors. With regard to the rate at which new processes and products are introduced commercially, the evidence is mixed: If innovations require large amounts of capital, the substitution of fewer large firms for more smaller ones may lead to more rapid introduction; if they require small amounts of capital this may not be the case. Finally, with regard to the rate of diffusion of new techniques, the limited amount of evidence that is available seems to suggest that greater concentration in an industry may be associated with a slower rate of diffusion; but the observed relationship is weak and could be due to chance.

Despite the views of Galbraith, Schumpeter,[13] and others, there is little evidence that industrial giants are needed in most industries to ensure rapid technological change and rapid utilization of new techniques. (There is no statistically significant relationship between the extent of concentration in an industry and its measured rate of productivity change.) Of course, this does not mean that industries composed only of small firms would necessarily be optimal for the promotion and diffusion of new techniques. On the contrary, there seem to be considerable advantages in a diversity of firm sizes, no single firm size being optimal in this respect. Moreover, the optimal average size is likely to be directly related to the costliness and scope of the inventions that arise.[14]

8. The Role of the Government

The federal government plays an extremely important role in the support of technological change and scientific advance in the United States. As noted in section 3, the federal government financed about 55 percent of the research and development carried out in the United States in 1970. The federal agencies that support the largest amounts of research and develop-

13. Joseph Schumpeter, *Capitalism, Socialism, and Democracy* (New York: Harper & Row, 1942).

14. Mansfield, *The Economics of Technological Change, op. cit.,* Chap. 7.

ment are the Department of Defense, the National Aeronautics and Space Administration, and the Atomic Energy Commission. Other agencies that support significant amounts of research and development are the Department of Health, Education, and Welfare, the Department of Transportation, the National Science Foundation, and the Department of Agriculture. Most of the federal government's expenditures for research and development are related to two fields: defense and space. Table 1.5 shows the percentage of

TABLE 1.5

*Percent of Total R and D Expenditures Devoted to
Defense, Space, and Other Federal Activities,
1953–1970*

PERCENT OF NATION'S R AND D EXPENDITURES

YEAR	DEFENSE	SPACE	OTHER FEDERAL ACTIVITIES	TOTAL FEDERAL ACTIVITIES
1953	47.5	0.8	4.7	53.0
1954	48.2	0.9	5.6	54.7
1955	47.4	1.0	7.5	55.9
1956	48.6	0.9	7.7	57.3
1957	52.2	1.0	8.5	61.7
1958	52.0	1.0	9.5	62.5
1959	53.3	2.5	8.5	64.3
1960	51.6	3.1	9.0	63.7
1961	49.2	5.5	9.0	63.7
1962	44.6	8.8	10.0	63.4
1963	40.2	14.7	9.7	64.6
1964	36.0	19.6	9.7	65.3
1965	32.0	21.6	10.1	63.7
1966	30.9	20.7	11.2	62.8
1967	31.6	18.0	11.4	61.0
1968[a]	30.7	16.7	11.8	59.2
1969[b]	30.7	13.8	12.1	56.6
1970[b]	30.5	12.7	11.9	55.0

Source: *National Patterns of R and D Resources* (National Science Foundation, 1969).

[a] Preliminary.
[b] Estimated.

the nation's R and D supported by government outlays for defense, space, and other activities. During the fifties and early sixties, 80 percent or more of the federal R and D expenditures were for defense. Beginning in the early sixties, space was assigned a larger and larger percentage of federal R and D expenditures, until in 1965 it accounted for over one-third of these expenditures. In recent years, there has been a tendency for nondefense, nonspace activities to get a greater share of federal R and D funds, this being part of a shift of resources toward the investigation of domestic problems.

Not all of the federal R and D programs are designed to promote technological change in goods and services provided by the public sector of the economy. Some programs are aimed at offsetting imperfections in the system that would otherwise lead to an underinvestment in research and development. Examples are the programs of the National Science Foundation and the National Institutes of Health. To justify these programs, it is asserted that there are considerable discrepancies between the private and the social benefits (and costs) of R and D in these areas. These discrepancies occur because the results of R and D can be appropriated to only a limited extent and because of the riskiness and costliness, in some areas, of the research and development.[15] Obviously, existing government R and D programs are based only partly on purely economic criteria. Also, it is important to note that only about one-fifth of the R and D financed by the federal government is actually done in government laboratories. The tremendous increase in federal contracting has resulted in a blurring of the distinction between the private and the public sectors.

9. Recent Changes in the Public's Attitude Toward Science and Technology

Beginning in the late sixties, the public's attitude toward science and technology seemed to change, enthusiasm waning and wariness growing. In part, this has been due to antiwar sentiments, with many observers, following the example of President Eisenhower in his last address to the nation, fearing undue power and influence by a "military-industrial complex" allied with—and having considerable control over—the nation's scientists and technologists. To an increasing degree, science and technology have been pictured as the handmaidens of the cold warriors. In addition, more and more emphasis has been placed on the costs associated with technological change in the civilian economy. For example, it is frequently pointed out that the application of modern technology has resulted in air and water pollution. Technological advances that were once heralded as modern miracles are now viewed with suspicion, and sometimes banned, as their unexpected side effects cause problems, damage, and even death. For example, insecticides turn out to kill birds and fish as well as harmful insects; and synthetic sweeteners may result in cancer.

15. Edwin Mansfield, "The Contribution of Research and Development to Economic Growth in the United States," *Symposium on the Relationship between Research and Development and Economic Growth and Productivity,* National Science Foundation, 1971 (to appear in *Science*).

This growing skepticism toward science and technology has coincided with the tightening of federal fiscal constraints caused by the Indochina war and the accompanying inflation, the result being that federal expenditures on research and development have remained essentially constant at about $16 billion per year from 1967 to 1971.[16] After the long period of spectacular increases, this leveling off has forced painful readjustments in many firms, government agencies, and universities. It has contributed to a marked slowdown during the late sixties and early seventies in the rate of increase of total R and D expenditures in the United States. Moreover, coupled with the increased supply of engineers and scientists being graduated by the nation's universities, it has helped to bring about an apparent surplus of some kinds of scientists and engineers.

The skepticism of the late sixties and early seventies is probably a healthy reaction to some of the naïveté and self-serving optimism of the earlier years. But it would be a tragic mistake to carry this reaction too far. Modern technology is a tremendously powerful force that can allow man to lead a fuller, longer, happier life. If we use this force with care, we can better our own lot as well as that of our less fortunate neighbors. Modern technology is no panacea, but used with wisdom it can accomplish a great deal.

10. Purpose of this Book

During the past fifteen years, economists have devoted a considerable amount of attention to technological change. After many years of comparative neglect, technological change has become a fashionable area for economic research. In large part this surge of interest has been due to the growing awareness that our nation's rate of economic growth depends heavily on our rate of technological change, to the increasing realization of the full importance of competition among firms through new products and processes rather than through direct price rivalry, and to the widespread concern over the adequacy of our national policies toward science and technology. Because of the work carried out in recent years, our understanding of the economics of technological change has progressed considerably. We know a great deal more about the way in which new products and processes are invented, commercialized, and accepted than we did fifteen years ago. Nonetheless, we have a long way to go before our understanding of these processes is at all close to being adequate. Despite the work that has gone on, many important areas remain unstudied and many areas have been studied in only a superficial fashion.

The purpose of this book is to report the findings of a number of studies

16. *Science Resources Studies Highlights* (National Science Foundation, August 14, 1970).

designed to throw light on various relatively unexplored aspects of the economics of technological change. The principal focus is on the individual firm and its attempts to develop and utilize new technology. We look in considerable detail at the characteristics, organization, and outcome of industrial research and development projects, the factors influencing the cost of developing a new product, the magnitude and determinants of the time and cost overruns in commercial development, the total cost and time involved in product innovation, the nature and determinants of the time-cost trade-off in product innovation, the problems encountered by small business in obtaining federal R and D contracts, the extent to which the largest firms tend to be the innovators, the lag between invention and innovation, and the rate of diffusion of a very important manufacturing innovation.

2 RESEARCH AND DEVELOPMENT:

CHARACTERISTICS, ORGANIZATION,

AND OUTCOME

1. Introduction

As pointed out in the previous chapter, recent years have witnessed a very great interest among economists in industrial research and development, a considerable number of studies of this facet of business activity having been carried out.[1] Although these studies have promoted a much clearer understanding of this area, we still have very little information concerning many important aspects of industrial research and development, one of the most obvious gaps being the lack of studies indicating the characteristics of research and development in various industries, the effect of various characteristics of a firm on the nature of the R and D it undertakes, and the effects of various characteristics of a firm on the effectiveness of a firm's R and D efforts.

One purpose of the research reported in this chapter is to investigate these aspects of R and D in two of the most research-intensive industries in the United States—chemicals and petroleum. Using data obtained from over twenty large chemical and petroleum firms, we begin by describing the expected chance of technical success of the R and D projects they undertake, the distribution of their R and D expenditures between research and development, the extent to which their R and D projects are expected to be relatively long-term, and the expected profitability of these projects if they

---

1. For example, see Edwin Mansfield, *Industrial Research and Technological Innovation*, (New York: W. W. Norton for the Cowles Foundation for Research in Economics at Yale University, 1968); Richard Nelson, Merton Peck, and Edward Kalachek, *Technology, Economic Growth, and Public Policy* (Washington, D.C.: The Brookings Institution, 1967); and Thomas Marschak, Thomas Glennan, and Robert Summers, *Strategy for R and D* (New York: Springer-Verlag, 1967). For a review of the literature, see Edwin Mansfield, *The Economics of Technological Change* (New York: W. W. Norton, 1968), Chap. 3.

are technically successful. Then we study the relationship between a firm's size and the characteristics of the R and D it carries out, as well as the relationship between the proportion of a firm's R and D expenditures devoted to research and the apparent technical riskiness of its R and D portfolio. In addition, we present the results of a small-scale experiment aimed at developing crude measures of the relative effectiveness of various firms' R and D establishments, these measures being similar in construction to Cartter's measures of the effectiveness of various graduate schools.[2]

Then, to obtain information concerning the actual—as opposed to estimated—technical risks encountered in industrial research and development, we report the results of an investigation of the work carried out in a sample of nineteen industrial laboratories in the New Jersey-Pennsylvania-Delaware area, these laboratories being in the chemical, drug, electronics, and petroleum industries. We present data concerning the actual technical risks involved, and the degree to which the actual probability of technical success is related to the extent to which a laboratory specializes in research or development. In addition, we study the origin of project proposals and the organization of these laboratories. Finally, we present the results of a very detailed study of the characteristics of technically successful and unsuccessful projects in three of these laboratories. For example, data are provided concerning the relationship between cumulated expenditures on a project and the actual probability of technical completion, as well as concerning the causes of project termination.

2. Characteristics of Research and Development Programs in Chemical and Petroleum Firms

To obtain some impression of the characteristics of the research and development programs carried out by various firms in the chemical and petroleum industries, we contacted most of the major firms in these industries, and requested information concerning (1) the distribution of the firm's 1964 R and D expenditures among basic research, applied research, and development;[3] (2) the distribution of R and D projects in progress during 1964 by expected rate of return, if technically successful; (3) the distribution of projects in progress during 1964 by expected chance of technical success—technical success being defined, roughly speaking, as

---

2. See Allan Cartter, "Economics of the University" (*American Economic Review*, May 1965); and his *An Assessment of Quality in Graduate Education* (American Council on Education, 1966).
3. We used the National Science Foundation's definitions of basic research, applied research, and development. For example, see *Basic Research, Applied Research, and Development in Industry, 1962* (National Science Foundation, 1965).

achievement of the project's *technical* objectives;[4] (4) the distribution of projects in progress during 1964 by the expected length of time before they would be completed and have an effect on profits; and (5) the firm's total expenditure on R and D, its total payroll for scientists and engineers, and the total number of scientists and engineers it employed in 1964. Data of this sort were obtained from thirteen chemical firms and eight petroleum firms. This sample includes over half of the chemical firms with 1963 sales of $100 million or more, and over half of the petroleum firms with 1963 sales of $500 million or more.

The results, shown in Tables 2.1 and 2.2, seem to indicate at least four things. First, they suggest that the bulk of the R and D projects carried out by these firms is regarded as being relatively safe from a technical point of view. In practically all firms in our sample, half of the projects are regarded as having at least a 50-50 chance of technical success. Second, only a small percentage of the money spent on R and D by these firms goes for basic research. About half of the money goes for development.[5] Third, most of the R and D projects are expected to be quite profitable if they are technically successful, the median expected rate of return for a firm's projects generally being about 30 percent.[6] Fourth, the bulk of the R and D projects are expected to be finished and have an effect on profits in five years or less. However, for reasons discussed in Chapter 5, these estimates of time are likely to be quite optimistic.

Taken at face value, these findings seem to support the hypothesis, advanced by Hamberg[7] and others, that the bulk of the research and development carried out by large corporations—other than that financed by the federal government (and generally devoted to military or space purposes)—is relatively safe from a technical viewpoint. Judging from

4. More precisely, a project is defined as being a technical success if it attains its technical objectives in the budgeted time and within the budgeted cost; otherwise it is defined as being a technical failure. (The technical objectives may, of course, include production-cost objectives as well as performance aims.) Of course, such a simple classification can be misleading. For example, a project may not attain its technical objectives but may result in very valuable information. Nonetheless, the estimated probability of technical success is likely to be as good a measure of risk from the technical viewpoint as one can obtain.

5. On the average, the firms devoted about 9 percent of their R and D expenditures to basic research, 45 percent to applied research, and 46 percent to development. Of course, the distribution of expenditures among basic research, applied research, and development has been investigated in various publications by the National Science Foundation. (See note 3.) Our results seem quite consistent with those of the Foundation.

We promised the firms that we would not publish figures for individual firms. Hence, the identity of the firms is disguised in all tables.

6. These estimates are conditional on the projects' being technically successful. The unconditional estimates would, of course, be lower. In computing the medians, the projects classified in the "not known" category had to be omitted. This is legitimate, since there is no evidence that such projects were considered more or less profitable than the others. The same procedure was used in computing the median probability of technical success.

For various reasons, one might expect the firms' estimates of profitability to be on the high side. But it is interesting to note that other studies also indicate that the estimated rate of return of R and D projects, if technically successful, tends to be high. See Mansfield, *Industrial Research and Technological Innovation, op. cit.,* Chaps. 3 and 4.

7. Daniel Hamberg, "Invention in the Industrial Research Laboratory," *Journal of Political Economy* (April 1963).

Tables 2.1 and 2.2, models or policies based on the common supposition that the bulk of the R and D in the industrial laboratory is very risky, far-out work are likely to be misconceived and misleading. This is an important point, for both analysis and policy.[8] But before jumping to conclusions, it is also important to note that firms may tend to be optimistic in their appraisal of the chances of success of their projects. In subsequent sections of the chapter, we shall see whether this is the case. To anticipate, we shall find that results based on *actual* probabilities of technical success, like those based on these firms' *estimates,* indicate that the bulk of the industrial R and D projects tend to be relatively safe from a technical point of view.

Another noteworthy finding that emerges from Tables 2.1 and 2.2 is the extent of the interfirm diversity in the characteristics of the R and D programs. In each of these industries, there is a great deal of variation on this score. For example, one chemical firm devotes 18 percent of its R and D expenditures to basic research, whereas another devotes none. Some chemical firms devote over 60 percent of their R and D expenditures to research, both basic and applied, whereas others devote less than 30 percent. Some chemical firms spend $47,000 on R and D per scientist and engineer, whereas others spend $25,000. The variation in the petroleum industry is no less than in chemicals; indeed, in some respects it is greater.[9] Moreover, to the extent that we could determine, this variation is not due to different definitions of terms.[10]

In addition, there is also considerable variation among firms in the median expected rate of return from projects (if successful) and the median expected length of time before completion of projects (and effect on profits). The median expected rate of return is about 40 percent for some chemical firms and less than 20 percent for others. The median expected length of time before completion is about two years for some chemical firms and about four years for others. Only in the case of the

8. Of course, since technical success by no means ensures commercial success, the total risks are considerably greater than is indicated by the probability of technical success. For a discussion of commercial risks, see Chapter 3. Needless to say, we are not saying that R and D is not a risky process. Including the probability of commercial as well as technical failure, the risks are greater than in most other aspects of business. But relative to the risks in very far-reaching R and D projects, the technical risks taken in most of these projects do not seem to be very great. This remains true when, in subsequent sections, we look at data regarding actual probabilities not estimates.

One large oil firm, Gulf Oil Corporation, has published information concerning some aspects of its R and D program in 1966. See J. Hirsch and E. Fisher, "The Alternative Service Concept in Research Project Evaluation," *Research Management* (January 1968).

9. Some petroleum firms devote at least 15 percent of their total R and D expenditures to basic research; one firm devotes none. One petroleum firm devotes over 80 percent of its total R and D expenditures to research, whereas others devote less than 50 percent. Some petroleum firms spend $60,000 on R and D per scientist and engineer, whereas others spend $25,000. For some petroleum firms, the median estimated length of time to completion for R and D projects is about 5 years; for others it is about 1.5 years. With regard to the latter figure, note that estimates of time to completion tend to be very optimistic. See Chapter 5.

10. Clearly, there could be differences among firms in the interpretation of the definitions of research and development, basic research, applied research, development, scientist, engineer, and so on. We questioned a number of the respondents to be sure that they were fully aware of the definitions and that they interpreted them properly. We could find no evidence that they were interpreting the definitions in significantly different ways.

TABLE 2.1
Characteristics of the R and D Programs of Thirteen Major Chemical Firms, 1964

CHARACTERISTICS	FIRM												
	1	2	3	4	5	6	7	8	9	10	11	12	13
Percent of total R and D expenditures devoted to													
Basic research	6	8	5	7	16	12	6	0	15	5	5	18	5
Applied research	n.a.	56	10	44	n.a.	23	42	56	30	77	37	25	35
Development	n.a.	36	85	49	n.a.	65	52	44	55	18	58	57	60
Percentage distribution of projects by expected rate of return, if successful													
0–19 percent	0	n.a.	5	a	n.a.	30	0	0	n.a.	72	20	50	50
20–29 percent	20	n.a.	25	a	n.a.	40	0	25	n.a.	0	20	15	50
30–39 percent	50	n.a.	30	a	n.a.	20	30	25	n.a.	0	20	5	0
40–100 percent	20	n.a.	10	a	n.a.	0	40	50	n.a.	0	20	5	0
Not known	10	n.a.	30	a	n.a.	10	30	0	n.a.	28	20	25	0
Percentage distribution of projects by estimated probability of technical success													
0–24 percent	80	n.a.	0	10	n.a.	36	20	25	15	0	20	15	5
25–49 percent	10	n.a.	0	20	n.a.	18	20	25	15	50	20	35	20
50–74 percent	0	n.a.	0	40	n.a.	18	30	25	30	50	20	35	60
75–100 percent	0	n.a.	80	20	n.a.	18	10	25	20	0	40	15	15
Not known	10	n.a.	20	10	n.a.	10	20	0	20	0	0	0	0
Percentage distribution of projects by expected number of years to completion and an effect on profits													
Less than 2 years	10	n.a.	40	25	n.a.	10	20	50	35	0	40	10	50
2 to 5 years	60	n.a.	40	60	n.a.	60	50	50	40	100	30	80	35
More than 5 years	30	n.a.	20	15	n.a.	30	30	0	25	0	30	10	15

a Some data are available, but too little to be of use for our purposes. Five percent of the firm's projects are in the 0–19 percent category, 15 percent are in the 20–29 percent category, and 80 percent are not known.

n.a. Not available.

TABLE 2.2

Characteristics of the R and D Programs of Eight
Major Petroleum Firms, 1964

CHARACTERISTICS	FIRM							
	1	2	3ᵃ	4	5	6	7	8
Percent of total R and D expenditure devoted to								
Basic research	2	0	11	6	15	9	7	24
Applied research	54	n.a.	87	65	45	39	n.a.	33
Development	44	n.a.	2	29	40	52	n.a.	43
Percentage distribution of projects by expected rate of return, if successful								
0–19 percent	n.a.	n.a.	n.a.	20	0	n.a.	60	13
20–29 percent	n.a.	n.a.	n.a.	20	10	n.a.	5	5
30–39 percent	n.a.	n.a.	n.a.	10	10	n.a.	5	5
40–100 percent	n.a.	n.a.	n.a.	20	30	n.a.	5	33
Not known	n.a.	n.a.	n.a.	30	50	n.a.	25	44
Percentage distribution of projects by estimated probability of technical success								
0–24 percent	11	n.a.	n.a.	25	0	n.a.	10	5
25–49 percent	11	n.a.	n.a.	5	10	n.a.	5	10
50–74 percent	22	n.a.	n.a.	10	10	n.a.	5	30
75–100 percent	36	n.a.	n.a.	50	30	n.a.	60	40
Not known	20	n.a.	n.a.	10	50	n.a.	20	15
Percentage distribution of projects by expected number of years to completion and an effect on profits								
Less than 2 years	40	50	n.a.	50	25	n.a.	65	54
2 to 5 years	40	25	n.a.	30	25	n.a.	25	11
More than 5 years	20	25	n.a.	20	50	n.a.	10	35

ᵃ There is evidence that in 1966 this firm devoted about 60 percent of its total R and D expenditures to applied research and about 30 percent to development. Thus, the figures shown below for the firm may be too high for applied research and too low for development.
n.a. Not available.

median estimated probability of technical success of projects is the interfirm variation in each industry relatively small. In all but three firms it lies between 50 and 62 percent in chemicals. In all firms it lies between 70 and 83 percent in petroleum.

3. Size of Firm and Characteristics of Research and Development Programs

To what extent are the differences observed in the previous section associated with differences in size of firm? The answer to this question is important since it may help us to understand the differences between the largest firms and their somewhat smaller competitors with regard to the characteristics of their R and D programs. Previous studies[11] have indicated that the largest firms in most industries spend no more, as a percentage of sales, on research and development than do somewhat smaller firms. However, these findings ignore the possibility that the largest firms may be doing a somewhat different kind of R and D than their somewhat smaller competitors, the result being that although total R and D expenditures might not be reduced, some types of R and D expenditures might decrease substantially if the largest firms were broken up—or that some types might increase substantially if more firms were to grow to their size. This section provides some needed information on this score.

One would expect that the largest firms would devote a larger proportion of their R and D expenditures to relatively basic research than their smaller competitors and that their R and D programs would lean more heavily toward more risky and longer-term R and D projects than those of their smaller competitors. To what extent are these hypotheses consistent with the estimates provided by the firms in the chemical and petroleum industries? To find out, we assume that

$$(2.1) \qquad B_i = \alpha_0 + \alpha_1 S_i + \alpha_2 S_i^2 + Z_i,$$

$$(2.2) \qquad P_i = \phi_0 + \phi_1 S_i + \phi_2 S_i^2 + Z_i',$$

$$(2.3) \qquad T_i = \theta_0 + \theta_1 S_i + \theta_2 S_i^2 + Z_i'',$$

where B_i is the percent of the ith firm's R and D expenditures devoted to basic research, P_i is the median estimated probability of technical success of the ith firm's projects, T_i is the median estimated number of years to completion of the ith firm's projects, S_i is the ith firm's size (measured in terms of 1964 [chemicals] or 1963 [petroleum] sales), the α's, ϕ's, and θ's

11. Mansfield, *Industrial Research and Technological Innovation*, op. cit.; and Nelson, Peck, and Kalachek, op. cit.

are parameters, and the Z's are random variables. Then we estimate the α's, ϕ's, and θ's—which differ, of course, from industry to industry.

The results are generally quite consistent with the hypothesis that up to some point, increases in size of firm are associated with increases in the proportion of total R and D expenditures devoted to basic research, decreases in the median estimated probability of technical success, and increases in the median expected time to completion. For example, consider a chemical firm with sales that are one-tenth of the sales of the largest firm in the sample. According to the regression, such a firm would be expected to devote to basic research a percentage of total R and D expenditures that is about one-tenth of the percentage devoted by the largest firm in the sample. Similarly, such a firm would be expected to have a median estimated probability of technical success that is about 20 percent higher, and a median estimated length of time that is 15 percent lower, than the largest firm in the sample.

However, it is very important to note that although the largest chemical firm in the sample differs significantly from the relatively small firms in these respects, the difference between the largest firm and a firm that is one-half its size is generally small, if it exists at all. With regard to the percentage of total R and D expenditures devoted to basic research, the regression indicates that the difference is only a couple of percentage points. With regard to the median estimated probability of technical success and the median estimated length of time to completion, the regressions suggest that the median estimated probability is higher (not lower), and the median estimated length of time to completion is lower (not higher) in the largest firm in the sample than in a firm that is one-half its size.[12]

Among the petroleum firms too, increases in size of firm generally tend to be associated with decreases in the median estimated probability of technical success and increases in the median estimated length of time to completion. However, only in the case of median estimated length of time to completion does the regression suggest that there is a substantial difference between the largest firm in the sample and a firm about one-half its size. The regression pertaining to the median estimated probability of technical success suggests that the median estimated probability decreases up to a point with increases in size of firm, and then increases, the result being that the median estimated probability of technical success is no lower for the largest firm than for a firm that is considerably smaller. Finally, in this size range, there seems to be no statistically significant relationship

---

12. Of course, the results would be somewhat different if the form of the equation used in equations (2.1)–(2.3) were altered. To see how sensitive the results are, we ran a linear regression of B_t on S_t, P_t on S_t, and T_t on S_t; but we included only the larger chemical firms (those with 1964 sales of $500 million or more), since this is the only range of firm size we are concerned with here. The results obtained from these regressions are essentially the same as those in the text. Note too that none of these linear correlations is statistically significant.

among the petroleum firms between a firm's size and the percentage of its total R and D expenditures devoted to basic research.

Thus, the results indicate that firm size is associated with a substantial part of the variation in B_i, T_i, and P_i that we observed in section 2. They also indicate that although the differences between the largest firms and relatively small firms are sometimes considerable, the differences between the biggest firms in the sample and firms one-half their size are seldom large, if they exist at all. Consequently, to the extent that the sample is trustworthy and the errors and biases in the estimates are not correlated with size of firm (which seems reasonable), the results suggest that in these industries at least, firms as large as the largest firms in the sample are not required to ensure that the existing amount of R and D of a more basic, technically risky, and long-term nature is carried out. If these assumptions hold, it appears that firms that are one-half the size of the largest firms in the sample invest about the same proportion of their R and D budget in more basic, technically risky, and long-term projects as do the largest firms.[13]

4. Research, Development, and the Estimated Technical Riskiness of a Firm's Research and Development Program

Tables 2.1 and 2.2 indicate some variation (but less than for some of the other variables shown there) in the estimated technical riskiness of firms' R and D programs, as measured by the median expected probability of technical success of their projects. To some extent, this variation may be due to the fact that the proportion of the total R and D program devoted to research, rather than development, is much larger for some firms than for others. It is interesting from several points of view to investigate the extent to which the estimated technical riskiness of a firm's R and D program seems to be related to the extent to which it emphasizes research rather than development. For one thing, the results are a partial test of whether the

13. Of course, the basic assumption here, as in the studies cited in note 11, is that if the largest firms were replaced by a suitable number of somewhat smaller firms (the total sales of the industry being held constant), these somewhat smaller firms would allocate funds to various types of R and D in approximately the same way that such firms (i.e., the somewhat smaller ones) do now. Or if the smaller firms were merged, they are assumed to act like the largest firms.

It is important to note that we do not have complete data for all of the largest firms in these industries. Although there is no obvious bias, the results pertain to only a sample of the firms, and it is always possible that this sample is unrepresentative. However, as noted above, a large proportion of the firms are included—over 50 percent of the chemical firms with 1963 sales of $100 million or more and over 50 percent of the petroleum firms with 1963 sales of $500 million or more.

Of course, nothing can be deduced from these results concerning other industries. Whether or not the same kind of results holds for other industries can only be determined by obtaining this sort of data for them.

Finally, estimates of the regression coefficients in equations (2.1)–(2.3) are not given because it would be easy to use them to estimate the characteristics of the portfolios of individual firms. See Note 5.

classification of projects as research or development is useful in distinguish-
ing more technically risky projects from less technically risky ones. Also,
they help to indicate whether the percent of a firm's total R and D expenditures devoted to research is useful as a surrogate for the average riskiness
from a technical point of view of the firm's projects. In a subsequent section
of this chapter, we shall perform a similar test using measures of actual, not
estimated, technical risk.

Letting U_i be the percent of the ith firm's R and D expenditures devoted
to research (rather than development), Q_{ri} be the mean estimated probability of technical success of research projects in the ith firm, Q_{di} be the
mean estimated probability of technical success of development projects in
the ith firm, and Q_i be the mean estimated probability of technical success
for all R and D projects in the ith firm, it follows that

(2.4) $$Q_i = [U_i Q_{ri} + (100 - U_i)Q_{di}] \div 100$$
$$= Q_{di} + U_i(Q_{ri} - Q_{di}) \div 100.$$

Thus, if Q_{di} and $(Q_{ri} - Q_{di})$ are statistically independent of U_i,

(2.5) $$Q_i = Q_d + \frac{(Q_r - Q_d)}{100} U_i + Z''''_i,$$

where Q_d is the mean estimated probability of technical success for development projects in all of the included firms in the industry, Q_r is the mean
estimated probability of technical success for research projects in all of the
included firms in the industry, and Z''''_i can be treated as a random error
term.

Using equation (2.5), one can employ least squares to estimate Q_d
and Q_r, as well as to determine the extent to which the interfirm variation
in Q_i can be explained by variation in U_i. The results for the chemical
firms are

(2.6) $$Q_i = 76 - 0.44\ U_i. \qquad (\bar{R}^2 = 0.27)$$
$$(10)\quad (0.21)$$

The results are quite consistent with the hypothesis that the mean estimated
probability of technical success is inversely related to the percent of a
firm's R and D expenditures devoted to research, the estimated values of
Q_d and Q_r being 76 and 32, respectively.[14] Because of the small number of
observations it is impossible to make such an estimate for the petroleum
firms.

14. We use the mean estimated probability of technical success, rather than the median
estimated probability of technical success, in this section because the sort of analysis expressed
in equations (2.4) and (2.5) can only be carried out in terms of the mean. Actually, the means
(which were computed from the broad frequency distributions in Tables 2.1 and 2.2) differ only
slightly from the medians.
Note too that U_i, Q_i, and A_i are measured on a scale from 0 to 100, rather than 0 to 1,
in equations (2.6) to (2.9). In other words, they are percentages, not fractions.

Further study shows that equation (2.6) does not fit the data as well as a curvilinear function,

$$(2.7) \qquad Q_i = 139 - 0.22 \ln U_i, \qquad (\bar{R}^2 = 0.40)$$
$$(0.07)$$

suggesting that the difference between the mean estimated probability of technical success of research projects and that of development projects may be smaller in firms with high values of U_i than in firms with low values of U_i. A result of this sort may arise if firms that devote a relatively large proportion of their R and D expenditures to research do not support as risky research projects, on the average, as firms that devote a small percentage of their R and D expenditures to research.[15] (Except when stated to the contrary, figures in parentheses are standard errors. This is true throughout this book.)

It is also of interest to see the extent to which U_i can explain the observed variation in the percent of a firm's R and D projects that have an expected probability of technical success of 75 percent or more. Using a linear form, the result is

$$(2.8) \qquad A_i = 83.9 - 1.24 \, U_i, \qquad (\bar{R}^2 = 0.53)$$
$$(0.37)$$

where A_i is the percent of the ith firm's R and D projects that have an expected probability of technical success of 75 percent or more. Using a nonlinear form, we have

$$(2.9) \qquad \ln A_i = 566 - 6.11 \, U_i. \qquad (\bar{R}^2 = 0.74)$$
$$(1.18)$$

In either case, a substantial portion of the variation in A_i can be explained in this way.

Thus, it appears that the estimated technical riskiness of a firm's R and D program is related to the percent of its R and D expenditures devoted to research. The latter variable can explain almost half of the interfirm variation in the mean estimated probability of technical success and about three-quarters of the interfirm variation in the percent of projects with an estimated probability of technical success of 75 percent or more. Of course, these results pertain entirely to the firms' estimates of the chances of success of R and D projects, which may be unreliable for a variety of reasons. But as we shall see in subsequent sections, one obtains essentially the same results when the actual figures concerning chances of success in

15. Also, firms that classify a relatively large percentage of their total R and D expenditures as research may include projects that other firms would regard as development. If so, this too would result in the observed tendency for Q_{r_i} to increase with increases in U_i. In addition, the mean estimated probability of technical success of development projects may be lower in firms with high values of U_i than in those with low values of U_i. This too could result in the observed tendency.

various laboratories are used instead. These results illustrate the usefulness of a breakdown of total R and D expenditures between research and development, since (among other reasons) the percent of a firm's R and D expenditures devoted to research is apparently a reasonably good surrogate for the riskiness from a technical standpoint of the firm's R and D program.[16]

5. Effectiveness of Research and Development Program, Size of Firm, and Research and Development Expenditures

It is extremely difficult to measure the productivity—the output per unit of input—of a firm's research and development. The situation appears somewhat similar to that of the nation's colleges and universities: There is considerable agreement among knowledgeable observers that the faculty and education provided by one university are better than those provided by another university (with the same tuition), but it is extremely difficult to formulate suitable objective measures of these variables. The comparison with universities suggests an interesting experiment: Why not obtain subjective rankings by knowledgeable observers of the relative productivity of various firms' R and D establishments, in much the same way that Cartter and others[17] have obtained them in connection with graduate schools? Needless to say, the results would be extremely crude, but they might prove interesting. In this section, we describe the results of an experimental effort along these lines.

In both the chemical and petroleum industries, we asked the research director (or some major R and D executive) of each of a sample of major firms to rank each of the firms listed in Table 2.3 by four aspects of their R and D programs: (1) the general effectiveness (output per dollar) of their R and D establishments, (2) the quality of their scientists and engineers, (3) the quality of their R and D management, and (4) top management's receptivity and orientation to R and D. In addition, we asked a number of professors in relevant fields at major universities to rank each of these firms by three of these four criteria. In all, twenty-three people formulated such rankings: eleven for the chemical industry (six R and D executives and five academicians) and twelve for the petroleum industry (five R and D executives and seven academicians).

To what extent is there agreement among the rankings formulated by

16. In addition, we looked at the relationship between λ_i—the percentage of the ith firm's projects with expected length of time to completion of less than two years—and U_i. Using the linear form, the result is

$$\lambda_i = 48.0 - 0.438 \ U_i.$$
$$(0.336)$$

Thus the relationship is inverse, as expected, but it is not statistically significant. Of course, only the chemical firms could be included.

17. See Cartter, op. cit., and the references contained in Cartter's studies.

TABLE 2.3
*Chemical and Petroleum Firms Included
in Effectiveness Rankings*

CHEMICAL	PETROLEUM
Allied Chemical Corporation	Atlantic Refining Company
American Cyanamid Company	Gulf Oil Corporation
Atlas Chemical Industries	Sinclair Oil Corporation
Dow Chemical Company	Socony Mobil Oil Company
Du Pont de Nemours and Company	Standard Oil Company of California
General Aniline and Film Corporation	Standard Oil Company (New Jersey)
Hercules Power Company	Sun Oil Company
Hooker Chemical Corporation	Texaco Incorporated
Monsanto Chemical Company	Union Oil Company
Union Carbide Corporation	

TABLE 2.4
*Average Ranking of Ten Major Chemical Firms
by Four Aspects of Their R and D Programs*[a]

ASPECTS OF R AND D PROGRAM	FIRM 1	2	3	4	5	6	7	8	9	10
	Average Ranking by Industrial Executives									
General effectiveness (R and D output per dollar spent on R and D)	8.2	4.0	8.3	3.0	2.2	7.8	6.2	7.7	4.3	3.3
Quality of R and D scientists and engineers	7.8	3.8	8.6	3.8	1.8	8.0	5.8	7.2	4.8	3.2
Quality of R and D management	8.2	4.3	7.1	3.3	2.2	8.3	5.3	7.1	4.5	4.7
Receptivity of top management	7.8	3.8	6.8	3.8	1.6	9.0	6.8	7.2	4.4	3.8
	Average Ranking by Academic Personnel									
General effectiveness (R and D output per dollar spent on R and D)	7.7	6.1	5.3	3.5	1.6	8.6	5.5	9.1	4.9	2.4
Quality of R and D scientists and engineers	7.7	5.5	6.0	5.0	2.0	9.0	4.5	8.0	4.0	2.7
Quality of R and D management	7.5	6.1	7.0	4.5	1.7	9.2	4.1	8.3	3.5	2.5
	Overall Average Ranking									
General effectiveness (R and D output per dollar spent on R and D)	8.0	5.0	6.8	3.2	1.9	8.2	5.8	8.4	4.6	2.8
Quality of R and D scientists and engineers	7.8	4.6	7.3	4.4	1.9	8.5	5.2	7.6	4.4	3.0
Quality of R and D management	7.8	5.2	7.0	3.9	2.0	8.8	4.7	7.7	4.0	3.6

[a] Note that 1 is the *highest* possible average rank and 10 is the *lowest* possible average rank.

the various experts included in the sample? Rank-correlation techniques indicate that the agreement is generally quite close, the coefficient of correlation between a pair of rankings generally being .60 or more. Tables 2.4 and 2.5 show that there is little difference between the average ranking

TABLE 2.5

Average Ranking of Nine Major Petroleum Firms by Four Aspects of Their R and D Programs[a]

| | FIRM | | | | | | | | |
ASPECTS OF R AND D PROGRAM	1	2	3	4	5	6	7	8	9
Average Ranking by Industrial Executives									
General effectiveness (R and D output per dollar spent on R and D)	7.2	4.2	8.5	3.3	1.9	3.8	7.0	4.0	5.0
Quality of R and D scientists and engineers	7.7	4.5	7.9	3.8	1.8	1.8	6.9	4.1	6.3
Quality of R and D management	7.7	4.7	8.4	3.3	1.5	2.6	6.9	4.3	5.5
Receptivity of top management	7.5	4.7	8.1	3.4	1.8	2.6	7.1	4.7	4.9
Average Ranking by Academic Personnel									
General effectiveness (R and D output per dollar spent on R and D)	7.9	4.6	7.1	3.6	2.7	1.9	4.8	5.3	6.7
Quality of R and D scientists and engineers	7.5	5.2	7.2	2.6	3.2	1.3	5.0	5.4	5.8
Quality of R and D management	7.7	4.3	7.1	3.5	3.0	1.9	5.0	5.2	6.8
Overall Average Ranking									
General effectiveness (R and D output per dollar spent on R and D)	7.6	4.4	7.8	3.4	2.3	2.8	5.9	4.6	5.8
Quality of R and D scientists and engineers	7.6	4.8	7.6	3.2	2.5	1.6	6.0	4.8	6.0
Quality of R and D management	7.7	4.5	7.8	3.4	2.2	2.2	6.0	4.8	6.2

[a] Note that 1 is the *highest* possible average rank and 10 is the *lowest* possible average rank.

provided by the industry experts and the average ranking provided by the academicians.[18] Regardless of which of the criteria is chosen, the coefficient of correlation between the two average rankings is about 0.85 or more. Thus, despite the great difficulty in obtaining suitable objective measures of the effectiveness of a firm's R and D establishment, there appears to be considerable agreement among the sample of experts.

It is also interesting to note that firms that rank high with regard to one of these criteria also tend to rank high with regard to the others. Tables 2.4 and 2.5 show that for any particular firm there is little difference between the average rankings (whether industrial or academic) for the various criteria. The coefficient of correlation between the overall average

18. In view of the experimental nature of the results, we do not think it advisable to publish them for each firm. Hence, the identity of firms 1, 2, and so on, is not divulged. However, the names of the three highest-ranking firms in each industry are given below. Incidentally, it should not be assumed that the firms are numbered in the order given in Table 2.3.

ranking based on one criterion and that based on another is about 0.95 or more. Thus, if these opinions are correct, there is a very high correlation between the general effectiveness of a firm's R and D establishment, the quality of its scientists and engineers, the quality of its R and D management, and the receptivity and orientation of top management to R and D. In part this high correlation may be due to the fact that the people who formulated the rankings could not separate these variables, which obviously are closely intertwined.

In terms of the estimated general effectiveness of a firm's R and D program, the highest-ranking firms (when the overall averages are used) are Du Pont, Union Carbide, and Dow in the chemical industry, and Standard Oil of California, Standard Oil (New Jersey), and Socony Mobil in the petroleum industry. What is the relationship between a firm's average ranking, on the one hand, and its expenditures on R and D and its size, on the other hand? Previous studies based on other measures of the productivity of the R and D programs of large chemical firms indicate that increases in a firm's R and D expenditures result in increases in productivity, while increases in size of firm (when R and D expenditures are held constant) are associated with decreases in productivity. Among large petroleum firms, the results are much the same, but not statistically significant.[19]

To see whether the same sort of relationship holds for the average rankings presented in this section, we assume that

$$(2.10) \qquad E_i = a_0 + a_1 R_i + a_2 S_i + Z'''_i,$$

where E_i is the overall average rank of the ith firm by the general effectiveness (output per dollar) of its R and D program, R_i is the total R and D expenditure of the ith firm, S_i is the size of the ith firm (measured in terms of 1964 [chemical] or 1963 [petroleum] sales), and Z'''_i is a random error term. When least squares are used to estimate the a's, the results for the chemical firms are

$$(2.11) \qquad E_i = 7.509 - 0.171\,R_i + 0.049\,S_i, \qquad (\bar{R}^2 = 0.86)$$
$$(0.059) \qquad (0.025)$$

and the results for the petroleum firms are

$$(2.12) \qquad E_i = 6.806 - 0.182\,R_i + 0.080\,S_i, \qquad (\bar{R}^2 = 0.45)$$
$$(0.116) \qquad (0.079)$$

the numbers in parentheses being the standard errors of the coefficients.

19. Mansfield, *Industrial Research and Technological Innovation, op. cit.* Also, see Jacob Schmookler's testimony before a subcommittee of the Senate Judiciary Committee in 1965, which is contained in *Monopoly Power and Economic Performance,* ed. by Edwin Mansfield, revised edition (New York: W. W. Norton, 1968).

(Note that E_i varies *inversely* with the effectiveness of the ith firm's R and D program.)

The results in equations (2.11) and (2.12) are entirely consistent with the results of the previous studies. In chemicals, the estimate of a_1 is significantly negative and the estimate of a_2 is significantly positive, as would be expected.[20] In petroleum, the estimate of a_1 is negative and the estimate of a_2 is positive, but as in the previous studies, neither is statistically significant. Of course, the average rankings are extremely crude measures, and they suffer in this context from the fact that they are based on ordinal measurements. Nonetheless, the striking similarity of these results to those of the previous studies (which were based on entirely different and independent data) is impressive.

6. Characteristics of Research and Development Programs: Nineteen Laboratories in Four Industries

Previous sections have been concerned with the research and development programs of entire firms; at this point, we turn to various questions concerning the R and D programs of individual laboratories. For example, what are the sources of proposals for R and D projects? How are laboratories organized? What characteristics of a project seem to be associated with whether or not it is technically successful? In the next few sections, we report some results concerning nineteen industrial laboratories—seven chemical laboratories, five drug laboratories, four petroleum laboratories, and three electronic laboratories. The laboratories were chosen from a geographical area including New Jersey, the Philadelphia metropolitan area, and the Wilmington metropolitan area, the selection being more or less at random (within the specified industries) from *Industrial Research Laboratories of the United States*.[21] For each of the four industries, the sample includes a substantial proportion of the laboratories in the geographical area.[22]

The annual expenditures of these laboratories vary from $500,000 to over $16 million, while the parent firms have annual sales ranging from

20. Note once again that low values of E_i mean high values of effectiveness. Thus, a negative value of a_1 means that increases in R_i result in increases in effectiveness, and a positive value of a_2 means that increases in S_i result in decreases in effectiveness. As in section 3 (and for the same reason) we do not divulge the scale in which S_i is measured.

21. This geographical area includes a substantial proportion of the laboratories in these industries. Since we are interested in this chapter in R and D in the major corporation, very small laboratories were excluded. (For some discussion of the problems of small R and D firms, see Chapter 3.) Also excluded were laboratories where government-sponsored research and development constitute over half of the laboratory program: This chapter is concerned with privately financed R and D.

22. The sample includes, for this area, about 15 percent of the electronics and chemical laboratories, about 40 percent of the drug laboratories, and about 80 percent of the petroleum laboratories which equaled or exceeded the size of the smallest participating laboratory.

slightly under $20 million to over $5 billion. Table 2.6 shows the proportion of expenditures devoted by these laboratories to basic research, applied research, and development. The proportions are very close to those given for these industries as a whole by the National Science Foundation (the only differences being that, in the petroleum, chemical, and drug industries, the laboratories in the sample seem to perform somewhat more development, and less research, than is found in the industry as a whole). Thus, in this important respect, the sample seems reasonably representative.

TABLE 2.6

Average Annual Company-Sponsored Laboratory Expenditures, with the Proportion Spent on Basic Research, Applied Research, and Development, by Industry, 1966

| INDUSTRY | AVERAGE ANNUAL EXPENDITURES (MILLIONS OF DOLLARS) | AVERAGE PERCENT OF EXPENDITURES SPENT ON | | | |
		BASIC RESEARCH	APPLIED RESEARCH	DEVELOPMENT	TOTAL[a]
Sample Laboratories					
All laboratories	4.7	7	29	65	100
Chemical	2.7	7	37	55	100
Drug	9.2	5	33	62	100
Electronics	0.6	3	13	83	100
Petroleum	6.0	10	20	70	100
National Science Foundation Laboratory Survey Data[*]					
All laboratories	n.a.	8	26	66	100
Chemical, including drug	n.a.	13	40	48	100
Electronics	n.a.	4	14	82	100
Petroleum	n.a.	8	38	54	100

[*] *Source: Reviews of Data on Science Resources*, No. 12 (National Science Foundation, (January 1968).
[a] Because of rounding, sums of individual items may not equal totals.
n.a. Not available.

7. Evidence Regarding Technical Risks

Before taking up new questions, we provide additional evidence concerning two important matters discussed in previous sections. First, the results in section 2 seem to indicate that the bulk of the industrial research and development projects carried out by the firms covered there are relatively safe from a technical viewpoint. To test this hypothesis further, we computed the average probability of technical completion for each laboratory on the basis of its records and the administrator's experience. (Technical completion means the achievement of the stated technical goal or goals of an R and D effort.) For each laboratory, the probability of technical completion was the actual proportion of its R and D projects that succeeded in fulfilling the established technical objectives during 1963–1965. The average probability of technical completion and the range among laboratories is shown for each industry in Table 2.7. Note that the average proba-

TABLE 2.7
*Average Probability of Technical Completion,
by Industry, for Sample Laboratories*

| INDUSTRY | PROBABILITY OF TECHNICAL COMPLETION | |
	AVERAGE	RANGE AMONG LABORATORIES
All laboratories	0.56	0.10–0.99
Chemical	0.70	0.37–0.99
Drug	0.32	0.12–0.62
Electronics	0.73	0.20–0.99
Petroleum	0.50	0.10–0.74

bility of completion tends to be greater than one-half, and that the chemical and electronics laboratories have a higher average probability of technical completion than the drug and petroleum laboratories. The results are in striking agreement with those in section 2, where we saw that the estimated probability of technical success almost always averages at least 0.50 in the firms included there. Table 2.7 shows that the probability of technical completion usually is 0.50 or more in these laboratories as well—and it is important to note once again that these are *actual* probabilities not *estimates*.

Another hypothesis put forth in previous sections is that much of the variation among firms in the average probability of technical success can be explained by differences among firms in the extent to which they are engaged in research rather than development. This hypothesis should hold for the average probability of technical completion as well as the average probability of technical success. Thus, the average probability of completion of a laboratory's R and D projects should be inversely related to the proportion of laboratory expenditures devoted to research, as opposed to development. Letting Q'_i and U_i equal, respectively, the ith laboratory's average probability of technical completion and the proportion of its expenditures spent on research, and letting C_i represent a dummy variable that is 1 if the ith laboratory is a chemical laboratory and 0 otherwise, we find that a regression of log Q'_i on log U_i and C_i equals

(2.13) $$\log Q'_i = 2.28 + 0.34\, C_i - 0.52 \log U_i. \qquad (\bar{R}^2 = 0.38)$$
$$(0.26) \quad (0.13) \qquad (0.18)$$

While other industry dummies were tried, only C_i was statistically significant. Clearly, Q'_i is inversely related to U_i. Thus, the results provide important additional evidence supporting the hypothesis set forth in section 4 —and it should be noted again that these are *actual* probabilities not *estimates*.[23]

8. Origin of Research and Development Suggestions

Research and development projects can be initiated by suggestions from laboratory personnel, from others within the firm, or from outside sources such as suppliers, customers, universities, and others.[24] It is of interest to study the relative importance of these groups as originators of R and D projects and programs. To what extent does R and D result from suggestions from outside the firm? How important is the research and development staff in providing acceptable suggestions? Our data for these nineteen laboratories indicate, as shown in Table 2.8,[25] that the R and D staff suggests the majority of accepted projects, and that sources within the firm are responsible for practically all suggestions that are accepted: Eighty-nine percent

TABLE 2.8

Percent of R and D Program
Suggested by Selected Groups, by Industry,
for Sample Laboratories, 1966

| INDUSTRY | GROUPS WITHIN THE FIRM | | | GROUPS OUTSIDE THE FIRM | TOTAL[a] |
	R AND D STAFF	MARKETING STAFF	OTHER		
	(percent)				
All laboratories	62	20	7	11	100
Chemical	59	22	7	12	100
Drug	63	24	6	7	100
Electronics	n.a.	n.a.	n.a.	n.a.	n.a.
Petroleum	65	9	13	13	100

[a] Because of rounding, sums of individual items may not equal totals.
n.a. Not available.

23. Some industry spokesmen claim that drug development is more risky than development in most other industries. Although the results in Table 2.7 seem to bear out this view, equation (2.13) seems to deny it. With U_i held constant, Q_i is no lower in drugs than in electronics and petroleum; but it is lower than in chemicals. See Edwin Mansfield, "Comment," in *The Economics of Drug Innovation*, ed. by J. Cooper (Washington: American University, 1970).
24. Mansfield, *The Economics of Technological Change, op. cit.*, Chap. 3.
25. Needless to say, it is not easy—or sometimes even possible—to identify exactly where particular ideas have come from; and in some cases there is no single source. The laboratory managers provided the best estimates they could of the proportions coming from various sources. However, it is quite possible that they exaggerated somewhat the share of ideas coming from their laboratories.

of R and D work is initiated by suggestions from internal sources. Also, note how little difference there is between industries in the relative importance of different sources. Our results agree very well with a study made by Robert Seiler. He found, for 117 firms surveyed, that an average of 60 percent of the R and D activity was initiated by suggestions from the R and D staff, 17 percent came from the marketing staff personnel, 9 percent from "management sources," and 8 percent from sources outside the firm.[26] These findings are in very close agreement with those in Table 2.8.

What causes variation among laboratories in the relative importance of the research and development staff as a source of accepted project suggestions? One factor that may be important is the size of the laboratory. In general, one would expect the R and D staff to be a more important source of projects in large laboratories than in small ones, because the number of suggestions coming from the R and D staff is likely to increase more rapidly with increases in the size of the laboratory than the number of suggestions coming from other sources. To test this hypothesis, we regressed V_i (the proportion of the ith laboratory's R and D projects originating from suggestions of the R and D staff) on E_i (the total expenditures of the ith laboratory), the result being

$$(2.14) \qquad \log V_i = 1.33 + 0.26 \log E_i. \qquad (\bar{R}^2 = 0.21)$$
$$ (0.20) \quad (0.12)$$

Thus, the evidence seems to bear out this hypothesis.

Another factor that may influence V_i is U_i, the proportion of the ith laboratory's total expenditures devoted to research, since one might expect research to lead to a greater number of acceptable proposals for further R and D work than development. Including U_i as an additional variable, we have

$$(2.15) \qquad \log V_i = 1.05 + 0.22 \log U_i + 0.24 \log E_i. \qquad (\bar{R}^2 = 0.28)$$
$$ (0.26) \quad (0.14) \qquad\quad (0.11)$$

The coefficient of $\log U_i$ has the expected sign but is not statistically significant. Whether or not U_i is included, the relative importance of the R and D staff in suggesting its own program appears to be directly related to the size of the laboratory.

To prevent misunderstanding, a further point should be noted. The fact that most of the successful suggestions for R and D projects come from the R and D staff is no contradiction of the hypothesis, advanced by many economists, that R and D projects are to a very considerable extent triggered by developments in the market (or the plant) that make it profitable

26. Robert Seiler, *Improving the Effectiveness of Research and Development* (New York: McGraw-Hill, 1965), p. 133.

to seek a particular type of technological change. Good management requires that the R and D personnel be made aware of the problems and needs of the company and the changing pattern of demand for its products. Also, although the final suggestions may come from the R and D staff, ideas may derive partly from various other sectors of the firm. As noted in Chapter 1, the R and D department should be integrated in various ways with the other parts of the firm. Unfortunately, however, for reasons discussed in detail in Chapter 10, one does suspect that there may be room for better coordination between the R and D department and the marketing and other departments in some of these firms.

9. Organization of Research and Development

In the organization of these laboratories, how often is research separated from development? Fifty-eight percent of the laboratories in this sample have separate research functions and development functions, each with its own staff and facilities.[27] Seiler's findings are identical: Research and development had been separated in 58 percent of the laboratories included in his study.[28] Under what circumstances does a laboratory tend to separate research from development? A relevant explanatory variable is the relative equality of research expenditure and development expenditure. As research expenditure and development expenditure become more nearly equal, the need for the separation of research from development intensifies, while if research expenditure or development expenditure is very small compared to the other, there is much less need for separation. If U_i equals the percentage of laboratory i's expenditure devoted to research, the variable $D_i = U_i (100 - U_i)$ increases as research expenditure and development expenditure become more nearly equal, and it decreases as either research expenditure or development expenditure tends to dominate.[29]

To test the usefulness of D_i in explaining the separation of research and development, we construct a statistical discriminant function based on D_i.[30] To estimate the discriminant function, let F_i equal 1 if the ith laboratory's research and development functions are separated, and 0 if they are combined. The regression of F_i on D_i results in the discriminant function. We

27. For some discussions of the reasons for, and the advantages of, separating research from development, see William Kornhauser, *Scientists in Industry: Conflict and Accommodation* (Berkeley: University of California Press, 1962); and A. Stanley and K. White, *Organizing the R and D Function* (American Management Association, 1965).

28. Seiler, *op. cit.*

29. Of course, one could find variables other than D_i that have this property, but D_i seems good enough for present purposes.

30. A statistical discriminant function is optimal in the sense that under specified conditions, it minimizes the proportion of incorrect predictions. See T. Anderson, *An Introduction to Multivariate Statistical Analysis* (New York: Wiley, 1958).

would expect that the regression coefficient of D_i would be positive. The results are

$$(2.16) \qquad F_i = -0.06 + 0.0004\ D_i.$$
$$(0.025)\ (0.0001)$$

The equation predicts that if research expenditure or development expenditure accounts for between 24 percent and 76 percent of the laboratory's expenditure, research and development will be separated. This prediction is correct in about three-quarters of the cases.

How are a laboratory's research activities organized? How are a laboratory's development activities organized?[31] We would expect research activity to be organized mainly along traditional disciplinary lines, and development to be structured according to the product market. Table 2.9 indicates that these expectations agree with the facts. Moreover, Seiler's data agree closely with ours.[32] To analyze why some laboratories organize their research activities along disciplinary lines, while others do not, we can construct a discriminant function, with G_i equaling 1 if the ith laboratory has research organized by discipline, 0 otherwise. As an explanatory variable, the percentage of expenditures devoted to research, U_i, should be relevant, since

TABLE 2.9

Organization of R and D, by Industry,
for Sample Laboratories, 1966

INDUSTRY	ORGANIZATION OF LABORATORY BY				
	FUNCTION	DISCIPLINE	PRODUCT	OTHER	TOTAL[a]
	(percent of laboratories)				
Research					
All laboratories	11	47	42	0	100
Chemical	0	57	43	0	100
Drug	0	80	20	0	100
Electronics	33	33	33	0	100
Petroleum	25	0	75	0	100
Development					
All laboratories	11	16	68	5	100
Chemical	0	29	71	0	100
Drug	20	20	60	0	100
Electronics	33	0	33	33	100
Petroleum	0	0	100	0	100

[a] Because of rounding, sums of individual items may not equal totals.

31. For some discussions of the organization of research and of development, see Kornhauser, *op. cit.* and Stanley and White, *op. cit.*
32. Seiler, *op. cit.*

more research should increase the probability of organization along traditional scientific lines. One would expect that laboratories oriented to research rather than development would be more likely to preserve scientific specialties as a basis of research organization—as in the academic environment.[33] The regression of G_i on U_i yields

$$(2.17) \qquad G_i = 0.14 + 0.0095\ U_i.$$
$$(0.08)\quad(0.0049)$$

The equation predicts a discipline-organized research department whenever U_i exceeds 34 percent. The relationship is statistically significant.

Why do some laboratories organize development along disciplinary lines while others do not? If development activity is small compared to research, the development organization may be dominated by the structure of research. Hence a discriminant function including the relative amount of research work performed may be useful in explaining the way development is organized. Only the sample from the chemical industry is large enough to be at all useful in testing this hypothesis. A regression of H_i (equal to 1 if the ith laboratory's development department is organized by discipline, 0 otherwise) on U_i for the chemical laboratories yields

$$(2.18) \qquad H_i = -0.66 + 0.015\ U_i.$$
$$(0.15)\quad(0.003)$$

The proportion of laboratory expenditures spent on research must exceed 44 percent for the equation to predict discipline-organized development. The organization of each chemical laboratory is correctly predicted by this equation.

10. Characteristics of Technically Completed and Uncompleted Projects: Three Laboratories

In this section, we turn to an analysis of the technical outcome of individual research and development projects. A project either succeeds in fulfilling the technical objectives of the project proposal, or is terminated short of success.[34] If a project is not completed successfully, the incompletion may be due primarily to intractable technical problems, or it may occur because new market conditions make continuation of the project less profitable. We shall label the first as technical incompletion due to technical problems and the second as technical incompletion due to nontechnical problems. What factors seem to influence the probability that a project will

33. Kornhauser, op. cit.
34. Of course, a project may sometimes provide valuable information even if it is not technically completed. See note 4.

be technically completed? What factors seem to influence the probability that a project will be scrapped due to technical problems rather than non-technical problems?

To find out, we gathered detailed data concerning over two hundred R and D projects completed during a period of several years in the sixties in three laboratories—a chemical laboratory (laboratory X) and two proprietary drug laboratories (laboratories Y and Z). Table 2.10 shows that the three laboratories have similar probabilities of technical completion, if all projects are lumped together. About 60 percent of each laboratory's projects were technically completed. In laboratory Z, most of the projects that were not technically completed were scrapped due to nontechnical, not technical, problems; but the opposite was true in laboratories X and Y.

As shown in Table 2.10, the probability of technical completion seems to be higher for projects that attempt relatively small advances in the state of the art, that are concerned with areas of technology with which the laboratory is familiar, and that are directed toward product improvements rather than entirely new products.[35] This is what would be expected. More-

TABLE **2.10**

Outcome of R and D Projects of Various Kinds,
Laboratories X, Y, and Z

LABORATORY AND TYPE OF PROJECT	PROBABILITY OF TECHNICAL COMPLETION	PROBABILITY OF AN INCOMPLETION DUE TO TECHNICAL REASONS
Laboratory		
X	0.68	0.80
Y	0.66	0.60
Z	0.52	0.27
Extent of technical advance sought		
Small	0.66	0.29
Medium	0.42	0.45
Large	0.26	0.57
Type of project		
Product improvement	0.72	0.32
New product	0.49	0.40
Familiarity with technical area		
Familiar	0.59	0.38
Unfamiliar	0.46	0.38
All projects	0.57	0.38

35. We asked the laboratory managements to rate each project as an attempt at a small, medium, or large advance in the state of the art. We also asked them to classify each project by whether or not it was concerned with an area of technology with which the laboratory was familiar, and by whether it was an attempt at a product improvement or an entirely new product. There is little point in belaboring the fact that the results are crude. For present purposes, they are useful despite this crudeness.

over, if a project is not technically completed, it is more likely that the failure is due to technical problems (rather than nontechnical problems) if the project attempts a relatively great advance in the state of the art and if it is directed toward a new product rather than a product improvement. This too is what would be expected.

According to the judgment of the laboratory managements, about 70 percent of the projects carried out in these laboratories were aimed at small advances in the state of the art, whereas less than 10 percent were aimed at large advances. Given the results in Table 2.10—which indicate that the probability of technical completion is much higher for projects attempting small advances than for those attempting large advances—it seems clear that the high probabilities of technical success in these laboratories are due to the fact that they devote most of their resources to projects aimed at small advances in the state of the art. In other words, the technical risks tend to be low because most of the projects aim at rather small technical advances. It seems likely that this is an important reason for the high probabilities of technical success found in sections 2 and 7 as well.

Finally, it is interesting to compare the costs of technically completed and technically incomplete projects in these three laboratories. The results differ from one laboratory to another. As shown in Table 2.11, projects

TABLE 2.11

Average Expenditure on an R and D Project,
by Outcome of Project, Laboratories X, Y, and Z

PROJECT OUTCOME	AVERAGE EXPENDITURE ON A PROJECT		
	LABORATORY X	LABORATORY Y	LABORATORY Z
	(*percent of average expenditure for all projects*)		
Technical completion	126	131	104
Incompletion due to technical problems	37	63	177
Incompletion due to nontechnical problems	77	6	63
All projects	100	100	100

that were technically incomplete cost less, on the average, than those that were technically completed in laboratories X and Y; but in laboratory Z, projects that were technically incomplete due to technical problems cost considerably more, on the average, than did technically completed projects. In laboratories Y and Z, projects that were technically incomplete due to technical problems cost more, on the average, than those that were technically incomplete due to nontechnical problems; but in laboratory X, the opposite was true.

11. Project Outcome and Cumulated Project Expenditures

To laboratory administrators, an ongoing R and D project requires a series of decisions over time. As more and more money is spent on a project, more and more information is obtained, some having to do with the technical progress of the project, some having to do with the value of the project's objectives to the firm. Given that a certain amount of money, X, has been spent on a project, one of three things must happen in the period during which an additional amount of money, $\triangle$, is spent on it: (1) the project may be terminated short of successful completion, (2) it may be successfully completed, or (3) it may be continued.

Our data for laboratory Z are sufficiently rich so that we can compute, for various values of X, the probability that a project already costing X dollars will reach successful completion if an additional \$5,000 is spent on it, and the probability that a project already costing X dollars will be terminated unsuccessfully in the interval before an additional \$5,000 is spent on it. Let the former probability be $S(X)$ and the latter probability be $F(X)$. For this laboratory, what is the relationship between $S(X)$ and X? What is the relationship between $F(X)$ and X? The relevant least-squares regressions are

$$(2.19) \qquad S(X) = 0.093 - 0.00049\ X,$$
$$(0.017)\quad (0.00019)$$

$$(2.20) \qquad F(X) = 0.12 - 0.0020\ X + 0.000010\ X^2,$$
$$(0.03)\quad (0.0007)\quad (0.000005)$$

where X is expressed in thousands of dollars. A quadratic term was tried in equation (2.19) but was not statistically significant.

Both functions are graphed in Figure 2.1. Note that the probability of unsuccessful termination exceeds the probability of completion for $X < \$20,000$ and $X > \$130,000$. There seems to be a "weeding out" process, many projects being terminated after small amounts have been spent on them. There follows a wide range where the probability of unsuccessful termination is much lower than the probability of completion (the latter also decreasing with increases in X). Only at relatively high project cost levels does the chance of unsuccessful termination begin to increase and eventually exceed the probability of completion. Apparently, in this laboratory at least, management chops off many projects after small amounts have been spent on them and tends to allow the survivors to go on until substantial amounts have been spent on them before the probability of unsuccessful termination becomes high once again.

Is there a correlation between the total past expenditure on a project

FIGURE **2.1**
Graph of $S(X)$ and $F(X)$, Laboratory Z

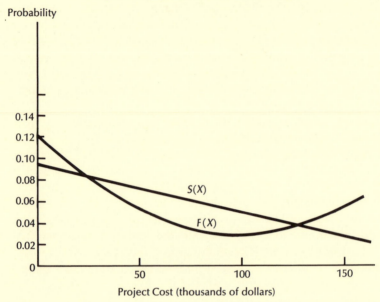

and the probability that the project, if it is discontinued unsuccessfully, will be discontinued due to technical rather than nontechnical problems? If we define $t(X)$ as the proportion of projects discontinued when a sum between X and $(X + \$5,000)$ has been spent on them that are discontinued due to technical problems, the regression of $t(X)$ on X in laboratory Z is

$$(2.21) \qquad\qquad t(X) = 0.16 + 0.0040\ X,$$
$$\qquad\qquad\qquad (0.16)\quad (0.0025)$$

the regression coefficient being significant at the 0.07 level. Apparently, in this laboratory at least, there may be some tendency for incomplete projects on which a considerable amount has been spent to fail more often due to technical problems than do incomplete projects on which relatively little has been spent.

12. Summary

The principal findings of this chapter can be summarized as follows: First, according to *estimates* made by about twenty chemical and petroleum firms and data regarding the *actual* past experience of nineteen laboratories in four industries, the bulk of the research and development projects carried out by the firms in our sample seem to be relatively safe from a technical point of view. Most of the projects seem to be technically successful. To a considerable extent, this appears to be due to the fact that the bulk of the R and D projects are aimed at fairly modest advances in the state of the art. For example, in the case of three laboratories in the sample, about 70 percent of the projects carried out were regarded by the laboratory management as being aimed at only small advances. This is in contrast with major government-financed projects—particularly in the military area—where large advances are often sought.

Second, increases in size of firm are associated in the chemical and petroleum industries with increases in the proportion of R and D expenditures devoted to basic research, decreases in the median estimated probability of technical success, and increases in the median expected time to completion. However, the difference between the largest firm (in our sample) and a firm that is one-half its size is generally small, if it exists at all. Thus, to the extent that the sample is trustworthy and the errors and biases in the estimates are not correlated with size of firm (which seems reasonable), the results suggest that, in these industries at least, firms as large as the largest firms in the sample are not required to ensure that the existing amount of R and D of a more basic, technically risky, and long-term nature is carried out.

Third, the variation among firms in the average estimated probability of technical success of R and D projects can be explained in considerable part by variation in the percentage of R and D expenditures devoted to research. Also, the variation among laboratories in the actual probability of technical completion can be explained in considerable part by this same variable. Apparently, the proportion of a firm's, or laboratory's, R and D expenditures devoted to research is a reasonably good surrogate for the riskiness from a technical standpoint of the firm's R and D program.

Fourth, a small-scale experiment aimed at developing crude measures of the effectiveness of some major firms' R and D programs (similar to Cartter's measures of the quality of graduate schools) indicates that there is very close agreement among the rankings formulated by the various experts in the sample. Highest ranking were Du Pont, Union Carbide, and Dow among the chemical firms, and Standard Oil of California, Standard Oil (New Jersey), and Socony Mobil among the petroleum firms. There is a significant tendency among the chemical companies for a firm's ranking to increase with the level of its R and D expenditures; in petroleum, the evidence for this tendency is not statistically significant. When R and D expenditures are held constant, there is no tendency for a firm's ranking to increase with its size.

Fifth, in our sample of nineteen industrial laboratories, the R and D staff seems to be responsible for about 60 percent of the suggestions or proposals leading to accepted R and D projects. In general, the R and D staff tends to be a more important source of projects in large laboratories than in small ones. Most of the laboratories separate research from development, the probability of such a separation increasing as research expenditures and development expenditures become more nearly equal. Usually, a laboratory's research activities are organized along disciplinary lines, while its development activities are organized along product lines.

Sixth, detailed data were gathered concerning the characteristics and outcome of each R and D project completed during several years in the sixties in three laboratories, results being obtained for over two hundred projects. According to these data, the probability of technical completion seems to be higher for projects that attempt relatively small advances in the state of the art, that are concerned with areas of technology with which the laboratory is familiar, and that are directed toward product improvements rather than entirely new products. Moreover, if a project is technically incomplete, it is more likely that the failure is due to technical problems (rather than nontechnical problems) if the project attempts a relatively great advance in the state of the art and if it is directed toward a new product rather than a product improvement.

Seventh, our data for one laboratory are rich enough to allow us to compute, for various values of X, the probability that a project already costing X dollars will reach successful technical completion if an additional $5,000 is spent on it, as well as the probability that it will be terminated unsuccessfully in the interval before an additional $5,000 is spent on it. In this laboratory, there seems to be a "weeding out" of projects after a relatively small expenditure. There follows a wide monetary range where the probability of unsuccessful termination is much lower than the probability of technical completion. Only at relatively high project cost levels does the chance of unsuccessful termination begin to increase and eventually exceed the probability of technical completion.

3 PROJECT SELECTION, COMMERCIAL RISKS, AND THE ALLOCATION TO SMALL BUSINESS OF FEDERAL RESEARCH AND DEVELOPMENT CONTRACTS

1. Introduction

The previous chapter was concerned with the nature, organization, and technical outcome of industrial research and development. In this chapter, we continue to focus on industrial research and development, but our attention shifts to different, though related, aspects of this topic. Specifically, we are interested in the extent to which firms are using various quantitative techniques to select R and D projects. These techniques have been the object of considerable investigation by operations researchers and management scientists. Also, we are interested in the extent of the *commercial* risks —as distinct from *technical* risks—involved in research and development. The previous chapter dealt only with technical risks.

In addition, we present the results of some research bearing on the allocation of federal R and D contracts. It is often asserted that small business is not getting its proper share of such contracts. In this chapter, we include some data indicating how the situation appears to some of the people most clearly affected—the owners of small R and D firms. Information is presented concerning their attitudes toward federal contracts, the problems they have encountered in dealing with government agencies, and their suggestions for ways to reduce these problems. In view of the fact that this is a perennial issue in Congress, the results should be of interest.

2. Project-Selection Techniques

Quantitative techniques—generally adaptations of well-known capital-budgeting techniques—have been proposed by many authors to help industrial laboratories in project selection. How widespread is their use, and how does their application vary among industries? What type of technique is used most often? To answer these questions, the administrators of the nineteen laboratories described in Chapter 2 were asked to indicate which, if any, of the following techniques their laboratories used as an aid in project selection: pay-out period, rate of return (or discounted cash flow), or composite index for project ranking.[1] The responses show that about three-quarters of our sample were using one or more of these techniques in 1969. This result may be compared with Seiler's finding that in 1964, 52 percent of the firms in his study used one or more of these techniques in project selection.[2] According to the data shown in Table 3.1, a calculation of estimated rate of return is the most widely used technique, except in the drug industry.

To prevent misunderstanding, it is important to note that the laboratories where these techniques are used do not rely entirely on them to select projects. On the contrary, intuition and "gut reaction" seem to continue to play a very important role. Moreover, these techniques are much more often employed in connection with development than with research. Where these quantitative techniques are used, it is difficult to tell how significant they are in the decision-making process. In some laboratories, they are taken much

TABLE 3.1

Use of Quantitative Techniques in R and D Project Selection, by Industry, for Sample Laboratories, 1969

	PERCENT OF LABORATORIES USING A QUANTITATIVE TECHNIQUE	PERCENT OF LABORATORIES PRIMARILY USING			
		RATE OF RETURN	PAYOUT PERIOD	RANKING INDEX	TOTAL
All laboratories	74	72	14	14	100
Chemical	86	67	33	0	100
Drug	20	0	0	100	100
Electronics	100	100	0	0	100
Petroleum	100	75	0	25	100

1. For descriptions of each kind of technique, see N. Baker and W. Pound, "R and D Project Selection: Where We Stand," *IEEE Transactions in Engineering Management* (June 1964); and Robert Seiler, *Improving the Effectiveness of Research and Development* (New York: McGraw-Hill, 1965). These three techniques were the only quantitative selection techniques used by any of the firms.
2. Seiler, *ibid.*, pp. 174–176. Note that the difference between Seiler's figure and ours seems to be due to the difference in year. In 1964—the year to which Seiler's figure pertains—58 percent of our laboratories used one or more of these techniques. This result is quite similar to Seiler's.

more seriously than in others. Indeed, one suspects strongly that in some laboratories these techniques are little more than window dressing, the real determinants of project selection—professional hunch, intrafirm politics, as well as a host of other factors—being at work behind the facade.

What factors are likely to influence the chance of a laboratory's using some quantitative technique? For two reasons, the size of the laboratory should be positively related to the probability of some such technique being employed. First, larger laboratories have more projects, and the laboratory management has more difficulty keeping informed of all facets of activity through direct personal observation. Second, a larger laboratory can more readily afford to employ personnel to collect the necessary data and make the calculations involved over time. Regressing X_i, the dependent variable showing whether or not the ith laboratory used some quantitative technique (X_i equals 1 if the ith laboratory used some quantitative project-selection technique in 1966, 0 otherwise), on the dollar size of R and D expenditures, E_i, yields

$$(3.1) \qquad X_i = 0.66 - 0.36\ D_i + 0.064\ E_i,$$
$$ (0.076) \quad\ (0.023)$$

where D_i equals 1 if the ith laboratory is in the drug industry, 0 for all other industries.[3] The negative coefficient of this variable reflects the much lower use of these project-selection techniques in the drug industry. The significant positive coefficient of E_i supports the hypothesis that the probability that a laboratory uses any formal quantitative technique for project selection is directly related to E_i, the laboratory's size.

3. The Rate of Diffusion of Quantitative Project-Selection Techniques

How rapidly has the use of quantitative project-selection methods of this sort spread among industrial laboratories? How does this rate of diffusion compare with that of other innovations? In early 1970, we asked each laboratory administrator to give the calendar year during which some quantitative selection method was first adopted as an aid to project-portfolio selection. Five laboratories do not use a quantitative method, while the other fourteen laboratory managements began routinely employing such a technique during the period from 1950 to 1967. The rate at which the use of these quantitative techniques spread among the fourteen laboratories was not uniform over the eighteen-year period. Only four of the laboratories were utilizing quantitative selection methods by the end of 1959, while in

---

3. Note that the dependent variable indicates whether or not the laboratory used a quantitative project-selection technique in 1966. Thus, it pertains to the same year as the data in Chapter 2 concerning these laboratories. On the other hand, Table 3.1 pertains to 1969.

the four years from 1960 to 1963, seven more laboratories introduced quantitative techniques for project selection.

According to a model used in our previous studies (and discussed at length in Chapter 9), there is reason to expect that the proportion of laboratories using this innovation will grow in accord with the logistic curve, a particular kind of S-shaped growth curve.[4] To see whether this is the case, let V_t equal the proportion of the nineteen laboratories using a quantitative project-selection method at the end of the tth year, and t equal the calendar year, less 1,949. The logistic function takes the form of

$$\ln\left(\frac{V_t}{1 - V_t}\right) = \alpha_0 + \alpha_1 t.$$

Inserting least-squares estimates of the α's based on our data, the resulting equation is

$$(3.2) \qquad \ln\left(\frac{V_t}{1 - V_t}\right) = -3.13 + 0.22\, t. \qquad (\bar{R}^2 = 0.95)$$
$$(0.01)$$

The actual values of V_t, as well as those predicted by the equation, are plotted in Figure 3.1. The agreement is reasonably good. The regression coefficient of t is statistically significant. This regression coefficient is a measure of the rate of diffusion.

Relative to the rate of diffusion of the major manufacturing innovations studied in our previous work, the rate of diffusion of quantitative project-selection methods is relatively slow, exceeding that of only five of the twelve innovations for which data are available.[5] The relatively slow rate of diffusion of quantitative project-selection methods—despite the smallness of the investment required to introduce them—may be due to the existence of considerable skepticism concerning the usefulness of these quantitative methods. Much more will be said about the reasons for this skepticism in subsequent chapters.

4. Commercial Risks in Industrial Research and Development

At this point, let us turn from project selection to the extent of the commercial risks in industrial research and development. It is both convenient and meaningful to divide the risks of industrial research and development into two categories—technical and commercial. First, a project may fail to achieve its technical objectives. The previous chapter was concerned with

---

4. Edwin Mansfield, *Industrial Research and Technological Innovation* (New York: W. W. Norton for the Cowles Foundation for Research in Economics at Yale University, 1968), Chap. 7.
5. *Ibid.*

FIGURE **3.1**

Actual and Predicted Proportion of Laboratories
Using Quantitative Project-Selection Techniques
1949–1969

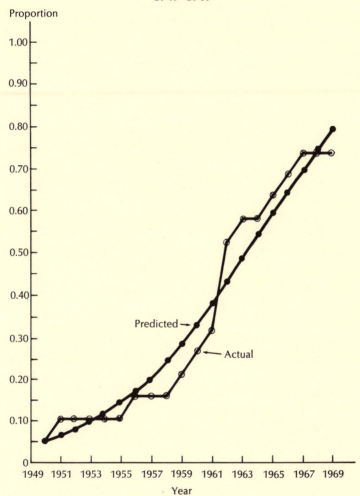

this risk of incompletion. Second, of those projects which are completed from a technical point of view, some are commercially applied and others are not. Of those commercialized,[6] moreover, some are regarded as market

---

6. Commercialization means the progression of the product beyond the test-market or pilot-plant stage. It means that the product was marketed on a scale similar to that of other products marketed by the firm.

successes,[7] and others are not. The second—or commercial—risk is that a technically completed project may not be commercially applicable or that it may not be commercially successful if applied.

We can divide all technically completed projects into two categories— those that are commercialized and those that are not. By commercialization, we mean the full-scale marketing or application of a new or improved product or process beyond a test-market or pilot-plant trial. Let us consider the three laboratories—X, Y, and Z—described in the previous chapter. What proportion of the technically completed projects was commercialized in each of these laboratories? Does the proportion of completions commercialized vary significantly with various project characteristics? These are important questions—and there exist practically no published data concerning them.

Table 3.2 shows that about 55 percent of the technically completed projects in our laboratories were commercialized—this percentage varying from 49 percent in laboratory Z to 71 percent in laboratory X. These results are quite similar to Meadows' finding that 62 percent of the completed projects[8] were commercialized in the three laboratories he studied.[8] The electronics laboratory in his study commercialized 73 percent (the highest proportion of completions), while a chemical laboratory in his sample com-

TABLE 3.2

Proportion of Technically Completed Projects
That Are Commercialized, Various Kinds of Projects,
Laboratories X, Y, and Z

	LABORATORY			
KIND OF PROJECT	X	Y	Z	ALL
	(*proportion of completed projects commercialized*)			
Size of technical advance				
Small	0.64	0.55	0.44	0.50
Large or Medium	0.86	0.71	0.75	0.77
Type of project				
Product improvement	0.78	0.54	0.64	0.64
New product	0.75	0.63	0.38	0.49
Familiarity with market				
Familiar	0.69	0.70	0.53	0.59
Unfamiliar	0.75	0.17	0.14	0.38
All projects	0.71	0.59	0.49	0.55

7. A market success is defined here as a commercialized product that earns a higher rate of return on its R and D and market-introduction costs than the rate available from comparable alternative investment opportunities. The product, in other words, earns an economic profit.
8. Dennis Meadows, "Estimate Accuracy and Project Selection Models in Industrial Research," *Industrial Management Review* (Spring 1968).

mercialized only 52 percent. Thus, both the average and the range of proportion of projects commercialized are very similar in our three laboratories
and in those studied by Meadows. Table 3.2 also contains data for projects
classified by size of technical advance, type of project, and the firm's famil-
iarity with the market area. The probability of commercialization seems
higher (1) for large or medium technical advances than for small technical
advances, (2) for product improvements than for new products, and (3)
for products intended for familiar markets than for products aimed at unfamiliar markets. It is particularly noteworthy that in each of the laboratories, a substantially higher proportion of large and medium technical
advances are commercialized than small technical advances. More will be
said on this score in Chapter 10.

Given that a project is begun, what is the probability that it will be
commercialized? To obtain this probability, one must multiply the probability of technical completion by the probability of commercialization (given
technical completion). For laboratories X, Y, and Z, the respective products
of the probability of completion and the probability of commercialization
(given completion) are 0.48, 0.39, and 0.25, the average for the three laboratories being 0.31. The corresponding proportions for Meadows' three
laboratories are 0.53, 0.52, and 0.40, the average being 0.49. Thus, in the
laboratories for which data are available in these studies, somewhere between one-quarter and one-half of the projects that are begun result in
marketed new or improved products. The rest are either not completed or
judged inapplicable due to a changed market situation or for some other
reason.

Returning to the probability of commercialization (given technical completion), what are the combined effects of various project characteristics on
this probability? Let V_i, as the dependent variable, be 1 if the ith project is
commercialized and 0 if it is not. As independent variables, let T_i be 1 if the
ith project is a large or medium technical advance and 0 if it is a small
technical advance, N_i be 1 if the ith project is a new product and 0 if it is a
product improvement, and M_i be 1 if the ith project is intended for an unfamiliar market area and 0 if it is intended for a familiar market. Only the
sample of completed projects from laboratory Z contains sufficient observations for a meaningful regression. According to the results of Table 3.2, we
would expect the coefficients of N_i and M_i to be negative and the coefficient
of T_i to be positive. The resulting equation is

(3.3) $$V_i = 0.60 + 0.22\,T_i - 0.27\,N_i - 0.30\,M_i.$$
$$(0.15)\quad(0.11)\quad(0.19)$$

All the signs conform to our expectations, although only the coefficient
of N_i is statistically significant.

5. Commercialization and Project Cost

How does the average cost of a commercialized project compare with the average cost of a project that is technically completed but not commercialized? Meadows[9] found that commercialized projects cost less, on the average, than those technically completed but not commercialized. Our data, found in Table 3.3, indicate just the opposite—that, on the average, commercialized projects cost more than those completed but not commercialized. Moreover, as shown in the table, we have sufficient data to compute the differences between average costs for projects classified by various characteristics. From the table, note that the difference between the average cost of commercialized projects and the average cost of technically complete but noncommercialized projects is greater (1) for large or medium technical advances than for small technical advances, (2) for new products than for product improvements, (3) for projects involving unfamiliar tech-

TABLE 3.3

*Difference Between Average Cost of Commercialized
Projects and Average Cost of Noncommercialized
Completed Projects, Various Kinds of Projects,
Laboratories X, Y, and Z*

	AVERAGE COST OF COMMERCIALIZED PROJECTS MINUS AVERAGE COST OF NONCOMMERCIALIZED PROJECTS			
	LABORATORY			
KIND OF PROJECT	X	Y	Z	ALL
	(thousands of dollars)			
All projects	124.3	37.4	24.2	53.0
Size of technical advance				
Small	50.0	31.7	16.5	28.2
Large or medium	191.0	21.4	19.3	69.6
Type of project				
Product improvement	110.0	20.5	19.7	34.7
New product	135.1	44.1	32.5	73.6
Familiarity with technology				
Familiar	98.2	a	17.8	33.1
Unfamiliar	148.0	a	114.9	138.2
Familiarity with market				
Familiar	117.6	26.4	17.0	40.1
Unfamiliar	130.7	64.8	205.9	160.3

a Insufficient data.

9. *Ibid.*

nology than for those involving familiar technical areas, and (4) for projects intended for unfamiliar markets than for those intended for familiar markets.

6. Market Performance of Commercialized Projects

As we observed earlier, commercialization does not imply market success, as exemplified by the Edsel. The Edsel may have been the largest, most costly, commercial failure, but it is by no means unique. We have seen that only about one-half of the completed projects are commercialized. What proportion of those commercialized actually succeed commercially? How does the probability of market success vary among projects with differing characteristics? To answer these questions, we gathered data from the three laboratories regarding the market performance of each of their commercialized projects. Each laboratory administrator was asked to rate each commercialized project in his laboratory's sample as either a "success" or a "nonsuccess," according to its actual market performance. For a product to qualify as a "success," its profits had to yield a rate of return on the investment in it (research and development costs, plus any additional costs incurred in the product's market introduction) in excess of a rate of return available to the firm from an investment elsewhere. Each "success," therefore, brought the firm an economic profit. Each "nonsuccess," while perhaps earning a positive return on the money invested in it, did not yield as high a rate of return as was available from another investment. Relative profit information was gathered to permit the study of the variability of market-success probabilities among projects grouped according to different characteristics. Obviously, the results may not be entirely comparable from one laboratory to another.

Table 3.4 shows the proportion of commercialized projects judged to be successes in various classifications of projects. Thirty-eight percent of all commercialized projects earned an economic profit. Note that the proportion of market successes is higher (1) for large or medium technical advances than for small advances, (2) for new products than for product improvements, and (3) for projects aimed at unfamiliar markets than for those intended for familiar market areas (but note that information was available on only very few projects intended for unfamiliar market areas). We must be extremely cautious in interpreting these figures on the relationships between market success and project characteristics, for at least two reasons. First, the dichotomy of projects into "successes" and "nonsuccesses" is very crude, although sufficient time had elapsed between commercialization and this evaluation to give ample market experience. Second, the proportions presented in Table 3.4 are influenced by the screening used by the

TABLE 3.4

Proportion of Commercialized Projects Rated
Market Successes, Various Kinds of Projects,
Laboratories X, Y, and Z

| KIND OF PROJECT | LABORATORY | | | |
	X	Y	Z	ALL
	(proportion of commercialized projects rated successes)			
Size of technical advance				
Small	0.38	0.25	0.30	0.30
Large or medium	0.86	0.60	0.33	0.57
Type of project				
Product improvement	0.57	0.57	0.14	0.31
New product	0.63	0.20	0.57	0.47
Familiarity with market				
Familiar	0.50	0.37	0.29	0.34
Unfamiliar	0.71	a	a	0.67
All projects	0.60	0.35	0.31	0.38

[a] Insufficient data.

firms to determine whether or not to commercialize a project. For example, a higher proportion of new products were successful than were product improvements: This may be the result of a more careful and stringent screening of potential new products, such projects having to exhibit higher potential returns than product improvements in order to be commercialized.

We have now derived three sets of probabilities pertaining to three outcomes of research and development projects: the probability of technical completion, the probability of commercialization (given technical completion), and the probability of market success (given commercialization). The product of these three probabilities gives us the probability that an R and D project, once started, will turn out to be a market success. These probabilities are shown in Table 3.5. For all 220 projects, the three probabilities, in the same sequence as above, are 0.57, 0.55, and 0.38, and their product is 0.12. Thus, for every 100 projects that were begun, 57 were technically completed and 43 were not completed. Of those successfully completed, 31 were commercialized and 26 were not. Of those commercialized, 12 were market successes (earning an economic profit), and 19 were nonsuccesses (either earning a lower accounting profit or incurring a net loss on the investment in them). Therefore, the odds in these laboratories were about 1 out of 8 that a project would return an economic profit on its investment.

Finally, it is important to note two things. First, the probability of technical completion is much higher, for each laboratory sample, than the

TABLE **3.5**

Probabilities of Technical Completion, Commercialization
(Given Completion), Market Success (Given Commercialization),
and Market Success (Given that the Project Is Begun),
All Projects, Laboratories X, Y, and Z

LABORATORY	PROBABILITY OF TECHNICAL COMPLETION	PROBABILITY OF COMMERCIAL- IZATION (GIVEN COMPLETION)	PROBABILITY OF MARKET SUCCESS (GIVEN COMMER- CIALIZATION)	PROBABILITY OF MARKET SUCCESS (GIVEN THAT THE PROJECT IS BEGUN)
All laboratories	0.57	0.55	0.38	0.12
Laboratory X	0.68	0.71	0.60	0.29
Laboratory Y	0.66	0.59	0.35	0.14
Laboratory Z	0.52	0.49	0.31	0.08

probability of market success (given technical completion). Market risks, according to these figures, seem much higher than the risks involved in attaining technical completion.[10] This is an important finding, the implications of which are discussed in Chapter 10. Second, the probability of market success (given commercialization) and the probability of commercialization (given technical success) are higher in laboratory X than in laboratories Y and Z. (Also, recall from Chapter 2 that the probability of technical incompletion due to nontechnical reasons is smaller in laboratory X than in laboratories Y and Z.) These differences may be due to the fact that there is much better coordination between the marketing people and R and D in firm X than in firms Y and Z. Estimates of potential market and other commercial factors are fed into the decision-making process earlier in laboratory X than in laboratories Y and Z. More will be said on this score in Chapter 10.

7. *Federal Research and Development Contracts and Small Business*

Up to this point, we have been concerned with company-financed research and development. Let us turn now to R and D by the federal government. As we saw in Chapter 1, the federal government finances a large percentage of the nation's R and D, industrial firms commonly acting as

---

10. Of course, attrition rates, although often used for this purpose, are very crude measures of risk. See Edwin Mansfield, "Comment" in *The Economics of Drug Innovation*, ed. by J. Cooper (American University, 1970). However, it is important to note that the attrition rates evaluated there are *not* the same as those used here and that some of the problems discussed there are *much* less pronounced in the present measures.

Also, it should be noted once again that a project that is not completed technically—or if completed, is not a commercial success—may yield important benefits to the firm. For example, information may be obtained that will prove useful in connection with other projects.

contractors for the government. One question that is frequently raised by congressmen and others concerning the allocation of federal R and D contracts is whether or not small business is getting its proper share. In the rest of this chapter, we present some information about the opinions of a sample of officers of small R and D firms concerning this and related questions. More specifically, we set forth the views of officers of twenty-two small R and D firms in the Philadelphia area, these firms having been chosen with the assistance of the Small Business Administration. For a variety of reasons, a random sample could not be drawn; but a major effort was made to ensure that the sample was reasonably representative of small R and D firms in the Philadelphia area that have some interest in obtaining government R and D contracts. Intensive interviews were conducted in late 1969 with the president, or other major executive, of each firm.

Table 3.6 shows the field of technology or type of product of each of

TABLE 3.6
Field of Technology or Type of Product of
Each of the Firms in Our Sample

Applied Industrial Chemical Research	Environmental Science and Sanitary Engineering
Custom Electronic Instruments (Medical and Industrial)	Polymer-Related Chemical Research
Automated Systems	Metal Fabrication
Character-Recognition Equipment	Fabricated Rubber Goods
Hydraulics	Telemetry Ground Equipment
Process-Control Electronics	Munitions and Gun-Care Products
Measuring Devices	Strain-Gage Instrumentation
Pressure Measurement	Containers
Systems Analysis	Metal Containers
General Scientific Research	Telemetering Equipment
Cathode Ray Tubes	Applied Ultrasonics

the twenty-two firms whose officers were interviewed. Clearly these enterprises represent a wide range of fields. There is considerable variation in the extent to which they specialize in research and development: About one-third have more than 70 percent of their professional work force engaged in research and development, while almost one-half have less than 30 percent engaged in research and development. They tend to be relatively young firms, about 60 percent having been in existence for ten years or less, and about 25 percent having been in existence for four years or less. They also tend to be quite small; over half employ a total of 100 people or less, and about 40 percent employ a total of 40 or less. On the average, half of their sales go to the federal government, but there is considerable variation among the firms in the extent to which they rely on the federal government as a customer for their goods and services. Nine of the firms currently have no federal R and D contracts at all.

8. Attitude Toward Their Share of Federal Contracts

To what extent do these firms believe that they are getting their fair share of federal research and development contracts? Since small business is sometimes portrayed as very dissatisfied with its share, it is interesting that only 27 percent of the firms think that they are getting less than they should.[11] To some extent, this figure may be somewhat misleading, since a number of these firms have made little or no attempt to get government R and D work: Whether they would continue to be satisfied with their share if they tried harder to get government work is, of course, unknown. On the other hand, however, the percentage of firms that are dissatisfied with their share may be swollen somewhat by the fact that one firm had been in existence for less than a year at the time of the interviews and had not received any contracts of any kind as yet, perhaps in part because insufficient time had elapsed for some of its proposals to be evaluated.

It is interesting to compare the characteristics of the firms that feel they are not getting their fair share of federal R and D contracts with those of firms that think they are getting their fair share. The firms that feel they are getting less than they should tend to be smaller than the others (their median number of employees being 22); they submitted more proposals for federal contracts in 1968 than the others (their median number of proposals being 6); and the percentage of their proposals that were accepted tended to be lower than for the others (their median percentage being 40). Because the sample is relatively small, these differences may not be statistically significant. With regard to age of firm and percent of sales accounted for by the federal government, there is little difference between these firms and the others.[12]

9. Problems in Dealing with Government Agencies

What are the most important problems that the 22 firms believe are present in their dealings with government agencies? First, 40 percent of the firms said that, in too many cases, the agency had—for all practical purposes—already chosen the source before requesting proposals. These

11. The standard error of this percentage would be about 0.1 if this were a random sample. Although there is no way to calculate the standard error here, the reader should be reminded that the results are subject to errors due to sampling.

12. The Department of Defense and NASA were cited most often as agencies that the firms had tried unsuccessfully to do business with. These agencies have the largest budgets, and are probably approached by more firms than other agencies. Thus it is not surprising that they turn down more firms than other agencies.

firms felt strongly that small firms should not be encouraged to spend a considerable amount of time and money to help an agency maintain the appearance of competition. Second, 40 percent of the firms said that there was often insufficient time to respond to requests for proposals. Often, unless a firm had contacts with the agency and knew in advance that a request was going to be made, it would not have time to formulate a proper proposal. Third, 40 percent of the firms said that there was too much paper work, which discourages small firms and which is not necessary in their opinion. The paper work seems geared to the large firm, not the small one.[13] In addition, there was considerable criticism directed at the government's bringing in of "marginal" suppliers, at an alleged bias against small business on the part of government personnel, at unfair use by government of ideas generated by small business, at statements of requirements by government agencies that are too vague and ill-specified, and at the government's patent policies.

Let's look in somewhat more detail at each of the three most frequently mentioned problems. With regard to the nature of the bidding process—which was one of the most frequently mentioned problems—the following quotation from an officer of one firm illustrates the sentiment: "If you are remote from the agencies and don't contact the agencies, and if you look at the *Commerce Business Daily*, you will be looking at unreality. Really the thing is a farce. It is predominantly the case that contracts are 'wired' to particular bidders. There is nothing so bad about this, but why not be more forthright about it? Lots of inefficiency and wasted motion result from the maintenance of this farce."[14] In this connection, it should be noted that, according to their estimates, the average cost of preparing a proposal is in the neighborhood of two thousand dollars for these firms.

As for insufficient time to respond to proposals—another of the most frequently mentioned problems—this quotation from an executive of another firm illustrates the sentiment: "Too little time is given. They fool with these things too long at the point of origin." An executive of still another firm said: "In many cases a contract is slanted to a great extent to a particular company. The government gives you only sixty days to do something that would take a hundred and twenty days for anyone except the favored firm." With regard to the paper-work problem—another of the most frequently mentioned difficulties—many firms complained that although the paper work might be appropriate for larger firms and contracts, it was a very substantial impediment to them.

In the course of analyzing the results, it became apparent that the problems regarded as most important by the larger firms in our sample (those

13. The standard error of each of the percentages quoted in this paragraph would be about 0.1 if this were a random sample.
14. The man speaking was the firm's director of research. The firm is among the larger ones in the sample.

with 100 or more employees) tend to be quite different from those regarded as most important by the smaller firms in our sample (less than 100 employees). Among the smaller firms, the biggest problems seem to be to find out what is going on in various agencies, to make themselves known to the agencies, and to handle the paper work. On the other hand, among the larger firms, these problems do not loom so large. Instead, the larger firms complain that bidders' lists are often too large and that too many "marginal" firms are included, there being inadequate monitoring of technical capability.

10. Suggested Improvements

It is by no means clear that small business is getting too small—or too large—a share of federal R and D contracts. But whatever the case may be, it is of interest to determine how, according to these firms, the government could—if it wanted to—help small business to participate more fully in the competition for federal R and D contracts. The most frequent reply given by the firms was that small business needs earlier and more information concerning agency needs. Big firms can maintain liaison people who keep track of what is going on in various agencies, what the agencies' personnel are interested in, and what the agencies' needs are likely to be. Small firms often are unable to do this. Unless small firms can somehow be acquainted earlier and more accurately with what the agencies want, they cannot compete with the large firms, in the opinion of a great many of the interviewed firms. However, it should be noted once again that the views of the larger firms in the sample differ considerably from those of the smaller ones. Although the smaller firms (those with less than 100 employees) tend to feel that small business needs earlier and more information concerning agency needs, this factor does not seem so important to the larger firms in the sample (those with 100 or more employees). The larger firms seem to feel that they are generally able to obtain the information they need. Apparently, the larger firms are big enough to afford the necessary liaison work.

A number of other suggestions were made by the firms. For example, some said that a major way to increase participation by small business was to simplify and reduce the amount of paper work. (Unfortunately, however, the suggestions did not include any specific recommendations concerning how this objective should be accomplished.) Others suggested that big prime contracts be broken into pieces, and that the government return to cost-plus contracts, which they feel are preferable for small firms because the risks are smaller. Also, there was considerable criticism of the bidding process. Of course, much of this criticism may be self-serving or ill-informed. But it is worthwhile to observe that, based on his studies of military research and development, Roberts[15] has concluded that the social costs of the procurement process are unnecessarily high, due in part to the encouragement of many firms to bid even though they in fact have little or no chance of getting the contract.

11. Summary

The major conclusions of this chapter are as follows: First, quantitative techniques—generally adaptations of well-known capital-budgeting techniques—are used as a guide for project selection by about three-quarters of the laboratories in our sample. The probability of such a technique being used is directly related to the size of the laboratory. The laboratories that presently use such techniques began using them in the fifties and sixties, the bulk of them having adopted this innovation since 1960. The rate of diffusion of this innovation is relatively slow, probably because there is considerable skepticism concerning the usefulness of these techniques.

Second, if a project is technically completed, the probability of its being commercialized is about 55 percent in laboratories X, Y, and Z. For all three laboratories, the probability of commercialization is higher for large and medium technical advances than for small technical advances. Moreover, the probability of commercialization is generally higher for product improvements than for new products and for projects aimed at familiar markets than for those intended for unfamiliar markets. Commercialized projects cost more, on the average, than those that are not commercialized.

Third, if a project is commercialized, the probability of its being a market success—economic profits being earned—is about 40 percent in these laboratories. The probability of market success is higher for large or medium technical advances, new products, and products involving unfamiliar markets than for small technical advances, product improvements, and products involving familiar markets. Combining the probability of technical completion, the probability of commercialization (given technical completion), and the probability of market success (given commercialization), we can estimate the following attrition rates for projects in these laboratories: On the average, for every 100 projects that are begun, 57 projects are completed technically, 31 of those completed are commercialized, and 12 of those commercialized are market successes.

Fourth, about 73 percent of the firms included in our sample of small

15. E. Roberts, "Questioning the Cost-Effectiveness of the R and D Procurement Process," in *Research Program Effectiveness*, ed. by M. Yovits, D. Gilford, R. Wilcox, E. Staveley, and H. Lerner (New York: Gordon and Breach, 1966).

R and D firms in the Philadelphia area feel that they are getting as many government R and D contracts as they reasonably can expect. The three problems in dealing with government agencies that the firms in the sample cite most frequently are bidding where it is felt that the agencies essentially have chosen the source before requesting proposals, insufficient time, and excessive paper work. The problems regarded as most important by the larger firms in our sample (those with 100 or more employees) tend to be quite different from those regarded as most important by the smaller firms in our sample (less than 100 employees). Among the smaller firms, the biggest problems seem to be to find out what is going on in various agencies, to make themselves known, and to handle the paper work. On the other hand, the larger firms complain that bidders' lists are often too long and that too many "marginal" firms are included.

Fifth, to the extent that it is felt that small business should be helped to increase its participation, the government—according to the suggestion made most frequently by the firms—should provide earlier and more information concerning agency needs. Big firms can maintain liaison people who keep track of what is going on in various agencies, what the agencies' personnel are interested in, and what the agencies' needs are likely to be. Small firms are often unable to do this. However, the provision of earlier and more information concerning agency needs was regarded as much more important by the smaller firms in our sample (under 100 employees) than by the larger firms (100 or more employees). Apparently, when a firm reaches an employment level of 100 or more, it is big enough to be able to afford much of the necessary liaison work.

4 THE DETERMINANTS

OF DEVELOPMENT COSTS

1. Introduction

Although a great many studies have been made of the costs of *production* in various firms and industries, there is surprisingly little information concerning the costs of *development*. Even the most basic sorts of data are generally unavailable. For example, we do not have even crude estimates of how much it cost to develop the individual new products that have arisen in recent years in various sectors of the economy. Beyond this, little attempt has been made to test various hypotheses concerning the determinants of development costs. Economists have hypothesized that the cost of developing a new product depends on the size and complexity of the product being developed, the extent of the advance in performance that is sought, the development time, the available stock of knowledge, components, and materials, and the development strategy that is pursued. But there has been little or no attempt to test these hypotheses or provide quantitative estimates of the effects of these or other factors.

In this chapter, we study the determinants of development costs in one large ethical drug firm. The firm allowed us complete access to its internal files, the consequence being that extraordinarily detailed and complete data have been assembled for all of the development projects it carried out during the fifties and early sixties. The analysis in this chapter represents the first econometric investigation of the determinants of commercial development costs.[1] Specifically, several questions will be explored in the chapter. First, we will examine how the characteristics of the product being developed affect development cost. For example, how do development costs vary

1. For some previous discussions of the determinants of development costs, see Edwin Mansfield, *The Economics of Technological Change* (New York: W. W. Norton, 1968); Richard Nelson, Merton Peck and Edward Kalachek, *Technology, Economic Growth, and Public Policy* (Washington, D.C.: The Brookings Institution, 1967); and J. Jewkes, D. Sawers, and R. Stillerman, *The Sources of Invention*, revised edition (New York: W. W. Norton, 1970). For a study of military aircraft, see Thomas Glennan, "Methodological Problems in Evaluating the Effectiveness of Military Aircraft Development," RAND Corporation, P-3357 (May 1966).

between innovative and imitative projects? Does the nature of the new drug and the extent of the technological advance have a significant effect on development costs? How do the number and types of uses for the product influence cost? We will also investigate the role of a second set of variables, which characterize the strategy used to develop the new product. In this regard, we will determine how the priority assigned to the project and the use of parallel development efforts affect development cost. Finally, we will study how development cost changes over time.

2. Description of the Data

The data to be used in this analysis pertain to seventy-five development projects conducted by the firm between 1950 and 1967.[2] All of the development projects were commercialized; that is, they resulted in marketed products. It is important to define development costs as they are used in this firm and industry. A development project is the final stage in the firm's R and D process, which consists of a research program, exploratory investigation, and a development project.[3] Development costs, as they are used here, refer to the costs of product formulation[4] and clinical testing.[5] Although the magnitude of these costs is substantial within the firm, and for the ethical pharmaceutical industry as a whole, they are not all of the R and D costs associated with a particular drug. There are also research-program and exploratory-investigation costs, which can be sizable for certain types of projects. This should be borne in mind in interpreting the results.

2. Most of the projects in the sample were completed prior to 1960. Only nine of the projects were completed between 1960 and 1967. Moreover, only three of the projects were completed after 1962, when some far-reaching amendments to the Food, Drug, and Cosmetic Act were passed. The significance of the sample's time dimension will be explained during the subsequent analysis.

3. Research and exploratory investigations are directed toward the discovery of drugs with desirable biological activity. They are the first stages in the process leading to a new marketed drug product. There is no single generalized approach to the identification of new chemical structures with biological activity. To some extent, knowledge concerning the underlying cause of disease is used, with attempts being made to synthesize drugs which inhibit the appropriate biological process. Often, biological test systems are used to identify the biological effects of diseases. After the new compound and its structural variants have been processed through the biological test system, the most promising version may be selected for development. We are concerned here with development costs.

4. "Product formulation" is a general term used to represent the series of laboratory activities which are required to convert the new chemical compound into a finished drug product. In industry terminology, these activities are often referred to as the "laboratory stage" of drug development. These various activities may be grouped into three categories: (1) determination of toxicity, (2) determination of optimal dosage quantity, and (3) determination of the mode of administration.

5. The final, and perhaps the most important, stage in the development process consists of clinical trials in human patents. Certainly it is the most persuasive phase of the process, since only clinical trials can indicate with the needed assurance that the new drug will accomplish its purpose with an acceptable level of side effects. Clinical trials proceed in three phases. Phase I is carried out by clinical investigation, small doses being tried upon limited numbers of volunteers. In Phase II, the drug is administered to a larger group of patients and for a longer period of time. In Phase III, the new drug is used by fifty or more physicians, the object being to establish the long-term safety and efficacy of the drug.

The De Haen classification[6] of new ethical drugs—into new chemical entities, compounded products, and alternate dosage forms—provides a useful way to distinguish the innovativeness, size, complexity, and technological advance of a development project. What is the definition of each of these project categories? *New chemical entities* are new, single chemical entities not previously known. *Compounded products*—products having more than a single ingredient—combine existing drugs. *Alternate dosage forms* are new forms (tablets, liquids, and so on) for existing products. These three project categories differ greatly with regard to the amount of information that is available concerning a compound when development begins. In particular, less is known about new chemical entities than about compounded products or alternate dosage forms. When development begins, a new chemical entity has never been subjected to large-scale clinical testing. This limited availability of clinical data contrasts markedly with the clinical picture at the beginning of compounded-product and alternate-dosage-form projects. In the case of a compounded product, a sizable body of clinical evidence frequently exists for one or more of the ingredients. Since the development of an alternate dosage form is the process of placing a previously marketed product (new chemical entity or compounded product) in a new dosage form, the scope and depth of clinical data is greatest at the beginning of such a project.

Drug-development projects can be viewed as efforts to systematically gather evidence concerning the performance of a particular compound in humans. The size and complexity of a project is, therefore, inversely related to the amount of accumulated information concerning a compound which exists when development begins. Since the least is known about new chemical entities at the start of a development project, undertakings in this category should generally be the largest and most complex, and require the greatest technological advances. Projects in the compounded-products category should, in turn, rank higher along these dimensions than alternate-dosage-form projects. Therefore, if development cost and time are increasing functions of size, complexity, and degree of technological advance, we would expect projects concerned with new chemical entities to be the most costly and lengthy, with compounded products and alternate dosage forms following, in that order.

In order to test this hypothesis, we grouped the seventy-five projects into the categories of new chemical entities, compounded products, and alternate dosage forms, on the basis of De Haen's classification of the new product developed during the project. Data regarding the mean and standard deviation of the development cost and duration suggest that the hypothesized relationships between the three categories do, in fact, hold for the seventy-

6. Paul de Haen, *Non-Proprietary Name Index,* Vol. VI (1967).

five development projects (Table 4.1).[7] The mean development time and cost for new chemical entities are higher than the mean development time and cost for compounded products, and the mean development time and cost for compounded products are higher than the mean development time and cost for alternate dosage forms. However, although the differences between new chemical entities and the other two categories are statistically significant, the differences between compounded products and alternate dosage forms are not.

TABLE 4.1

*Mean and Standard Deviation of Development Cost
and Development Time, for New Chemical Entities,
Compounded Products, and Alternate Dosage Forms*

TYPE OF PROJECT	NUMBER	COST		DURATION (MONTHS)	
		MEAN	STANDARD DEVIATION	MEAN	STANDARD DEVIATION
New chemical entities	17	$534,141	$499,800	24.8	12.8
Compounded products	29	160,828	223,560	16.4	10.2
Alternate dosage forms	29	83,310	338,200	14.5	7.6
All Projects	75	215,467	332,900	17.6	10.7

In subsequent sections, we shall treat each of these project types—new chemical entities, compounded products, alternate dosage forms—separately, because the nature of the development work differs from one project type to another. For example, product formulation is more important than clinical testing in the development of alternate dosage forms. We would therefore expect variables which affect the extent of product-formulation efforts to be more significant than clinical-testing variables in explaining the magnitude of development costs in this category. The reverse should hold true for new chemical entities. While compounded products should fall somewhere in between these two extremes, we might expect the development process for the firm's compounded products to be closer to that for alternate dosage forms than to that for new chemical entities. This seems reasonable when we consider that some of these compounded products involved the formulation of standard drugs, such as aspirin or phenobarbital, into timed-release capsules. Such products are not considered alternate dosage forms in the De Haen classification because they represent modifica-

7. There may be substantial differences between the figures in Table 4.1 and the present average cost and duration of development projects. In his paper "The Changing Costs and Risks of Pharmaceutical Innovation," in *The Economics of Drug Innovation*, ed. by J. Cooper (American University, 1970), Harold A. Clymer states that the average development time for a new chemical entity is now five to seven years, as compared to two years for our sample. He estimates the average development cost for a new chemical entity at $2.5–$4.5 million, while the average cost in Table 4.1 is $534,141.

tions of competitors' products rather than variations of existing products
marketed by the firm.[8]

3. Nature of the New Drug and the Extent of
the Technological Advance

We turn now to a description of the variables which will be used in a
regression analysis to explain differences in development costs among the
seventy-five development projects. This section describes the variables that
relate to the nature of the new drug and the extent of the technological advance.

Variable 1: Type of Dosage Form / The first variable introduced into the
analysis is the type of dosage form in which the new drug is formulated.
Drugs come in various dosage forms—tablets, liquids, sprays, and so forth.
For the compounded products and alternate dosage forms, dummy variables are used to represent the type of dosage form. The dosage-form categories for the twenty-nine compounded products are tablets, timed capsules,
oral liquids, nasal sprays, and tablets-timed capsules. Alternate dosage
forms are grouped into tablets, timed capsules, oral liquids, suppositories,
and tablets-injectables. The tablets-timed capsules and tablets-injectables
categories indicate that two dosage forms were developed during the project.
We would expect such projects to require greater product-formulation and
clinical-testing efforts than single-dosage-form projects and, hence, development of products in these categories should cost more. Also, development of timed-release capsules should be relatively costly because of the
need to ensure constant dosage release over extended periods of time.

(However, timed-release capsules may not be relatively costly in the

---

8. Some research executives within the firm expressed reservations concerning the
use of the De Haen classification. They contended that many drug products were not clearly
defined by De Haen; indeed, they believed that some of the firm's products were incorrectly classified. We experimented with some alternative categorizations suggested by the firm.
One classification scheme involved creating four categories—new chemical entities, compounded
products, alternate dosage forms, and timed-release capsules. Another alternative involved
eliminating from our sample all projects which the firm considered misclassified in the De Haen
listing. After careful consideration of the alternatives, we decided to use the De Haen classification
without eliminating any projects from our sample. We made this decision for the following
reasons: First, there is the important issue of the objectivity of our results. While the De Haen
classification is certainly not free of problems, it is widely accepted and used in the ethical
pharmaceutical industry. The classification of all new drug products is made by an objective and
independent third party. The availability of this uniform classification system makes it possible
to replicate our study in other ethical pharmaceutical firms as well as to replicate it at a future
date with new development-cost data. Second, we concluded that, of all the classifications suggested, the De Haen scheme was superior in providing interclass heterogeneity and intraclass
homogeneity. For this reason we rejected classification on the basis of dosage category. Third, we
reasoned that elimination of a substantial number of projects from our sample, as suggested by
the firm, would not provide a fair test of the models. In suggesting elimination of these projects,
the firm cited various "exceptional" characteristics of the projects. However, the independent
variables included in the model, such as technological advance, dosage category, and product
category, are designed to deal with such "exceptions."

case of compounded products: As noted earlier, a number of compounded products which were formulated in timed-release capsules involved the formulation of standard drugs, such as aspirin or phenobarbital, into this dosage form. Since these products had been marketed by other drug firms for some time, more knowledge concerning them was available at the start of development. The availability of this knowledge could make the development process for timed-release projects easier and cheaper than that for other projects in the compounded-product category.)

The dosage-form variable is included in the new-chemical-entity regression equation in a different manner. Since a number of the projects in this category involved more than one dosage form, it seemed more appropriate to use a variable measuring the number of dosage forms, rather than dummy variables. In the case of new chemical entities, the development of multiple dosage forms requires additional clinical work to demonstrate the equivalence of different dosage forms of the same product. We would therefore expect the cost of developing a new chemical entity to increase as the number of dosage forms increases.[9]

Variable 2: Product Category / A second variable which should influence the cost of developing a new drug is the product category represented by the drug. The precise nature of the clinical trials and product-formulation activities performed during the development project depends on the product category of the drug being developed. For example, the clinical study of an analgesic designed to eliminate mild-to-moderate pain can be considerably more complex than the evaluation of other types of drugs, the measurement of degrees of pain in human subjects being a particularly difficult task. Moreover, clinical studies designed to prove that the drug lacks addiction liability could take three to four years. Differences also exist among product areas with respect to the magnitude of product-formulation problems. In some areas, formulation problems may prove more difficult than clinical trials. For example, vitamins and hematinics, although relatively easy to evaluate clinically, pose formidable problems in the laboratory. Some multiple-vitamin products consist of ten different ingredients which must be carefully combined, while hematinics are frequently liquids with accompanying stability problems.

To determine if there are significant differences in development cost between product categories, the seventy-five development projects were classified on the basis of the system employed in the 1966 Census report entitled "The Value of Shipments of Pharmaceutical Preparations."[10] This

---

9. Of course, we could use dummy variables to represent whether or not each dosage form and each combination of dosage forms were required. But this would necessitate the inclusion of six variables plus the constant, with a resulting thinness of data in the dosage-form categories.

10. U.S. Department of Commerce, *Current Industrial Reports, Pharmaceutical Preparations, Except Biologicals* (1965).

system uses ten product categories, each of which is a five-digit SIC class. Five of these classes were needed to classify the firm's projects:

SIC 28342—pharmaceutical preparations acting on the central nervous system and the sense organs
SIC 28344—pharmaceutical preparations acting on the respiratory system
SIC 28345—pharmaceutical preparations acting on the digestive or the genitourinary system
SIC 28347—vitamin, nutrient, and hematinic preparations
SIC 28348—pharmaceutical preparations acting on parasitic and infective diseases

Dummy variables are used to represent the product category for each development project. Four dummy variables plus the constant are needed to represent the product categories of the seventy-five projects.

Of these five classes, central-nervous-system drugs (SIC 28342) are typically the most difficult to evaluate clinically. Vitamins and hematinics (SIC 28347) tend to require the largest product-formulation efforts. We would therefore expect central-nervous-system drugs to be the most expensive new chemical entities and vitamins and hematinics to be the most costly alternate dosage forms. If the development of compounded products is, in fact, very similar to that of alternate dosage forms, then vitamins and hematinics should also be the most costly product class among the compounded products.

Variable 3: Spectrum of Activity / The third variable measures the spectrum of activity of the drug being developed. The term "spectrum of activity" refers to the range of a drug's biological activity. The broader the spectrum of activity of a drug, the greater the number of therapeutic markets for it. Within each five-digit SIC product category, there are ten to twenty-five seven-digit classes. These seven-digit classes correspond to the standard therapeutic-market definitions adopted by firms and market-research agencies in the ethical pharmaceutical industry in 1957. As an example, the SIC class of central-nervous-system and sense-organ drugs includes, among others, the tranquilizer market, the analgesic market, the sedative and hypnotic market, and the general-anesthetic market.

While each new product is categorized into only one five-digit SIC class, it is possible for a product to compete in more than one therapeutic market within that SIC product category. For example, some products which are primarily promoted as diuretics are also marketed as antihypertensives. Some major tranquilizers derive a substantial portion of their total sales from the distinct nausea and vomiting market. In each case where a product is introduced into two or more distinct therapeutic markets, the efficacy and safety of the product must be established in the separate markets. Since the clinical cost component of drug development depends on the scope and extent of clinical trials, we would expect development costs to be higher for multiple-market products. Therefore, a dummy variable to indicate development for more than one therapeutic market was used for new chemical entities and compounded products.

While several of the alternate-dosage-form projects were modifications of multiple-market new chemical entities, the spectrum-of-activity variable was not considered relevant for alternate dosage forms. Usually, the alternate dosage form or product strength was developed with only one therapeutic market in mind. For example, a higher strength of a product which was marketed as both a tranquilizer and an antinauseant would be specifically designed to compete in the mental-hospital segment of the tranquilizer market. Even in those cases where an alternate dosage form was to be used in two therapeutic markets, the limited magnitude of all clinical efforts during alternate-dosage-form projects made it inappropriate to include this variable.

Variable 4: Technological-Advance Score / The magnitude of the technological advance sought in the development project is a fourth determinant of development cost. Projects which attempt large advances in the state of the art are characterized by more uncertainty than projects which seek less ambitious advances. During the course of development, money must be expended to reduce these uncertainties. Therefore, we would expect costs to be higher for projects that seek substantial technological advances. To test this proposition, a rough rating was made of the extent of the technological advance sought for each of the seventy-five projects in our sample. A survey of a number of experienced project administrators and scientists was conducted in which each respondent was asked to rate subjectively the magnitude of the improvement in the state of the art sought in each of the development projects. The survey results were then consolidated into a set of technological-advance scores which comprise the fourth variable in the three regressions.[11]

We would expect considerable differences in technological-advance score among the projects in the three categories. New chemical entities generally involve greater technological advances than compounded products, which, in turn, are more advanced than alternate dosage forms. Data on the mean and standard deviation of the technological-advance score for each category (Table 4.2) confirm that differences among the three project

11. The respondents were asked to rate the state-of-the-art advance represented by each development project on a five-point scale whose end points were "very much" (rating = 5.0) and "not at all" (rating = 1.0). The technological-advance score for each project was obtained by averaging all respondent ratings for the project. Essentially, this procedure is similar to that used by Peck and Scherer and by Summers. See Merton Peck and F. M. Scherer, *The Weapons Acquisition Process* (Cambridge: Harvard University Press, 1962) and Thomas Marschak, Thomas Glennan, and Robert Summers, *Strategy for R and D* (New York: Springer-Verlag), 1967.

TABLE **4.2**

Mean and Standard Deviation of
Technological-Advance Scores, for New Chemical Entities,
Compounded Products, and Alternate Dosage Forms

	TECHNOLOGICAL-ADVANCE SCORE	
PROJECT CATEGORY	MEAN	STANDARD DEVIATION
New chemical entities	3.16	0.88
Compounded products	2.13	.78
Alternate dosage forms	2.03	.74
All Projects	2.33	.90

groupings do, in fact, exist. The mean technological-advance score for new chemical entities is significantly higher than the mean technological-advance scores for compounded products and alternate dosage forms at the 5-percent level. However, as in Table 4.1, the difference between compounded products and alternate dosage forms is not statistically significant.

4. Development Strategy and Calendar Time

This section will describe three additional variables employed to explain the variations in development cost among the seventy-five projects. The fifth and sixth variables are used to characterize the development strategies utilized during the projects. The final variable attempts to measure how development costs have changed over time.

Variable 5: Parallel Development Efforts / The first of the development-strategy variables is a dummy variable indicating whether parallel development efforts were employed in the project. The use of parallel development efforts has received considerable attention in previous studies of military-aircraft development. For example, Nelson suggests that parallel development efforts are desirable in those projects where estimates of cost, time, and performance are subject to great uncertainty at the outset and become more reliable as development proceeds.[12] Research programs may well be the phase of this firm's research process where parallel strategies are most applicable. Certainly, during research the magnitude of the uncertainty is of a different order than at the start of development. The use of parallel strategies in a research program would imply the use of alternate sets of

12. See R. Nelson, "Uncertainty, Learning, and the Economics of Parallel Research and Development Efforts," *Review of Economics and Statistics* (1961) and B. Klein, "The Decision Making Problem in Development," in *The Rate and Direction of Inventive Activity* (National Bureau of Economic Research, 1962).

screening tests or the combination of theoretical and empirical approaches within the same research program. If parallel strategies are at all applicable for development projects, they should be most appropriate for new chemical entities. The uncertainties of cost, time, and performance are undoubtedly greatest for this category.

One type of parallel effort used in development pertains to the product which competes in more than one therapeutic market. In such an instance, separate sets of clinical studies must be designed to demonstrate the effectiveness and safety of the product in each distinct market. These studies may be conducted in parallel or, alternatively, the most promising market may be selected initially, with other studies to follow. Parallel strategies are also used when there is considerable uncertainty concerning the most effective strength or dosage form of a product after the limited clinical testing of the exploratory-investigation stage. In the parallel projects, separate sets of clinical studies and pre-market surveys are conducted on the strengths or dosage forms under consideration. For example, in the case of a drug where substantial variation exists between the biological activity of the tablet and of the capsule dosage forms, the original project to develop the drug may be conducted as two parallel subprojects.

During the development of compounded products, major questions concerning product strength often have to be resolved. In cases where two products are being combined, several alternatives exist for the combination ratio (e.g., 2:1 or 3:2). A parallel approach places the ratios in concurrent clinical studies. This may be contrasted with a "serial" approach, which selects the "best" ratio or dosage form for extended clinical studies and a pre-market survey. If problems develop with the stability of the dosage form, or the frequency of side effects is greater than anticipated, new studies are established for the product in a more stable dosage form or lower strength.

Finally, two additional points should be noted concerning our treatment of parallel efforts. First, although we distinguish between projects where parallel efforts are used and projects where they are not, it should be recognized that this characterization ignores a further question of importance: If parallel efforts are carried out, how many such efforts are used? For simplicity, this aspect of the firm's strategy has been ignored. Second, to a certain extent, a parallel research and development strategy may entail parallelism among several development projects of the sort considered here, as well as parallelism of efforts within each such project.

Variable 6: Project Priority / The second development-strategy variable is a dummy variable which describes the priority assigned to the development project. In the drug firm which we studied, when the development blueprint for a project was presented to the firm's Research and Development Executive Committee, a priority was assigned to the project by the committee. For the most part, this priority rating reflected the potential significance of the new product in terms of future profits and competitive considerations. For example, if it was known that other drug companies were completing development of drugs in the same therapeutic market, a premium was generally placed on being first to the market. Two priority ratings, A and B, could be assigned. An A priority meant that all efforts should be devoted to marketing the project as early as possible, whereas a B priority indicated that the product's marketing date was not that important. Operationally, the priority rating was interpreted to mean that nothing could interfere with the progress of A-priority projects, while B priority projects could be interrupted to meet the demands of A-priority projects or other pressing work, such as exploratory investigation or research programs.

We might expect A-priority projects to cost more than B-priority projects for two reasons. First, those projects which were regarded as more significant from the standpoint of the market tended to be bigger and more complex than those with less of a potential marketing impact. Second, we might expect development costs to be higher for A-priority projects than for B-priority projects because development costs might have been increased in order to reduce development time. Observers who have studied these time-cost trade-offs contend that, within a certain range, development time can be decreased only by increasing total cost.[13]

Variable 7: Calendar Year / The changes in development cost over time will be examined by including the calendar year in which the project commenced (minus 1950) as the seventh variable. We would expect development costs to increase with time for several reasons. First, there is the general rise in the cost of doing business that occurred during the 1950–1967 period. Therefore, even if the nature of the drug-development task remained constant over time, development costs would rise due to the increases in equipment and material costs and in salaries for scientists, technicians, and supporting personnel. One study of the increasing cost of R and D indicates that a dollar spent on R and D in 1958 purchased only 57 percent of the amount purchased in 1950.[14] The nature of the drug-

---

13. For a more detailed discussion of this relationship, see Peck and Scherer, *op. cit.*, and F. M. Scherer, "Government Research and Development Programs," in *Measuring Benefits of Government Expenditures,* ed. by R. Dorfman (Washington, D.C.: The Brookings Institution, 1965). More will be said on this score in Chapters 6 and 7.

14. See E. A. Johnson and H. S. Milton, "A Proposed Cost-of-Research Index," *IRE Transactions on Engineering Management* (December, 1961). The authors develop the following cost-of-research index, using 1950 as the base year:

1950—100	1954—139	1957—165
1951—109	1955—139	1958—176
1952—123	1956—151	1959—183
1953—126		1960—191

They suggest that the sources of these cost increases are rises in overhead, scientific salaries, skilled wages, and equipment and material costs, in that order.

development task has, however, changed dramatically during this time period. In particular, advances in knowledge of drug action and increased technical sophistication have resulted in clinical investigations that are more intensive and broader in scope. One veteran industry research executive has noted: "We do more today in proving the effectiveness and safety of a potential drug than in the past, the greatest change having occurred during the past five years. The processes of a decade ago for taking potential drugs to the clinic and releasing new drugs to the physician have changed."[15]

Ethical pharmaceutical firms have also changed their objectives somewhat. Increasingly, firms have focused their research and development efforts on the search for therapeutic breakthroughs rather than improvements of existing therapy.[16] This shift in research strategy results in a more complex and costly process for discovering and developing new drugs. In addition, the drug-development process has been significantly affected by the 1962 amendments to the Food, Drug, and Cosmetic Act.[17] Several observers have attributed decreases in new drug products, decreases in the number of drugs in clinical trials, and increases in the costs and risks of drug development to these amendments.[18] It is important to emphasize that only three of the seventy-five projects in our sample were completed after the passage of the 1962 amendments. Consequently, we are not in a position to measure, with any accuracy, whatever increase in costs occurred in response to the 1962 amendments.

In summary, we hypothesize that development costs have increased over time due to the rising costs of doing business and the more complex

15. Max Tischler and R. G. Denkewalter, "Drug Research—Whence and Whither," in *Progress in Drug Research,* ed. by Ernest Jucker (Basel, Switzerland, 1966), p. 12.

16. Schmookler provides some interesting comments in this regard. In speculating on the causes of a decline in inventive activity in certain fields, he notes that the decline may not be due to cost factors; instead, inventive activity in a field may decline because the value of another invention in the field begins to decrease. He cites the case of horseshoe inventions, noting that they only began to decline when their value decreased because of the reduction in the use of horses. This latter factor probably explains why drug firms now seek breakthroughs rather than relatively minor product improvements in some fields. It is not that the minor improvements are prohibitively expensive, but rather that the value of minor improvements in many product categories has decreased. See J. Schmookler, *Invention and Economic Growth* (Boston: Harvard University Press, 1962).

The dramatic increase in development costs in the twentieth century has been noted by Jewkes, Sawers, and Stillerman. They identify two sets of factors—market and technical—which are responsible for these cost increases. The market factors they identify seem most relevant to the situation in the ethical pharmaceutical industry. One such market factor is the rapid technical progress which results in one invention's supplanting another. A second market factor which they identify is management's greater caution in confirming the quality and reliability of a new invention before introducing it to an increasingly sophisticated market. See Jewkes, Sawers, and Stillerman, *op. cit.*

17. Two major changes resulted from these 1962 amendments to the Food, Drug, and Cosmetic Act. First, manufacturers were now required to prove the efficacy of new drug products, in addition to their safety, before marketing. Second, the Food and Drug Administration was provided with the authority to oversee the clinical-testing phase of drug development. Manufacturers were now required to obtain approval before beginning clinical trials, through submission of an Investigational New Drug (IND) application. See "Clinical Testing: Synopsis of the New Drug Regulations," *FDA Papers* (March 1967), pp. 21–25.

18. See, for example, B. H. Minchew, "Problems and Trends in IND and NDA Preparation and Review," a paper presented to the PMA Research and Development Section Annual Meeting, October 20–23, 1968; and Harold A. Clymer, "The Changing Costs and Risks of Pharmaceutical Innovation," *op. cit.*

development procedures. The sample of post-1962 projects is, however, too limited to be a basis for valid conclusions with regard to the impact of the 1962 amendments to the Food, Drug, and Cosmetic Act. Since new chemical entities require the most extensive clinical investigations, the cost increases produced by more extensive clinical trials should be greatest for this class of development projects. Similarly, cost increases over time for compounded products should exceed those for alternate dosage forms.

5. Results of Regressions

Separate regression equations based on the variables in sections 3 and 4 were run for new chemical entities, compounded products, and alternate dosage forms. The results are shown in Table 4.3. In each category the regression appears to explain the observed variation in development cost quite well, $\bar{R}^2$ being 0.88 for new chemical entities, 0.72 for compounded products, and 0.76 for alternate dosage forms.[19] In part, of course, these high correlations may be due to the fact that the data pertain to only one firm. However, not all of the independent variables turn out to be statistically significant. Among new chemical entities, the number of dosage forms and the calendar year are significant variables. For compounded products, the type of dosage form, the product category, the spectrum of activity, the technological-advance score, the use of parallel development efforts, and the calendar year are significant. In the case of alternate dosage forms, all seven variables are statistically significant.

Why are fewer of the independent variables statistically significant in the case of new chemical entities than in the case of compounded products or alternate dosage forms? There is first the matter of sample size. The new-chemical-entity sample of seventeen projects is smaller than the compounded-product and alternate-dosage-form samples, each of which contains twenty-nine projects. A second explanation is that project characteristics that we have not measured—such as the available stock of knowledge at the beginning of the development phase—are likely to vary more from project to project and to be more important in explaining the variations in cost among new-chemical-entity projects. Finally, there is likely to be a bigger random component in the development of projects which are larger, more complex, and attempt greater technological advances. That is, pure chance may play a more critical role in the development of new chemical entities than it does for compounded products and alternate dosage forms.

---

19. In interpreting the regression results in Table 4.3, note that many of the type-of-dosage-form and type-of-product dummy variables were omitted after they were found not to be significant. The other variables that were excluded—such as, in the case of new chemical entities, which dosage form was being developed—were excluded because they were inappropriate, or for reasons given above.

TABLE 4.3

Regression Coefficients, Regression of Development Cost on Selected Project Characteristics, for New Chemical Entities, Compounded Products, and Alternate Dosage Forms

INDEPENDENT VARIABLES[a]

TYPE OF PROJECT	NUMBER OF DOSAGE FORMS	TYPE OF DOSAGE FORM		PRODUCT CATEGORY		TECHNO-LOGICAL ADVANCE SCORE	PARALLEL EFFORTS	PROJECT PRIORITY	CALENDAR YEAR	CONSTANT	$\bar{R}^2$	DEGREES OF FREEDOM
		TIMED-RELEASE CAPSULES	TABLETS-INJECT-ABLES	VITAMINS AND HEMATINICS	SPECTRUM OF ACTIVITY							
New chemical entities	139.1 (1.91)	—	—	—	6.24 (0.04)	72.7 (0.94)	−44.2 (−0.37)	54.9 (0.38)	100.2 (5.86)	−341.6 (−1.18)	0.88	10
Compounded products	—	−123.9 (−2.28)	—	109.7 (1.99)	424.2 (4.51)	69.6 (2.11)	163.0 (2.92)	−8.5 (−0.13)	27.6 (3.37)	−150.4 (−1.41)	0.72	21
Alternate dosage forms	—	106.5 (2.66)	226.3 (3.49)	53.6 (1.83)	—	35.9 (2.92)	107.8 (3.33)	85.7 (2.28)	7.15 (2.34)	−131.3 (−2.83)	0.76	21

[a] *t* values are shown in parentheses.

6. Empirical Results: Nature of the New Drug and Extent of the Technological Advance

Let us turn to a discussion of the individual regression coefficients. The coefficients of the dosage-form, product-category, and spectrum-of-activity variables indicate that these factors do influence development cost, at least in most project categories. Development cost increases with the number of dosage forms, and projects with broad spectra of activity (i.e., projects which develop multiple-market products) cost more than projects with narrow spectra of activity (i.e., projects which develop single-market products). This, of course, is in line with the hypotheses set forth in previous sections.

The size of these differences is interesting. According to the results, each additional dosage form in the new-chemical-entity category increases development cost by about $140,000. The results concerning the type of dosage form suggest that it is inappropriate to generalize regarding the cost relationships among dosage forms without considering the particular project category. For alternate dosage forms, the multiple-dosage form—tablets-injectables—is most costly (about $225,000 greater than tablets or liquids); and timed-release capsules, while less expensive than tablets-injectables, cost about $105,000 more than other single-dosage forms. On the other hand, for compounded products, timed-release capsules cost $125,000 less than all other dosage forms. This occurs because several timed-release compounded products involve the formulation of standard drugs, such as aspirin or phenobarbital, in this dosage form. Since these products had been marketed by other drug firms for some time, more knowledge concerning these drugs was available at the start of development. Development was therefore easier and cheaper for these projects.

Vitamins and hematinics show up as $110,000 more expensive than other product categories among compounded products and $55,000 more expensive than other product categories among alternate dosage forms. Since this product category is marked by substantial product-formulation activity, these results lend support to the view that product formulation is relatively more important in the development process for compounded products and alternate dosage forms than it is for new chemical entities.[20] The results for the spectrum-of-activity dummy variable show that, among compounded products, broad-spectrum projects cost $420,000 more than narrow-spectrum projects.

Next, let's turn to the technological-advance variable. The regression coefficient for the technological-advance score is significant for both com-

---

20. Contrary to our hypothesis in section 3, central-nervous-system drugs do not turn out to be significantly more expensive than other new chemical entities.

pounded products and alternate dosage forms. These results, together with the correct sign for new chemical entities, indicate that projects attempting large advances in the state of the art cost more than less ambitious projects. This, of course, is in line with previous studies—and with what one would expect.[21] Note that the regression coefficients of the technological-advance scores for new chemical entities and compounded products are approximately twice that for alternate dosage forms. This means that the maximum possible expected cost difference between the most-advanced (technological-advance score equal to 5.0) and least-advanced (technological-advance score equal to 1.0) new chemical entity or compounded product is $280,000–$290,000, while the maximum possible cost differential of this type for alternate dosage forms is about $145,000.

We should note the roughness of the technological-advance score as a measure of the degree of technological advance attempted by a project. One difficulty is that respondents in our survey may have based their responses on the cost of the development project, reasoning that a more expensive project probably involved a greater technological advance. If this were the case, our technological-advance scores would be a function of development costs rather than vice versa. Because this possibility exists, we investigated the effects of omitting this variable from the three regressions. The results are presented in Table 4.4. Fortunately, the omission of the technological-advance score produces no major change in the explanatory power of the three regressions or in the value and significance of the other regression coefficients (although the regression coefficient of the vitamin-and-hematinic dummy variable is no longer statistically significant in both the compounded-product and alternate-dosage-form categories).

7. Empirical Results: Development Strategy and Calendar Time

In this section, we discuss the empirical results concerning the effects of development strategy and calendar time. The results concerning the effects on costs of using parallel development efforts are quite interesting. As hypothesized, it turns out that parallel development efforts are more likely to reduce costs for new chemical entities than for compounded products or alternate dosage forms. The effect of this variable is statistically significant among compounded products and alternate dosage forms, where parallel efforts appear to increase development costs by about $165,000 and $110,000, respectively. Parallel efforts appear to decrease costs by about $45,000 among new chemical entities, but this effect is not statistically significant. Of course, these results do not necessarily imply that in these

21. Marschak, Glennan, and Summers, *op. cit.*

TABLE 4.4

Regression Coefficients, Regression of Development Cost on Selected Project Characteristics (Omitting Technological-Advance Score), for New Chemical Entities, Compounded Products, and Alternate Dosage Forms

INDEPENDENT VARIABLES[a]

TYPE OF PROJECT	NUMBER OF DOSAGE FORMS	TYPE OF DOSAGE FORM		PRODUCT CATEGORY		PARALLEL EFFORTS	PROJECT PRIORITY	CALENDAR YEAR	CONSTANT	$\overline{R}^2$	DEGREES OF FREEDOM
		TIMED-RELEASE CAPSULES	TABLETS-INJECTABLES	VITAMINS AND HEMATINICS	SPECTRUM OF ACTIVITY						
New chemical entities	123.5 (1.75)	—	—	—	111.4 (1.03)	−86.8 (−0.79)	−33.6 (−0.30)	99.5 (5.85)	−88.4 (−0.81)	0.88	11
Compounded products	—	−106.9 (−1.85)	—	86.2 (1.49)	409.7 (4.05)	132.5 (2.28)	−43.1 (−0.65)	30.8 (3.57)	9.98 (0.12)	0.68	22
Alternate dosage forms	—	117.1 (2.54)	221.5 (2.95)	33.5 (1.0)	—	105.3 (2.81)	76.8 (1.77)	6.99 (1.98)	−53.5 (−1.2)	0.68	22

[a] *t* values are shown in parentheses.

projects the use of parallel development efforts for compounded products and alternate dosage forms was unwise. While parallel efforts increased development costs in these categories, the use of this strategy may have reduced development time or enhanced the quality of the product. Unfortunately, our data do not permit us to test this hypothesis.

Let's turn next to the effect of project priority on development cost. The results concerning the effects of project priority are surprising. In terms of the concept of time-cost trade-offs, we would expect A-priority projects to cost more than B-priority projects. The regressions suggest the opposite. While the coefficient of the variable representing project priority is only significant for alternate dosage forms, the signs are in the wrong direction for both new chemical entities and alternate dosage forms. The difficulties associated with the use of this priority variable in this context permit only the most tentative of explanations. However, if we accept the existence of the development possibility curve, such as that shown in Figure 4.1,[22] our results can perhaps be explained by assuming that B-priority projects

FIGURE **4.1**

Development Possibility Curve

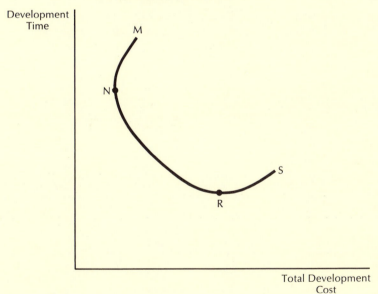

Source: F. M. Scherer, "Government Research and Development Programs," in *Measuring Benefits of Government Expenditures,* ed. by R. Dorfman (Washington, D.C.: The Brookings Institution, 1965).

22. Scherer, *op. cit.,* p. 35. For some estimates of time-cost trade-off functions and an extended discussion of this topic, see Chapters 6 and 7.

operate on the *NM* portion of the curve.[23] In other words, such projects are carried out so slowly that important economies are lost. This assumption seems plausible when we consider that B-priority projects are frequently interrupted by the demands of higher-priority work. Another possibility is that B-priority projects are inefficiently carried out and that these projects lie above and to the right of the curve. Our results are interesting in that they imply that, if this firm is at all typical, a greater number of commercial R and D projects operate on the *NM* portion of the development possibility curve (or are off the curve) than had previously been supposed.[24]

Finally, we turn now to the effects of the calendar year on development cost. The coefficient of the calendar-year variable is highly significant in each category. As hypothesized, the annual cost increases for new chemical entities exceed those for compounded products and alternate dosage forms; the average annual increases in the three categories are about $100,000, $30,000, and $7,000, respectively.[25] These results provide new documentation of the dramatic increases in drug-development costs in recent years.[26] The cost-of-research index developed by Milton and Johnson for all industries as a whole suggests that costs for the same technical effort were 191 percent as great in 1960 as they were in 1950 (see footnote 14). To compare the increase in drug-development costs to this index, we selected a development project in each project category with representative characteristics, and holding these characteristics constant, we examined the cost increases between 1950 and 1960.[27] The results show that the ratio between 1960 and 1950 drug-development costs is 1,100:100 for new chemical

23. To estimate the development possibility curve, we would want to vary the way the development is carried out and observe the relationship between total development time and total development cost. We have not done this here, but estimates of roughly this sort are presented in Chapters 6 and 7 for several other industries.

24. However, the results in Chapters 6 and 7 do not suggest that this is the typical case. None of the projects studied there are on the *NM* portion of the curve. For a further discussion of this subject see Scherer, *op. cit.*, p. 36; and Scott C. Daubin, "The Allocation of Development Funds: An Analytic Approach," *Naval Research Logistics Quarterly* (September 1953), p. 263.

25. Earlier we noted that some observers contend that the 1962 amendments to the Food, Drug, and Cosmetic Act have substantially increased development cost. We noted that since only three of our seventy-five projects were completed after 1962 it was highly unlikely that we could draw any conclusions in this regard. We investigated the coefficient of the calendar-year variable when these three projects were omitted from the analysis. Since there were no post-1962 projects in the alternate-dosage-form category, these results were unchanged. When the three post-1962 projects were eliminated from the other two project categories, the average annual cost increase was $76,700 for new chemical entities and $22,400 for compounded products.

26. Jewkes, Sawers, and Stillermann, *op. cit.* provide an interesting discussion for the economy as a whole.

27. The characteristics of the projects selected for this comparison were as follows: For new chemical entities, we selected a project with two dosage forms, a broad spectrum of activity, a technological-advance score of 3.2, parallel development efforts, and an A priority. For compounded products, we selected a project with a tablet dosage form, a narrow spectrum of activity, a vitamin and hematinic product category, a technological-advance score of 2.1, parallel development efforts, and an A priority. For alternate dosage forms, we selected a project with a tablet dosage form, a vitamin and hematinic product category, a technological-advance score of 2.0, parallel development efforts, and an A priority.

entities, 202:100 for compounded products, and 170:100 for alternate dosage forms. Of course, these ratios for changing drug-development costs are not really comparable to the figures in the Milton-Johnson index because, in addition to cost increases for the same technical effort, they reflect changes in the nature of the drug-development task. The comparison does, however, highlight the dramatic increase in development costs for new chemical entities during this period.

8. Forecasts of Drug-Development Costs

How useful are the models in Table 4.3 for forecasting drug-development costs? In the case of forty-nine of the projects in our sample (thirteen new chemical entities, twenty-three compounded products, thirteen alternate dosage forms), we were able to obtain development-cost estimates prepared by the firm at the outset of each of the projects. These estimates are discussed in detail in Chapter 5.[28] The four most recent projects in each of the three project categories were separated from the forty-nine-project sample, and the three multiple-regression equations were fitted to the reduced sample (nine new chemical entities, nineteen compounded products, and nine alternate dosage forms). The resulting regression equations were then used to "forecast" development costs for the twelve projects separated from the sample.

The accuracy of the twelve model-generated "forecasts" was compared to the accuracy of the estimates prepared by the firm. The comparison is presented in Table 4.5. In order to compare the "forecasted" development costs with actual development costs, a cost factor

$$\left(\text{Cost Factor} = \frac{\text{Actual Development Cost}}{\text{Estimated Development Cost}}\right)$$ was computed. The average,

standard deviation, and root-mean-square deviation from 1 of the cost factors were calculated for both sets of "forecasts." Using the root-mean-square deviation from 1 as an overall measure of forecasting accuracy, we conclude that the model-generated "forecasts" are much more accurate than the firm-generated estimates for new chemical entities. For compounded products, the model's estimates are somewhat more accurate than the firm's, while the opposite is true for alternate dosage forms. Thus, this rough experiment does suggest that models of the type developed here may hold promise for forecasting development costs. However, we should emphasize that our model would require extensive refinement and testing before it could be used for this purpose.

28. For some data regarding the accuracy of these estimates, see Tables 5.1 and 5.2.

TABLE 4.5

*Parameters of Distribution of the Ratio of Actual
to Estimated Cost, Model-Generated and Firm-Generated
Forecasts, for Twelve Development Projects*

TYPE OF PROJECT AND STATISTIC	MODEL FORECASTS	FIRM FORECASTS
New chemical entities		
Mean	1.08	2.62
Standard deviation	0.03	0.51
Root-mean-square deviation from 1	0.03	1.70
Percent of cases where ratio exceeds 1	100	75
Number of projects	4	4
Compounded products		
Mean	0.64	1.39
Standard deviation	0.02	0.04
Root-mean-square deviation from 1	0.48	0.55
Percent of cases where ratio exceeds 1	0	75
Number of projects	4	4
Alternate dosage forms		
Mean	2.19	2.03
Standard deviation	1.26	0.81
Root-mean-square deviation from 1	2.06	1.46
Percent of cases where ratio exceeds 1	75	100
Number of projects	4	4

9. Summary

This chapter reports the findings of an econometric study of the determinants of development cost within one large ethical drug firm in 1950–67. Three categories of development projects—new chemical entities, compounded products, and alternate dosage forms—are examined. The major results are as follows: First, regression equations using as independent variables the dosage form, product category, spectrum of activity, and technological advance of drug-development projects; the development strategy used during the projects; and the calendar year, can explain a substantial portion of the observed variation in development costs. Moreover, in the case of compounded products and alternate dosage forms, most of these variables are statistically significant.

Second, there are interesting differences in the results for the three types of development projects—new chemical entities, compounded products, and alternate dosage forms. For example, fewer of the independent variables are statistically significant in the case of new chemical entities than in the case of compounded products or alternate dosage forms. This may be due to several factors, including the smaller sample size for new chemical entities. Also, pure chance may play a more critical role in the development of new chemical entities than it does for compounded products and alternate dosage forms.

Third, when we compare the accuracy of "forecasts" generated by the models with the accuracy of estimates of development cost prepared at the outset of each project by the firm, we find that the model-generated "forecasts" are much more accurate than the firm's forecasts for new chemical entities. For compounded products, the model's figures are somewhat more accurate than the firm's, but the reverse is true for alternate dosage forms. While this comparison is crude, it does suggest that models of the type developed here may hold promise for forecasting development costs. We emphasize, however, that our models would require extensive refinement and testing before they could be used for this purpose.

Fourth, when we compare the development cost and development time for the three project categories, we find that the development of innovative products (new chemical entities) is a longer and more costly process than the development of more imitative products (compounded products and alternate dosage forms). The average cost of projects in the former category was $534,141, while compounded products and alternate dosage forms cost an average of $160,828 and $83,310, respectively. The average length of the three types of projects was 24.8, 16.4, and 14.5 months, respectively. Within each of the project categories higher technological advance leads to higher development cost. Of course, our measure of technological advance is extremely rough.

Fifth, when we consider the effects of development strategy, we find that parallel development efforts are more likely to reduce costs for new chemical entities than for compounded products or alternate dosage forms. These results seem to support the contention that parallel efforts are most appropriate where estimates of cost, time, and performance are very uncertain, which is the case for new chemical entities. However, parallel efforts may have reduced development time or enhanced the quality of the product in the case of compounded products and alternate dosage forms. Time-cost trade-offs are considered by using the priority attached to a project as an independent variable. The results are not what one might expect; B-priority projects cost more than A-priority projects. The most reasonable explanation for this result seems to be that B-priority projects are carried out so slowly that important economies are lost. Finally, there has been a considerable increase in development costs over time, this increase being due largely to more complex development procedures and the general increase in the cost of doing business.

5 OVERRUNS AND ERRORS

IN ESTIMATING DEVELOPMENT COST,

TIME, AND OUTCOME

1. Introduction

In recent years, cost and time overruns in military development have made the front pages of newspapers. Long before these overruns reached the headlines, economists were interested in them. For example, studies carried out by the RAND Corporation in the late fifties showed that there were substantial errors in the estimates (made prior to development) of the costs of producing various types of military hardware. When adjusted for unanticipated changes in factor prices and production lot-sizes, the average ratios of actual to estimated cost were 1.7 (fighters), 3.0 (bombers), 1.2 (cargoes and tankers), and 4.9 (missiles). The extent to which costs were understated was directly related to the extent of the technological advance. In cases where a "large" technological advance was required, the average ratio was 4.2; in cases where a "small" technological advance was required, the average ratio was 1.3.[1]

Turning to development costs, Peck and Scherer reported an average ratio of actual to expected costs of 3.2 for twelve plane and missile development projects.[2] Both the RAND study and the study by Peck and Scherer also presented data on the average ratio of actual to estimated project length. The RAND study reported that schedule slippage on ten programs ranged from two to five years, with an average ratio of actual to estimated length of 1.5.[3] The corresponding ratio for the twelve programs examined

---

1. A. Marshall and W. Meckling, "Predictability of the Costs, Time, and Success of Development," in *The Rate and Direction of Inventive Activity* (Princeton, N.J.: Princeton University Press, 1962).
2. Merton Peck and F. M. Scherer, *The Weapons Acquisition Process* (Cambridge: Harvard University Press, 1962).
3. Marshall and Meckling, *op. cit.*

by Peck and Scherer was 1.36.[4] There also has been interest in the accuracy of various firms' estimates of a project's probability of technical success. The study by Mansfield and Brandenburg of a large electrical-equipment firm provides some indication of the difficulties involved in predicting the probability of technical success for research and development projects.[5] A comparison of estimates of the probability of a number of projects' technical success (made prior to the beginning of the projects) with the actual outcomes indicates that such estimates have some predictive value, but not much. A discriminant function based on these estimates predicted correctly in only 64 percent of the cases studied.

This chapter is divided into three parts. In the first part (sections 2–5), we analyze the accuracy of estimates of development cost and development time in the large ethical drug firm discussed in Chapter 4. How accurate are these cost and time estimates, and to what extent (and in what direction) are they biased? What factors seem to be associated with the size of the overrun for an individual project? How does the size of the overruns in this industry compare with the size of those in military procurement? Also, we study the size of the errors in sales estimates made by the firm before a new product is marketed. In the second part of the chapter (sections 6–8), we describe and analyze the accuracy of the estimates of the probability of technical completion, development cost, and development time made by one of the proprietary drug laboratories (laboratory Z) discussed in Chapters 2 and 3. Finally, in the third part of the chapter (section 9), we describe the results of a study of the attitudes of laboratory administrators in four industries toward estimates of this sort.

2. Data for the Ethical Drug Firm

The sample from the ethical drug firm consisted of the same development projects which were examined in Chapter 4. Using the development blueprints for the projects, we obtained cost estimates for forty-nine projects and time estimates for fifty projects. Estimates were unavailable for the remainder of the seventy-five commercialized development projects. Figures on estimated and actual sales were available for fifty-nine new products during their first twelve months on the market.[6] The sales estimates were

4. Peck and Scherer, *op. cit.*
5. Edwin Mansfield, *Industrial Research and Technological Innovation* (New York: W. W. Norton for the Cowles Foundation for Research in Economics at Yale University, 1968), Chap. 3.
6. The fifty-nine new products resulted from fifty-seven of the seventy-five development projects. Normally, each development project yielded one new product. Even in those cases where more than one dosage form was developed, one estimate was prepared in the marketing plan if all dosage forms were marketed at the same time. There were two projects which resulted in two products because the two dosage forms developed during the project were marketed at different times.

obtained from the marketing plan prepared by the appropriate product manager in the Marketing Division of the firm. In order to assess the accuracy of the estimates, the ratio of actual to estimate was computed to obtain a cost factor, a time factor, and a sales factor:

$$\text{Cost Factor} = \frac{\text{Actual Development Cost}}{\text{Estimated Development Cost}}$$

$$\text{Time Factor} = \frac{\text{Actual Development Time}}{\text{Estimated Development Time}}$$

$$\text{Sales Factor} = \frac{\text{Actual First-Year Sales}}{\text{Estimated First-Year Sales}}$$

The frequency distribution for each factor is shown in Table 5.1. Data on the mean, standard deviation, and root-mean-square deviation from 1 for the three types of factors are contained in Table 5.2. (The standard deviation measures the dispersion of the estimates around the mean, while the root-mean-square deviation from 1 measures the dispersion of the estimates from unity.)

TABLE **5.1**

*Frequency Distributions of Ratios of Actual
to Estimated Cost, Time, and Sales,
Ethical Drug Firm*

RATIO	COST	TIME	SALES
	(number of projects)		
00–0.50	1	0	12
0.51–1.00	5	16	21
1.01–1.50	18	17	12
1.51–2.00	6	9	8
2.01–2.50	6	2	2
2.51–3.00	10	3	1
3.01–3.50	3	1	1
3.51–10.00	0	2	2
Total	*49*	*50*	*59*

Several interesting characteristics of the estimates emerge from the two tables. First, the data indicate the extent of the bias and variability of the three types of estimates. If the estimates had been substantially correct, the cost, time, and sales factors would have been close to unity. The fact that the means of all three distributions are above 1 (average cost factor equals 1.78, average time factor equals 1.61, and average sales factor equals 1.29) would seem to indicate that the actual value is generally greater than the

TABLE 5.2

Parameters of Distributions of Ratios of Actual to Estimated Cost, Time, and Sales, Ethical Drug Firm

	COST	TIME	SALES
New chemical entities			
Mean	2.25	1.89	1.75
Standard deviation	0.72	0.97	2.24
Root-mean-square deviation from 1	1.38	1.32	2.36
Percent of cases where ratio exceeds 1	100	86	46
Number of projects	13	14	13
Compounded products			
Mean	1.70	1.60	1.11
Standard deviation	0.72	1.40	0.71
Root-mean-square deviation from 1	1.00	1.52	0.72
Percent of cases where ratio exceeds 1	83	56	50
Number of projects	23	23	24
Alternate dosage forms			
Mean	1.51	1.33	1.20
Standard deviation	0.71	0.44	1.54
Root-mean-square deviation from 1	0.88	0.57	1.55
Percent of cases where ratio exceeds 1	84	69	36
Number of projects	13	13	22
Total			
Mean	1.78	1.61	1.29
Standard deviation	0.74	1.15	1.38
Root-mean-square deviation from 1	1.09	1.34	1.58
Percent of cases where ratio exceeds 1	88	68	44
Number of projects	49	50	59

estimate in each of the three categories.[7] We might have expected substantial differences in the size and direction of errors for the three types of estimates. A number of studies have shown that the optimistic bias which exists in sales estimates frequently causes forecasted sales to be greater than actual sales.[8] On the other hand, the hazards involved in predicting the cost of complex, uncertain activities, such as the construction of a railroad or the

7. Of course, a mean factor above 1 does not necessarily indicate that most of the values are greater than 1. See Tables 5.1 and 5.2.

8. See, for example, R. Ferber, "Measuring the Accuracy and Structure of Businessmen's Expectations," *Journal of the American Statistical Association*, (September 1953), pp. 385–413; M. Hastay, "The Dun and Bradstreet Surveys of Businessmen's Expectations," *Proceedings of the Business and Economics Statistics Section of the American Statistical Association* (September 1954), pp. 93–123; H. Theil, *Economic Forecasts and Policy* (Amsterdam: North Holland Publishing Company), 1961, Chaps. 3 and 4; D. Tull, "The Relationship of Actual Sales to Predicted Sales for New Products," *Journal of Business* (July 1967), pp. 233–250.

development of a new fighter plane, usually result in actual costs exceeding original expectations.[9] Table 5.2 indicates that the estimates of cost and time conform to these expectations, the average ratio of actual to estimated values being well above 1. On the other hand, the average ratio of actual to estimated sales—but not the median ratio—also exceeds 1.

Second, there are differences in the average cost, time, and sales factors for new chemical entities, compounded products, and alternate dosage forms. However, the only statistically significant differences occur among the cost factors, the average cost factor for new chemical entities being significantly higher than the average cost factor for the other two categories (at the 5-percent level). The higher average cost and time factors for new chemical entities probably reflect the fact that such projects are marked by the greatest uncertainty. Sales-forecast errors are also highest for the most innovative products (new chemical entities), but the difference does not appear to be statistically significant.

Third, if we compare the extent of the time overruns in this ethical drug firm with the extent of the time overruns in weapons-system development, we find that the time overruns tend to be somewhat larger in drug development. The average ratio of actual to estimated development time in this firm is 1.61, whereas the average ratio reported by RAND is 1.5 (for ten weapons systems) and the average ratio reported by Peck and Scherer is 1.36 (for twelve plane and missile-development projects).[10] The average time overrun in this firm is also higher than the average estimated overrun reported by Mansfield and Brandenburg in their study of a large equipment and appliance manufacturer.[11]

Fourth, we can also compare the cost overruns in this firm with those in weapons development. As noted above, Peck and Scherer reported an average ratio of actual to estimated development cost of 3.2 for twelve weapons-system projects. Thus, since the average ratio in the ethical drug firm is 1.78, its cost overruns are not as large as those of the firms producing the weapons systems. But for the more innovative products—new chemical entities—the average cost overrun—125 percent—is closer to that for weapons systems This result is interesting, since it suggests that when commercial activity is devoted to distinctly new products, it begins to approximate weapons-system development in the extent of overruns. More will be said on this score in subsequent sections.[12]

9. See the discussion of military cost estimating errors in Thomas Marschak, Thomas Glennan, and Robert Summers, *Strategy for R and D* (New York: Springer-Verlag, 1967).

10. Marshall and Meckling, *op. cit.*, and Peck and Scherer, *op. cit.*

11. The Mansfield and Brandenburg data are not exactly comparable to our data. First, they measure an average "slippage factor" which is the revised estimated time to project completion divided by the original estimated time to completion. The drug-development time factors are ratios of actual time to estimated time. Second, they measure average slippage only for those projects which are delayed, while we compare actual time to estimated time for all completed projects. Our average time factor would be higher if all projects completed on time were excluded. See Mansfield, *op. cit.*

12. See Peck and Scherer, *op. cit.*, pp. 44–45.

Fifth, the sales-forecast errors for the fifty-nine new drug products are somewhat higher than those reported in Tull's study of sixty-three new products introduced by sixteen companies. Using the absolute relative error (defined as $ARE = \left| \dfrac{F-A}{A} \right| \cdot 100$ where F is the forecast and A is the actual value) as a measure of forecast accuracy, Tull found that the mean and median absolute relative errors for the sixty-three new products were 65 percent and 26 percent, respectively. The mean and median ARE for the fifty-nine new drug products are 76 percent and 45 percent, respectively. In terms of forecasting accuracy, the new drug products are more like the industrial products (mean ARE equal to 85 percent) in Tull's sample than the consumer products (mean ARE equal to 49 percent). There are also differences in the direction of the error between the Tull and the new-drug-product samples, the sales forecasts for the sixty-three new products in the Tull sample being more optimistic than the estimates for the new drug products.[13] In part, these differences may be due to the very rapid growth of the drug market during this period.

3. Analysis of Cost Overruns

What factors are associated with the size of the cost overrun for a particular project? To help answer this question, we construct a simple model in which the logarithm of the ratio of actual to estimated development cost is the dependent variable, and various project characteristics are the independent variables. In contrast to the analysis in Chapter 4, where three separate regression equations were used for new chemical entities, compounded products, and alternate dosage forms, we include all forty-nine projects in one regression equation.[14] The first project characteristic used as an independent variable is the degree of technological advance attempted by a project.[15] The magnitude of the technological advance sought in the development project will, in part, determine the degree of initial uncertainty and the frequency with which the original development plan is changed. Since these revised development plans generally result in actual costs and

13. Tull, op. cit.
14. It may seem logical to use a separate regression equation for each project category, as we did in Chapter 4. In subsequent sections, we shall examine the influence of project category on time and cost overruns by introducing dummy variables representing project category into our single multiple-regression equation. This approach, of course, assumes that the coefficients of the other variables in the regression are the same for all three project categories. Unfortunately, there is really no other way to deal with the influence of project category. Cost estimates were available for only forty-nine of the seventy-five successful development projects and time estimates were available for fifty development projects. If the projects were divided into three project categories, there would be only three degrees of freedom for new chemical entities and four degrees of freedom for alternate dosage forms. Interviews with research executives within the firm indicate that they generally agreed with this approach of pooling all projects in a single regression.
15. See Chapter 4 for details of how the technological-advance score was computed.

times which are above the estimates in the development blueprint, the over-runs in cost and time may tend to be relatively large when the attempted technological advance is great.

Turning to the next independent variable, we note that a project which attempts to develop a product with a broad spectrum of activity (i.e., a multiple-market product) is more likely to encounter unanticipated prob-lems than is a project which attempts to develop a product with a narrow spectrum of activity (i.e., a single-market product). Consequently, one might expect the cost overruns to be larger for products with a broad spec-trum of activity. Thus, the second variable included in the regression is a dummy variable denoting the product's spectrum of activity.[16] The third independent variable is the year the estimate was made. Calendar year proved to be a significant variable in explaining the magnitude of develop-ment cost (see Chapter 4), and we might expect it to be important here as well for two reasons. The data include estimates made as early as 1950 and as late as 1962. Since skills improved significantly in virtually all technical fields during that period, we might expect an improvement in estimating techniques as well. On the other hand, the effects of more complex develop-ment procedures and inflation probably increased the inaccuracies in cost and time estimates over time. The impact of these changes may well have outweighed any improvements in forecasting proficiency within the firm.

The fourth independent variable is the actual duration of the develop-ment project. The longer a project goes on, the more likely it is that changes will be made in the nature of the product being developed and that overruns will grow. This variable has proved useful in studies of military cost over-runs. The fifth independent variable is the estimated cost of carrying out the development project. Why? Because the absolute size, as well as the per-centage size, of the overrun is of importance. The percentage overrun in development costs is likely to be smaller, all other things being equal, for a big, expensive project than for a smaller one. A small absolute overrun is more likely to be tolerated than a big one, even if percentagewise it is the same or larger: As an overrun becomes larger in absolute terms, it becomes more and more likely to result in trouble for the relevant people in the firm.[17]

The specific form of the multiple regression model is

(5.1) $\ln R_c{}^i = \alpha_0 + \alpha_1 \ln A_i + \alpha_2 s_i + \alpha_3 \ln t_i + \alpha_4 \ln C_e{}^i + \alpha_5 \ln L_i,$

where $\ln R_c{}^i$ is the logarithm of the ratio of the ith project's actual to esti-mated development cost, α_0 is a constant, $\ln C_e{}^i$ is the logarithm of the ith

---

16. See Chapter 4 for a discussion of the significance and meaning of a product's spectrum of activity.

17. Of course, it should be noted that we are regressing the logarithm of a ratio on, among other variables, the logarithm of the denominator. It may be objected that this results in some spurious correlation. But the results change relatively little if $\ln C_e{}^i$ is omitted from the regression. This is true as well in the other cases of this sort in this chapter. Note, too, that $R_e{}^i$ can be greater or less than 1, the consequence being that under some circumstances, a "bigger overrun" is really a "smaller underrun."

project's estimated development cost, $\ln A_i$ is the logarithm of its technological-advance score, s_i is a dummy variable that equals 1 if the ith project
is meant for more than a single market and 0 otherwise, $\ln t_i$ is the logarithm
of the year the estimate was made (less 1,949), and $\ln L_i$ is the logarithm of
the actual duration of the ith project. The resulting regression equation is

$$(5.2) \qquad \ln R_c{}^i = -0.01 + 0.51 \ln A_i + 0.32 \, s_i + 0.39 \ln t_i$$
$$\qquad\qquad\quad (0.17) \qquad\quad (0.16) \quad\;\; (0.12)$$

$$- \, 0.38 \ln C_e{}^i + 0.40 \ln L_i,$$
$$(0.09) \qquad\quad (0.12)$$

R^2—corrected for degrees of freedom—being 0.34.

Equation (5.2) provides a considerable amount of information concerning the hypotheses presented in previous paragraphs. It appears that
all five of the variables discussed above have statistically significant effects
on the size of a project's cost overrun. In line with our hypotheses, the regression coefficients of the logarithm of the technological-advance score, the
spectrum-of-activity dummy variable, the logarithm of the project's duration, and the logarithm of calendar time are positive,[18] while the regression
coefficient of the logarithm of estimated cost is negative. According to
equation (5.2), cost overruns tend to be greater for projects attempting
considerable advances in the state of the art than for less ambitious projects.
Specifically a 1-percent increase in the technological-advance score is associated with a 0.51-percent increase in the size of the cost overrun.[19] Also,
cost overruns tend to be greater for products with a broad spectrum of
activity than for single-market products. The effect of this variable is quantitatively important, the average size of the cost overrun being about 38
percent greater for projects with a broad spectrum of activity than for
single-market products.

In addition, cost overruns seem to have increased over time, a 1-percent
increase in t_i being associated with a 0.39 percent increase in the cost overrun. Thus, the effects of changing development procedures and inflation
seem to have offset any improvements in forecasting accuracy. Cost overruns also seem to be smaller (in percentage terms) for bigger projects, a
1-percent increase in estimated costs being associated with a 0.38-percent
decrease in the average cost overrun. And cost overruns tend to be bigger
for longer projects, a 1-percent increase in a project's duration being associated with a 0.40-percent increase in the average cost overrun. Finally,
although these variables have a significant effect on the size of a project's
cost overrun, they cannot explain more than about one-third of the variation

---

18. Our hypotheses said nothing about the sign of the coefficient of $\ln t_i$, however.
19. These results concerning the effects of technological advance are similar to those reported
in the RAND study of production costs. See Marschak, Glennan, and Summers, *op. cit.* The cost
factors for the twenty-two weapons systems were directly related to the extent of the technological
advance.

among projects in cost overruns. This is not surprising, partly for reasons discussed in the final paragraph of this section.[20]

These results enable one to explain why cost overruns tend to be larger for new chemical entities than for compounded products and alternate dosage forms (Table 5.2): The highest proportion of projects with a broad spectrum of activity are in the new-chemical-entity category, and the average technological-advance score is highest for new chemical entities (Table 4.2). However, although the larger overruns among new chemical entities can be explained in this way, we can also obtain equally good results by simply using the project category—new chemical entity, compounded product, or alternate dosage form—as a surrogate for the extent of the technological advance and the risks involved. Specifically, if we modify equation (5.2) by eliminating $\ln A_i$, the logarithm of the technological-advance score, and s_i, the spectrum-of-activity dummy variable, and by substituting two dummy variables, n_{1i} and n_{2i}, which equal 1 for new chemical entities and compounded products respectively (and 0 otherwise), the results are

$$
(5.3) \qquad \ln R_c{}^i = -0.23 + 0.66\, n_{1i} + 0.27\, n_{2i} + 0.39\, \ln t_i \\
\qquad\qquad\qquad (0.16) \qquad (0.13) \qquad (0.17)
$$

$$
- 0.32\, \ln C_e{}^i + 0.43\, \ln L_i, \\
(0.08) \qquad\qquad (0.12)
$$

$\bar{R}^2$ being 0.36. Both of the new variables, n_{1i} and n_{2i}, are statistically significant, and the regression coefficients of both new variables have the expected signs. The logarithm of estimated development cost, the logarithm of duration, and the logarithm of calendar time, all of which were significant in equation (5.2), retain their significance in equation (5.3). While equation (5.3) seems to provide a slightly better fit to the data than equation (5.2), the results are not sufficiently different to permit a choice between the equations on the basis of goodness-of-fit.

Finally, we should note that the variation in the size of overruns is not due entirely to the uncertainty associated with certain project characteristics. Development costs and times may be deliberately underestimated in a project's development blueprint. Because of the intrafirm competition for resources, there may be incentives to use low estimates as a means of marshaling support for particular development projects. If all estimates were uniformly adjusted downward by, for example, 10 or 20 percent, $\bar{R}^2$ would be unaffected. It appears more likely, however, that some estimates may be cut by 25 percent, others by 10 percent, and some not at all. This variability would limit our ability to explain the observed variation in cost and time factors. This deliberate downward adjustment of estimates is not, of course,

---

20. There are many other factors affecting the size of overruns, among them the deliberate underestimation of costs and time.

a phenomenon unique to this firm. Many observers have noted that in-dustrial scientists sometimes pursue scientific and professional goals which may not be consistent with the strictly commercial objectives of the firm.[21] While the observed variation in the accuracy of estimates is probably a composite of uncertainty and deliberate underestimating, there is no effec-tive way to separate out the effects of deliberate underestimating.

4. Analysis of Time Overruns

What factors seem to be associated with the size of the time overrun for a particular project? To help answer this question, we construct a model similar to that discussed in the previous section. The same project char-acteristics make up the independent variables. However, the logarithm of the ratio of the actual to estimated project length is substituted, of course, for the logarithm of the ratio of the actual to estimated project cost as the dependent variable; and the logarithm of the estimated project length re-places the logarithm of the estimated cost among the independent variables. The resulting regression is

$$(5.4) \qquad \ln R_L{}^i = 0.81 + 0.21 \ln A_i + 0.46\, s_i - 0.01 \ln t_i - 0.29 \ln L_e{}^i,$$
$$\phantom{(5.4) \qquad \ln R_L{}^i = 0.81 +} (0.14) \qquad (0.16) \qquad (0.12) \qquad (0.16)$$

where $\ln R_L{}^i$ is the logarithm of the ith project's ratio of actual to expected length, and $\ln L_e{}^i$ is the logarithm of the ith project's estimated length. The fit for the time overruns is slightly poorer than for the cost overruns, $\overline{R}^2$ being 0.23.

As in the case of the cost overruns, the effects of s_i and $\ln L_e{}^i$ are statis-tically significant. Time overruns tend to be larger for products with a broad spectrum of activity than for single-market products, the overrun being about 60 percent greater among broad-spectrum products. As expected, time overruns tend to be smaller (in percentage terms) for projects expected to take a long period of time than for those expected to be completed quickly. On the average, a 1-percent increase in estimated time is associated with a 0.29-percent decrease in the time overrun. Also, there is some ten-dency for time estimates (like cost estimates) to be less accurate for projects with high technological-advance scores, but (in contrast to cost estimates) this tendency is not statistically significant. The case of time overruns is unlike that of cost estimates in that there is no evidence that time overruns have tended to increase over time. However, neither is there any evidence that they have tended to decrease over time.

---

21. For a discussion of this conflict see S. Marcson, *The Scientist in American Industry* (New York: Harper, 1960) and William Kornhauser, *Scientists in Industry: Conflict and Accommodation* (Berkeley: University of California Press, 1962).

As in the case of cost overruns, we can also compute the regression where dummy variables representing project categories are substituted for the spectrum-of-activity and technological-advance scores. When $\ln A_i$, the technological-advance score, and s_i, the spectrum-of-activity dummy variable, are replaced by n_{1i}, the new-chemical-entity dummy variable, and n_{2i}, the compounded-products dummy variable, the results become

$$(5.5) \qquad \ln R_L{}^i = 1.07 + 0.32\, n_{1i} - 0.01\, n_{2i} + 0.06 \ln t_i - 0.36 \ln L_i.$$
$$\phantom{(5.5) \qquad \ln R_L{}^i = 1.07 +} (0.17) \quad\;\; (0.12) \qquad (0.09) \qquad\;\; (0.19)$$

The effect of n_{1i} is significant, but that of n_{2i} is not. Equation (5.5) does not fit as well as equation (5.4), $\bar{R}^2$ being only 0.06.

5. Analysis of Errors in Sales Estimates

What factors seem to be associated with the extent of the "overrun" in the sales forecast for a particular project? A model similar to those employed in Sections 3 and 4 is used to analyze the "overruns" in the sales estimates. Three independent variables are used in this analysis: (1) the innovativeness of the new product, (2) the calendar year of the estimate (less 1,949), and (3) the identity of the forecaster. With regard to the first variable, it is often hypothesized that the degree of innovativeness of a product affects the accuracy of the sales forecast.[22] Since new chemical entities are more innovative than compounded products or alternate dosage forms, the two dummy variables n_{1i} and n_{2i} were used as independent variables.

Turning to the second variable, we might expect the accuracy of sales forecasts to improve over time. During 1950–1967, considerable progress was made in developing and refining techniques for new-product sales forecasting. In addition, increased knowledge and experience in specific therapeutic markets should have improved forecasting accuracy over time. Finally, turning to the third variable, we might expect knowledge of the source of a sales estimate to be helpful in judging its accuracy. Since five product managers were responsible for the fifty-nine sales forecasts, four dummy variables were introduced into the regression to account for the identity of the forecaster.

22. Tull hypothesized that a product's degree of innovativeness would affect forecast accuracy. He grouped the products in his sample into three categories: (a) innovative products—products which are new to the economy; (b) emulative products—products which the company has never marketed before, although they are marketed in essentially the same form by other companies; (c) adaptive products—products which result when the company makes a significant differentiation in an existing product which it now markets. The innovative and emulative products were combined and the mean absolute relative error of this class was compared to the mean absolute relative error of adaptive products. No significant difference was found. See Tull, op. cit., p. 245.

Of course, for some purposes, one is interested in the accuracy of the sales forecast (i.e., the size of the error, whether positive or negative) rather than the "overrun." For some discussion of the accuracy of the sales estimates, see Section 2. In addition, it clearly is useful to analyze the factors that determine sales "overruns"—or "underruns."

The following model is used:

$$(5.6) \quad \ln R_s{}^i = k + \gamma_1 \ln S_e{}^i + \gamma_2 \ln t_i + \gamma_3 I_{1i} + \gamma_4 I_{2i} + \gamma_5 I_{3i}$$
$$+ \gamma_6 I_{4i} + \gamma_7 n_{1i} + \gamma_8 n_{2i},$$

where $\ln R_s{}^i$ is the logarithm of the ratio of the ith product's actual to estimated sales, k is a constant, $\ln S_e{}^i$ is the logarithm of the ith product's estimated sales, $\ln t_i$ is the logarithm of its calendar year (less 1,949), I_{1i}, I_{2i}, I_{3i}, and I_{4i} are dummy variables indicating the identity of the forecaster, and n_{1i} and n_{2i} are dummy variables denoting new chemical entities and compounded products, respectively; $l_n S_e{}^i$ is included for obvious reasons.

The results are

$$(5.7) \quad \ln R_s{}^i = 0.94 - 0.18 \ln S_e{}^i - 0.18 \ln t_i + 0.33\, I_{1i} - 0.02\, I_{2i}$$
$$(0.13) \qquad\quad (0.67) \qquad\quad (0.31) \qquad\quad (0.29)$$

$$+ 0.31\, I_{3i} + 1.01\, I_{4i} + 0.19\, n_{1i} + 0.16\, n_{2i}.$$
$$(0.39) \qquad (0.48) \qquad (0.28) \qquad (0.24)$$

The value of $\bar{R}^2$—0.08—is lower than that achieved with the models concerning development cost and development time. Although new-product sales forecasting is generally more accurate in this firm than the forecasting of development time and cost, we are unable to explain the variation in sales overruns (on the basis of the variables considered here) as well as we could explain the variation in cost and time overruns. Moreover, our results, like Tull's,[23] provide no evidence of differences between more innovative and less innovative products in the size of the sales-forecast errors.

The only statistically significant variable in equation (5.7) is a dummy variable identifying one of the forecasters. However, this does not mean that the observed differences among the forecasters are due to differences in personal characteristics alone. The product managers who prepared the sales forecasts differed considerably in the number and diversity of the product lines they managed. The least accurate forecasts were generated by a product manager who had responsibility for the firm's entire product line during the early fifties. As the firm grew, the product-management and accompanying new-product sales-forecasting responsibilities were divided among three individuals. Under this arrangement each product manager prepared sales forecasts for products in one or two product categories. The allocation of greater resources to new-product sales forecasting and the increased market specialization that resulted may have contributed to the improved forecast accuracy among the other forecasters. The moral here is simple but important, and is frequently overlooked: The accuracy of a forecast is dependent on the amount of resources devoted to making it. Unfortunately, despite the obvious relevance of this variable, it is seldom included in studies of this sort.

23. *Ibid.*

6. Probability of Technical Completion in the Proprietary Drug Firm

In the proprietary drug laboratory described in Chapters 2 and 3 (laboratory Z), records of many completed projects include an estimate of the probability of achieving the technical objectives, as stated in the project proposal.[24] This estimate is made at the time of formal project proposal. How accurate are these estimates? Are they generally optimistic, perhaps to sell the project to management? What project characteristics are associated with the size of the error in the estimate? Since laboratory management uses these estimates in project selection, these questions are of practical importance as well as being interesting from an academic viewpoint.

Data for seventy-nine completed projects are used to help answer these questions. Each of the projects has records containing an estimated probability of successful completion, and each either succeeded or failed technically. For obvious reasons, projects that were not completed for non-technical reasons are excluded.[25] As Table 5.3 shows, the estimated probability of technical completion is, *on the average,* a very good indicator of

TABLE 5.3

Relationship Between Estimated Probability
of Technical Completion and Project Outcome,
Proprietary Drug Laboratory

ESTIMATED PROBABILITY OF TECHNICAL COMPLETION	TECHNICAL OUTCOME OF PROJECTS		ALL PROJECTS
	NOT COMPLETED	COMPLETED	
	(*proportion of projects*)		
Below 0.70	0.42	0.08	0.16
0.70–0.79	.16	.17	.16
0.80–0.89	.11	.17	.15
0.90–1.00	.32	.58	.52
Total[a]	*1.00*	*1.00*	*1.00*
Average estimated probability of technical completion			.81
Actual proportion of projects technically completed			.76

[a] Because of rounding, sums of individual items may not equal totals.

24. Note that project completion means that the original technical objectives are achieved but not necessarily within the estimated time and cost. Presumably these probabilities are based on the supposition that only certain cost and time overruns will be allowed, but no explicit maximum ratio of actual to expected cost or time is specified. Note too that attempts are sometimes made to adjust a project's objectives so as to make them conform with its results. For this reason, the original objectives are the relevant ones here.

25. The estimates are based on the supposition that the projects are carried out. If some projects are not carried out because their objectives no longer seem commercially worthwhile, it is not fair to expect the estimates to anticipate this eventuality.

actual outcome, the average estimated probability of technical completion (0.81) being very close to the actual proportion of projects that were completed (0.76). However, the fact that the *average* estimated probability of technical completion is close to the actual proportion of projects that were completed does not mean that the estimates are useful in predicting *which* projects are more likely to be completed. How useful are the estimates in predicting whether a particular project will be completed? Table 5.3 indicates that they are of some use, the average estimate clearly being higher for projects that were completed than for projects that were not completed.

To get a better idea of the usefulness of these estimates in predicting which projects will be completed, we construct a discriminant function. Defining U_i, the dependent variable, as 1 if the ith project is completed and 0 if it is not completed, and regressing U_i on the estimated probability of technical completion, P_i, yields the following equation:

(5.8)
$$U_i = 0.0001 + 0.94\,P_i.$$
$$\quad\;\;(0.216)\quad(0.26)$$

If the right-hand side of this equation is greater than 0.76, we should predict that the project will be completed; if not, we should predict that it will not be completed. According to well-known statistical theory, this procedure should, under particular circumstances, minimize the probability of an incorrect prediction. How well does this discriminant function "predict" the data? It correctly predicts 70 percent of the outcomes and is wrong 30 percent of the time.

Thus, the estimated probabilities of technical completion are of some use in predicting which projects will be completed and which ones will not. But they are not of much use. Even if they are employed in such a way that the probability of an incorrect prediction is minimized, they predict incorrectly in about 30 percent of the cases. (As shown in Chapter 10, one would expect to make incorrect predictions in only 36 percent of the cases *by chance.*) This result is very close to that obtained by Mansfield and Brandenburg.[26]

Table 5.4 compares the actual proportion of projects that are technically completed with the average estimated probability of technical completion for projects attempting small, medium, and large technical advances. For those attempting small technical advances, the estimated probability of completion, on the average, overstates the risk of failure. On the other hand, for those attempting medium or large technical advances, the estimated probability of completion, on the average, understates the risk of failure. These biases can be used to extend the discriminant functions. Let L_i be a dummy variable that is 1 if the ith project attempts a large technical advance and 0 otherwise, and M_i be a dummy variable that is 1 if the ith project

26. Mansfield, *op. cit.*, Chap. 3. Note that P_i runs from 0 to 100, not 0 to 1.

TABLE 5.4

*Actual Proportion of Projects Technically Completed
and Average Estimated Probability
of Technical Completion, for Small, Medium, and Large
Technical Advances, Proprietary Drug Laboratory*

SIZE OF TECHNICAL ADVANCE SOUGHT

	SMALL	MEDIUM	LARGE	ALL PROJECTS
Average estimated probability of technical completion	0.84	0.71	0.74	0.81
Actual proportion of projects technically completed	0.91	0.47	0.14	0.76

attempts a medium technical advance and 0 otherwise. Using L_i and M_i as additional independent variables,

$$(5.9) \qquad U_i = 0.43 - 0.71\,L_i - 0.37\,M_i + 0.57\,P_i.$$
$$\qquad\qquad (0.20)\quad (0.14)\quad\ (0.10)\quad\ (0.23)$$

This discriminant function predicts correctly in 80 percent of the cases.

Thus, it appears that the usefulness of the estimates may be increased by combining them with information concerning the size of the technical advance sought by the projects. However, further work must be carried out before this result can be accepted fully. It is possible that the people who rated the size of the technical advance attempted by a project were influenced by whether or not it was completed. (The ratings were made after the projects were terminated.) If there was a tendency to rate projects that were not completed as more ambitious than those that were completed, the results in equation (5.9) are spurious. One way to get around this difficulty in future work is to obtain the rating of the size of the attempted technical advance at the beginning of the project.

7. Cost Overruns in the Proprietary Drug Firm

In the proprietary drug firm, how accurate are the estimates of development cost made at the time of project proposal? Is there a persistent overoptimism in forecasting costs, resulting in overruns of actual above estimated expenditures? Is the size of the overrun associated with the characteristics of the project described in section 3? To help answer these questions, data regarding sixty-nine projects at laboratory Z are analyzed. (For obvious reasons, only projects that were technically completed could be included.[27]) Table 5.5 shows the frequency distribution of the projects by

27. It would make no sense to compare the estimated cost of doing something with the actual cost of not doing it.

TABLE 5.5

*Distribution, by Ratio of Actual
to Estimated Cost, Sixty-nine Projects,
Proprietary Drug Laboratory*

RATIO OF ACTUAL TO ESTIMATED COST	PERCENT OF PROJECTS[a]
0.39 and less	22
0.40–0.79	28
0.80–1.19	9
1.20–1.59	6
1.60–1.99	7
2.00–2.99	10
3.00 and above	19
Total	*100*

[a] Here and elsewhere, percentages may not sum to 100 because of rounding errors.

the ratio of actual to estimated cost. The distribution is quite skewed, the median ratio being 0.80 but the mean ratio being 2.11. Thus, most projects did not experience a cost overrun. But on the average, there was a large cost overrun, actual costs being 211 percent of estimated costs.

We have sufficient data to classify projects according to relative technical ambition and project type. This allows us to extend the findings in sections 2 and 3, as well as those of Klein, Summers, and Peck and Scherer.[28] We would expect the average ratio of actual to estimated cost to be higher, and the standard deviation of this ratio also to be higher, for new product developments than for product improvements, and for large and medium technical advances than for small technical advances. Table 5.6 shows that these expectations are fulfilled. For example, the average ratio of actual to estimated cost is 2.75 for new products and 1.41 for product improvements; it is 3.66 for large and medium technical advances and 1.82 for small technical advances.[29]

How does the size of these cost overruns compare with that described in section 1 for weapons systems? For those projects that aimed at new products, the average overrun in the proprietary drug firm—175 percent—is about four-fifths as large as the average overrun found by Peck and Scherer for airplane and missile development projects—220 percent. For those projects that aimed at medium or large technical advances, the average overrun

28. B. Klein, "The Decision Making Problem in Development," in *The Rate and Direction of Inventive Activity* (New York: National Bureau of Economic Research, 1962); Marschak, Glennan, and Summers, *op. cit.*; and Peck and Scherer, *op. cit.*
29. These differences may not be statistically significant, but equation (5.10) shows that the extent of a project's technical ambition is significantly related to the size of the cost overrun. As in the case of the ethical drug firm, the firm's executives rated all projects with regard to technical ambition; but in this firm they were asked to classify them into three groups: large, medium, and small technological advances. The crudeness of this procedure need not be belabored.

TABLE 5.6

*Average and Standard Deviation of Ratio of Actual
to Estimated Cost, by Project Type and Relative
Size of Technical Advance, Sixty-nine Technically
Completed Projects, Proprietary Drug Laboratory*

| | SIZE OF TECHNICAL ADVANCE | | |
PROJECT TYPE	SMALL	LARGE AND MEDIUM	TOTAL
	(ratio of actual to estimated cost)		
Product improvement			
Average	1.39	1.49	1.41
Standard deviation	1.39	1.64	1.41
Number of projects	28	5	33
New products			
Average	2.21	5.46	2.75
Standard deviation	3.56	5.86	4.11
Number of projects	30	6	36
Total			
Average	1.82	3.66	2.11
Standard deviation	2.74	4.73	3.18
Number of projects	58	11	69

in the proprietary drug firm is larger than the average for airplane and missile development projects. These findings add further weight to the conclusion in section 2 that the cost overruns for civilian projects begin to approximate those for military projects when entirely new types of products or larger technical advances are attempted.

Finally, we compute a regression similar to those in section 3, the dependent variable being $\ln R_c{}^i$, the logarithm of the ith project's ratio of actual to estimated cost, and the independent variables being $\ln C_e{}^i$, the logarithm of the ith project's estimated cost; W_i, a dummy variable that equals 1 if the ith project represented a medium or large technical advance and 0 otherwise; V_i, a dummy variable that equals 1 if the ith project is a new product and 0 if it is a product improvement; $\ln L_i$, the logarithm of the ith project's duration; and $\ln t_i$, where t_i is the year (less 1,960) when the ith project was started. The result is

$$(5.10) \qquad \ln R_c{}^i = -0.29 - 0.10\, V_i + 0.36\, W_i + 1.76 \ln t_i$$
$$\phantom{(5.10) \qquad \ln R_c{}^i = -0.29} (0.12) \qquad (0.17) \qquad (1.12)$$

$$-\, 0.56 \ln C_e{}^i + 1.30 \ln L_i,$$
$$(0.15) \qquad\qquad (0.29)$$

$\bar{R}^2$ being 0.31. The effects of W_i, $\ln L_i$, and $\ln C_e{}^i$ are statistically significant.

Their effects are in the expected direction, and are quantitatively important. On the average, a project attempting a large or medium technical advance had a 43 percent larger cost overrun than a project attempting a small technical advance. A 1-percent increase in estimated cost was associated with a 0.56-percent decrease in the cost overrun. And a 1-percent increase in the duration of a project was associated with a 1.3 percent increase in the cost overrun.

8. Time Overruns in the Proprietary Drug Firm

How great are the time overruns in the proprietary drug firm? Using data regarding the same sixty-nine projects discussed in the previous section, we attempt to answer this question. As in the previous section, the estimates were made at the time of project proposal. Table 5.7 shows the frequency

TABLE 5.7

Distribution, by Ratio of Actual
To Estimated Time, Sixty-nine Projects,
Proprietary Drug Laboratory

RATIO OF ACTUAL TO ESTIMATED TIME	PERCENT OF PROJECTS
0.79 and less	3
0.80–1.19	12
1.20–1.59	3
1.60–1.99	7
2.00–2.99	30
3.00–3.99	22
4.00 and more	23
Total	*100*

distribution of the projects by the ratio of actual to estimated time. Apparently, project durations almost always overran the estimates in the laboratory, the ratio of actual to estimated time exceeding 1 in 88 percent of the cases. On the average, the ratio of actual to estimated time is 2.95. For the same reasons as in the preceding section, we would expect the average ratio of actual to estimated time to be higher, and the standard deviation of this ratio also to be higher, for new products than for product improvements, and for large and medium technical advances than for small technical advances. Table 5.8 shows that there is some tendency for the average and standard deviation of this ratio to be higher for new products than for product improvements (although the differences are not statistically significant). However, although the standard deviation turns out to be somewhat higher,

TABLE **5.8**

*Average and Standard Deviation of Ratio of
Actual to Estimated Time, by Project Type and
Relative Size of Technical Advance,
Sixty-nine Technically Completed Projects,
Proprietary Drug Laboratory*

PROJECT TYPE	SIZE OF TECHNICAL ADVANCE		
	SMALL	LARGE AND MEDIUM	TOTAL
	(ratio of actual to estimated time)		
Product improvement			
Average	2.80	1.74	2.64
Standard deviation	1.28	0.84	1.27
Number of projects	28	5	33
New products			
Average	3.14	3.70	3.24
Standard deviation	1.74	2.19	1.80
Number of projects	30	6	36
Total			
Average	2.98	2.80	2.95
Standard deviation	1.53	1.93	1.58
Number of projects	58	11	69

there is no indication that the average of this ratio is higher for large and medium technical advances than for small technical advances. Perhaps the firm felt that the costs of schedule slippage were greater for the technically more ambitious projects and that, for this reason, it did not permit the ratio to be larger on the average, for large and medium advances than for small advances.

Comparing the size of these time overruns with that of the weapons systems described in section 1, we find that the average overrun in this proprietary drug firm is considerably greater than in weapons-system development. The average ratio of actual to estimated time was 1.5 in the RAND study and 1.36 in the study by Peck and Scherer, as contrasted with 2.95 in this firm (and 1.61 in the ethical drug firm discussed in sections 2–5). This result seems quite reasonable, since the pressure for meeting time schedules is almost certainly greater in weapons development than in proprietary (or ethical) drugs.

Finally, we regress the logarithm of the ith project's ratio of actual to estimated time ($\ln R_t^i$) on the logarithm of the ith project's estimated time ($\ln L_e^i$), a dummy variable indicating whether the ith project was a small or a medium-to-large technical advance (W_i), a dummy variable indicating whether the ith project was a new product or a product improvement (V_i), and the logarithm of its calendar year, less 1,960 (ln t_i). The results are

$$(5.11) \quad \ln R_t^i = 1.89 + 0.074\ V_i + 0.078\ W_i - 1.62 \ln t_i - 0.65 \ln L_e^i,$$
$$\qquad\qquad (0.048) \qquad (0.070) \qquad (0.41) \qquad (0.11)$$

$\bar{R}^2$ being 0.37. All of the regression coefficients have the expected signs.[30] The effects of calendar year and the estimated length of the project are statistically significant and quantitatively important. There is definite evidence that this firm, unlike the ethical drug firm discussed in section 4, has witnessed smaller time overruns as time has gone on. The effects of the dummy variables representing project type and the extent of technical advance are not significant, but the difference between new products and product improvements is nearly significant.

9. Use of Estimates, and Attitudes Toward Their Accuracy

Previous sections have presented and analyzed data concerning the accuracy of estimates of development cost, development time, and project outcome in a major ethical drug firm and a major proprietary drug firm. In addition, we have compared the size of the errors in these estimates with the size of the errors in the corresponding estimates in weapons-development firms and a large electrical-equipment firm. At this point, we turn to two further questions concerning estimates of this sort: First, how widely are such estimates used? Second, how reliable are these estimates considered by laboratory managers?

Table 5.9 shows the percentage of the nineteen laboratories described

TABLE 5.9

Use of Selected Estimates,
Nineteen Laboratories, 1966

TYPE OF ESTIMATE	RESEARCH PROJECTS	DEVELOPMENT PROJECTS
	(*percent*)	
Project cost	90	95
Manpower requirements	100	100
Project duration	84	100
Size of market	63	74
Probability of technical success	63	84
Probability of market success	58	79
Capital-facility requirements	42	74

PERCENT OF LABORATORIES MAKING AND USING ESTIMATES

30. Actually, the sign of the coefficient of ln t_i is not specified by our hypotheses.

in Chapters 2 and 3 that made and used various kinds of estimates concerning research projects and development projects in 1966. Several things are apparent from these data. First, laboratories more commonly make such estimates for *development* projects than for *research* projects. In view of the fact that development tends to be more predictable than research, this is what we would expect. Second, practically all of the laboratories make formal estimates of a project's manpower requirements, its cost, and its duration. Third, a somewhat smaller percentage—about 75 or 80 percent —estimate the probability of technical success, the probability of market success, the size of the market, and capital-facility requirements for *development* projects.[31] Fourth, a still smaller percentage—about 50 or 60 percent —estimate the probability of technical success, the probability of market success, the size of the market, and capital-facility requirements for *research* projects.

Thus, the bulk of these laboratories say that they make and use estimates of these types in evaluating and selecting development projects. However, as noted in Chapter 3, there is considerable skepticism among laboratory managers concerning the effectiveness of quantitative project-selection techniques. How reliable do the administrators of these laboratories feel these estimates are? The director of each of the nineteen laboratories was asked to rate the accuracy of each of the twelve types of estimate in Table 5.10 as totally unreliable, poor, fair, good, or excellent. Table 5.10 shows the percentage of administrators that rated each type of estimate as good or excellent and the percentage that rated each type of estimate as poor or totally unreliable. Also included are the findings of a similar survey by Seiler,[32] these findings being reasonably similar to our own.

The surprising thing is the number of laboratory directors who seem to regard these estimates as being reasonably reliable. About one-half or more of the laboratory directors in our sample—and about one-third or more in Seiler's sample—feel that estimates of a project's manpower requirements, its development cost, its capital requirements, its research cost, its probability of technical success, and its development time are good or excellent. Only about 10–20 percent of the laboratory directors in our sample—and about 5–20 percent in Seiler's sample—regard these estimates as poor or totally untrustworthy. Given the data provided in previous sections concerning the errors in estimates of development cost, time, and outcome, it appears that laboratory directors may be unduly optimistic about the accuracy of these estimates, unless, of course, they are able to

---

31. For a description of the way in which these estimates are made and used, see Mansfield, *op. cit.;* N. Baker and W. Pound, "R and D Project Selection: Where We Stand," *IEEE Transactions in Engineering Management* (June, 1964); and works cited there. Note that these results pertain to 1966 (as in the relevant part of Chapter 2), not 1969 (as in the relevant part of Chapter 3).

32. In this survey, similar questions were asked in a much larger sample of firms; see Robert Seiler, *Improving the Effectiveness of Research and Development* (New York: McGraw-Hill 1965).

TABLE 5.10
*Perceived Accuracy of R and D
Project Estimates, for Sample Laboratories
and Seiler Study*

| | JUDGMENT OF ESTIMATE ACCURACY | | | |
| | GOOD OR EXCELLENT | | POOR OR TOTALLY UNRELIABLE | |
TYPE OF ESTIMATE	SAMPLE LABORATORIES	SEILER STUDY	SAMPLE LABORATORIES	SEILER STUDY
	(percent of laboratory administrators)			
Manpower	79	37	11	10
Cost of development	69	41	16	12
Capital facilities required	63	n.a.	21	n.a.
Cost of research	53	31	16	17
Probability of technical success	53	55	16	6
Duration of development	47	36	21	22
Cost reduction	42	68	16	18
Duration of research	42	30	26	30
Probability of market success	32	37	37	25
Net profit	26	n.a.	37	n.a.
Market revenue	21	41	37	30
Market life	16	33	63	38

n.a. Not available.

make much better estimates than their colleagues in our two drug firms.[33]

Also, judging from both Seiler's and our findings, the estimates of market factors—probability of market success, revenue, profit, and market life—are regarded as poor or totally unreliable by a larger percentage of the laboratory administrators than are the estimates of development cost, development time, and the probability of technical success. If the estimates of market factors are less reliable than the estimates of development cost, development time, and probability of technical success—and we have no reason to question it—and if their estimates of development cost, development time, and the probability of technical success are as poor as those made by the drug firms, the errors in the estimates of the market factors must be very large indeed, since they must be even larger than the errors (described in previous sections) in the estimates of development cost, de-

33. There is a small amount of data for two other firms that suggest that our two drug firms are not unrepresentative. Dennis Meadows provides some data for two chemical firms. One of these firms (laboratory B) has cost overruns that seem to be larger, on the average, than the ones in our two drug firms, while the other (laboratory A) has smaller cost overruns than those in our drug firms. Meadows also compares the estimated probability of success in a chemical laboratory with actual results. Dennis Meadows, "Estimate Accuracy and Project Selection Models in Industrial Research," *Industrial Management Review* (Spring 1968). Also, see Mansfield, *op. cit.*

velopment time, and the probability of technical success. Given this evidence that the estimates of the market factors are less accurate than the estimates of development cost, development time, and probability of technical success, perhaps it is not surprising that as we found in Chapter 3, the probability of commercial failure is much greater than the probability of technical failure.

10. Summary

The principal conclusions of this chapter are as follows: First, very detailed data for a major ethical drug firm and a major proprietary drug firm indicate that there are sizable errors in the cost and time estimates made at the beginning of drug-development projects. For over 80 percent of the projects in the ethical drug firm, the actual cost and time exceed the estimated values. The average ratio of actual to estimated cost is 1.78; the average ratio of actual to estimated time is 1.61. Cost and time estimates are less reliable for new chemical entities than for compounded products and alternate dosage forms. In the proprietary drug firm, the average ratio of actual to estimated cost is 2.11, and the average ratio of actual to estimated time is 2.95. Again, the overruns are greater for more ambitious projects.

Second, when we compare the overruns in these two drug firms with those in weapons development, we find that the cost overruns for new drug products are less than those in weapons development and that the time overruns are greater than in weapons development. However, it is important to note that the cost overruns in the drug firms begin to approximate those for military projects when entirely new types of projects or larger technical advances are attempted. For example, the average ratio of actual to expected cost is 2.25 for new chemical entities in the ethical drug firms, 2.75 for new products in the proprietary drug firm, and 3.2 for a sample of airplane and missile projects. Turning to time overruns, we find the average ratio of actual to expected time is 1.89 for new chemical entities, 3.24 for new products in the proprietary drug firms, and 1.4 for the airplanes and missiles.

Third, in the ethical drug firm, we tested various hypotheses concerning the effects of certain factors on the size of a project's cost overrun. In accord with these hypotheses, it turns out that technically more ambitious projects tend to have greater cost overruns than technically less ambitious projects. Also, products with wider spectra of activity tend to have larger cost overruns than single-market products, and projects with small estimated costs or longer duration tend to have larger cost overruns than projects with large estimated costs or shorter duration. In the proprietary drug firm, there is also a significant tendency for technically more ambitious projects and projects with smaller estimated costs and longer duration to have larger cost overruns. In the ethical drug firm, and perhaps in the proprietary drug firm, cost overruns seem to have increased over time.

Fourth, when the same kind of model is used to analyze development time, the results are rather similar to those for development cost. In the ethical drug firm, there is a significant tendency for products with wider spectra of activity and projects with smaller estimated lengths to have greater time overruns. In the proprietary drug firm, there is also a significant tendency for projects with small estimated lengths to have greater time overruns; moreover, there is a nearly-significant tendency for new products to have larger time overruns than product improvements. In the proprietary drug firm, time overruns seem to have decreased significantly over time.

Fifth, in the ethical drug firm, the average ratio of actual to estimated sales of new products is 1.75. There is some tendency for this ratio to be higher for entirely new chemical entities than for compounded products or alternate dosage forms, but the difference is not statistically significant. The forecasts made by this firm seem to be somewhat less accurate than the average reported by Tull. An important reason why some of the firm's forecasts are more accurate than others is that some forecasters had more resources at their disposal than others. As would be expected, the accuracy of a forecast seems to be related to the amount of resources devoted to its preparation.

Sixth, in the proprietary drug firm, we studied the accuracy of the estimated probabilities of project completion. The average probability of technical completion (0.81) turns out to be very close to the actual proportion of projects successfully completed (0.76). Moreover, the estimated probabilities of technical completion are of some use in predicting which projects will be completed and which will not. But they are not of much use, since even if they are used in such a way as to minimize the probability of an incorrect prediction, they lead to an incorrect prediction in about 30 percent of the cases. There is some reason to believe that their accuracy may be increased if the extent of the technical advance is taken into account, but more work needs to be done before we can be at all sure of this.

Seventh, our sample of laboratories in four industries indicates that practically all laboratories make formal estimates of a project's manpower requirements, cost, and duration; and the bulk of them also make formal estimates of the probability of technical success, the probability of market success, and other such variables. Although there is considerable skepticism concerning the usefulness of quantitative project-selection techniques, it appears that the laboratory administrators may be unduly optimistic concerning the accuracy of the estimates of cost, time, and the probability of technical success. Also, if these administrators' judgment is correct, the errors in the estimates of various market factors may be very large indeed, since even they view these estimates as less accurate than those regarding development cost, time, and the probability of technical success.

6 THE ANATOMY OF THE PRODUCT-INNOVATION PROCESS: COST AND TIME

1. Introduction

In this chapter, we study the anatomy of the product-innovation process. Exactly what is involved in product innovation? What is the cost of the various activities that must be undertaken to develop a new product and introduce it to the market? How long do these activities take? To what extent can the time required to get the product to market be reduced by increasing the cost of the project? These questions are extremely important to economists and others. Yet the truth is that, except for a few areas, we have little or no information bearing on them.

We shall present and analyze data concerning the product-innovation process in three product groups—chemicals, machinery, and electronics. The product-innovation process is considered to begin when exploratory work is started by the firm with a particular new product in mind. Thus, it excludes basic research but includes applied research (if any) directed toward the product. The product-innovation process is completed when the new manufactured product is available for sale and delivery. An important word here is *manufactured*. Often trial models, prototypes, or pilot-plant output may be sold to customers for actual use or given out for evaluation, but this does not complete the innovation process. In order for a product to be a true innovation (a new element in the "commodity space" of economic theory), an acceptable quality level must be reached, and the firm must be in a position to produce enough of the product at a sufficiently low cost so that there is a reasonable chance of profit. Moreover, the product must be sold, not given away.[1]

---

1. Like the line between invention and innovation, the line marking the end of the innovation process is not very clearly defined. For example, Asher, Hirsch, and other writers on the "learning

In this chapter, we exclude innovations which are pure process innovations, whose sole effect is to lower the cost of manufacturing an already available product. However, since our concept of product innovation does include the application of technology to the problems of producing the product, our definition may encompass certain process innovations that are incidental to, or necessitated by, the emergence of a new product. Nevertheless, it should be clear at the outset that our attention is focused on innovation where a new commercial product is the primary result. There would be problems involved in extending our concepts and generalizing our conclusions to the case of pure process innovation. Also, it should be recognized that each of the innovations in our sample was carried to completion, without interruption, by a single firm. This is in contrast to cases where one firm begins a project but terminates it at a certain point, the project being completed by the same or another firm at a later date.

We begin by defining in some detail the various stages of the innovation process. Then the nature of our data and the sample used are presented, and the time and cost data are summarized. We compare our figures with those obtained in several previous studies, and also note apparent differences (and similarities) among product groups in the breakdown of cost and lead time among the stages of innovative activity. Next, we compare the rates of expenditure during various stages of the work. Finally, we discuss the time-cost trade-off function, the data we have gathered concerning this function, and some results concerning the shape of this function.

2. Stages of the Product-Innovation Process

Once the definition of the total innovation process, i.e., its starting and ending points, had been determined, as presented above, the next step was to break the process into stages. For our purposes, it was necessary that the classification scheme meet two major criteria. First, we wanted a scheme which would be meaningful when applied to fairly diverse types of products. This meant that the stage definitions had to be general enough so that the type of work in each stage would be necessary for most innovation projects and would be roughly comparable among products in different industries. Second, however, we needed a group of stages about which actual measurements of time and cost could be made. This meant that the stage definitions had to be specific enough so that they could be reconciled adequately with the accounting records of firms.

---

curve" have shown that even after an innovation is "in production" its cost function may shift. Our definition is conservative because we exclude from the innovation process this learning that goes on once the product is in production. See H. Asher, *Cost-Quantity Relations in the Airframe Industry,* RAND Corporation, R–291 (July 1956); and W. Hirsch, "Manufacturing Progress Functions," *Review of Economics and Statistics* (May 1956).

Two breakdowns presented in the previous literature were the basis for the scheme we employed. They—as well as our own breakdown—are shown in Figure 6.1. The first breakdown was used by the Panel on Invention and Innovation in its report to the Commerce Department.[2] It was employed not to obtain actual data but rather as a guide for estimates of cost which were made by the panel members for a "typical" product innovation. The second breakdown is that utilized by A. Yorke Saville, in his study of lead time in the mining-machinery industry,[3] to obtain lead-time data for actual product innovations.

FIGURE 6.1

Breakdowns of the Innovative Process

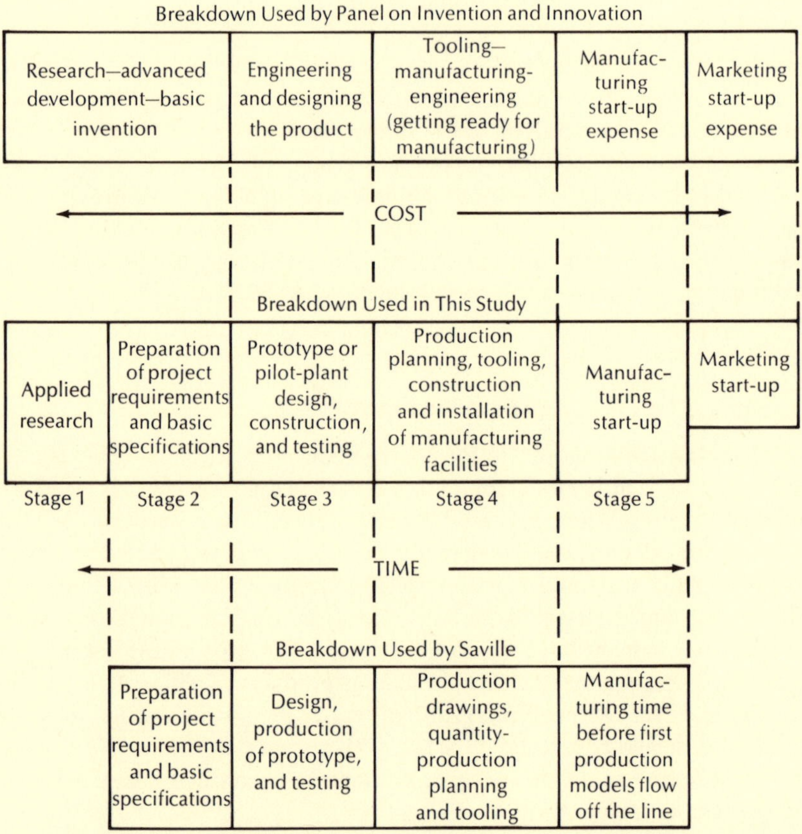

Breakdown Used by Panel on Invention and Innovation

Research—advanced development—basic invention	Engineering and designing the product	Tooling—manufacturing—engineering (getting ready for manufacturing)	Manufacturing start-up expense	Marketing start-up expense

←————————————————— COST —————————————————→

Breakdown Used in This Study

Applied research	Preparation of project requirements and basic specifications	Prototype or pilot-plant design, construction, and testing	Production planning, tooling, construction and installation of manufacturing facilities	Manufacturing start-up	Marketing start-up
Stage 1	Stage 2	Stage 3	Stage 4	Stage 5	

←————————————————— TIME —————————————————→

Breakdown Used by Saville

	Preparation of project requirements and basic specifications	Design, production of prototype, and testing	Production drawings, quantity-production planning and tooling	Manufacturing time before first production models flow off the line

2. See U.S. Department of Commerce, *Technological Innovation* (Washington, D.C., 1967).
3. A. Yorke Saville, "Mining Machine Industry," *Iron and Coal Trades Review* (September 19, 1958). Also see C. Freeman, "Research and Development in Electronic Capital Goods," *National Institute Economic Review* (November 1965).

The breakdown we use is the middle one in Figure 6.1. While it is quite similar to the Panel's and to Saville's, it is not precisely the same. In particular, the Panel's initial stage is too broad for our purposes, "research" and "basic invention" being very general terms. In contrast, our initial stage is "applied research," as defined by the National Science Foundation.[4] Saville did not include research at all in his scheme—perhaps because research is of relatively minor importance in the topics he is discussing. Our second stage is the same as Saville's first stage. Stages 2, 3, and 4 of Saville's breakdown and of the Panel's breakdown are the same as our stages 3, 4, and 5. We did not include marketing start-up as one of the stages, but did collect separate cost data for this activity.

Having compared our classification scheme with the schemes used in other studies, we must go on to describe in more detail the nature of each of our stages. Specifically, what activities are included in each stage? Stage 1 is composed of *applied research,* as defined by the National Science Foundation.[5] The nature of the research will, of course, depend on the particular product that the firm is trying to develop, but several general characteristics of this activity may be noted: First, the workers here are primarily scientific professionals. Second, the work generally involves experimentation, data collection, and testing of hypotheses. For example, research may be done on materials to be used in the product or on scientific principles which are important for its operation or design. Often the research will be aimed at determining the applicability of a basic scientific principle to the particular product innovation.

A few examples from the sample of projects on which our results are based may suggest the types of work included in applied research. One chemical innovation was based on a chemical which had been synthesized by a university scientist. His laboratory method was far too expensive to be used on a large scale, however. The applied-research problem for the firm was to determine if another method could be used to synthesize the chemical. For several innovations in the electronics group, applied research involved investigation of the properties of integrated circuits to see if such circuits were suitable for use in a particular type of device. Research on one project in the machinery group was in the area of hydraulics, since the product included a new type of fluid-drive clutch.

Preparation of project requirements and *basic specifications* is stage 2. This step often consists of routine planning and scheduling, but sometimes the preparation of specifications requires considerable effort. Where the marketing situation is such that the innovation's success depends critically on certain product characteristics, close coordination with the marketing

4. See *Methodology of Statistics on Research and Development* (National Science Foundation 1959).
5. *Ibid.*

staff at this point is important and specifications may be prepared with reference to market studies. In one of our sample projects—a chemical innovation to be used in food products—the preparation of specifications was particularly important because the innovation had to conform to FDA standards. Also, one machinery product was to be used in conjunction with other products and thus had to be designed compatibly.

Stage 3 represents the major product engineering and development work. Its effort is focused on the *prototype or pilot plant.* The goal of stage 3 is a complete product which meets desired specifications. Problems in chemical projects in this stage often are related to scale-up. Engineering difficulties which are not apparent when a chemical is at the bench-scale development phase become evident when a pilot plant is built. The prototype stage for machinery and electronics products often encounters problems associated with integrating individual components into a whole. Even if parts of a device are not themselves new, integrating them in new ways can present engineering problems. Finally, the prototype stage often involves the firm in new technological areas related to manufacture of the product. One electronic device, for example, involved a firm in the technology of ultrasonic welding, while another company needed to acquire a capability in microminiaturization in order to carry out prototype work successfully.

Stage 4 involves getting ready for manufacture. It includes preparation of detailed manufacturing drawings, *tooling,* and the design and construction of *manufacturing facilities.* While stage-4 work may lead to minor changes in the product in order to make it a more suitable object for manufacture, the focus is on the problems of manufacturing rather than on the product itself. This stage generally represents a transfer of responsibility from the research and development management to the production management. It is also quite often characterized by considerable investment in physical capital. In some cases the firm will have equipment which can be adapted to the manufacture of the new product. A chemical plant, for example, often requires simply the rearrangement of certain standard units of equipment. If the firm has some unused capacity this stage may involve the modification or adaptation of existing facilities. In other cases new equipment must be designed and built. In one electronics innovation, for example, an important part of stage 4 was the construction of test equipment to be used for quality control.

Stage 5 is *manufacturing start-up.* A number of things must be done before the production facility is ready to begin routine operation. Production workers must be trained. The assembly line or plant must be "debugged" and procedures set up for manufacturing. Often some production must take place before an acceptable quality level is reached. The cost and time of these tasks is included in stage 5. A final cost which is not included as a numbered stage, but which is important, is *marketing start-up cost.* Marketing start-up may include marketing studies undertaken to investigate demand for the product, advertising campaigns prior to its introduction, establishment of a system of distribution, and training of the sales force in the operation or characteristics of the product. Marketing start-up cost includes all expenditure of this nature before the first sale and delivery of the manufactured product.

3. The Data: Chemicals, Machinery, and Electronics Innovations

The data were almost all collected by means of personal interviews. Very little information regarding cost and time is available in published form for individual commercial product innovations. The specialized nature of the material requested was such that a mail survey was inappropriate, so in all cases the innovating firm was visited in person; in most instances two or three interviews were required in order to obtain the desired information. The basic source for choosing firms was *Industrial Research Laboratories of the United States,* 1966 edition. A sample of firms in the Philadelphia-New Jersey area which were doing work in the relevant product fields was selected, and contacts with the firms were initiated. Generally the first contact was made with a senior R and D executive. About 50 percent of the firms provided data which proved useful. The most common reasons given by firms which did not choose to participate were (1) that the information requested was confidential, or (2) that the information was not available or could be compiled only at too great an expense. Although each participating firm was asked to provide data on five recent innovations, very few could supply material on that many, the most important reason being that very few firms had introduced more than a few reasonably significant innovations during the early and middle sixties. In most cases a firm gave information on two or three new products.

Data were collected for the product innovations in terms of the above definitions of each stage of the innovation process. For each innovation, information was obtained concerning the costs incurred in each stage of the process (including marketing start-up). In most cases some of this information was available from accounting records, but these data were often supplemented by the respondents' estimates in order to reconcile the particular accounting system used by the firm with our definitions of the stages. For each innovation, information was also collected concerning the time taken to complete each stage of the process and the extent of the time overlap between stages. Note that while the sum of the costs in each stage (plus marketing start-up costs) does give a meaningful figure for total expenditure, the sum of stage times does not represent the total duration of the innovation process, since several stages may have been going on simultaneously. The total elapsed time is given by the sum of stage times minus the overlap. (The importance of overlap is stressed in the next chapter, which describes the extent of this overlap and its effect on a project's cost structure.) An illustration of a typical project is given in Figure 6.2. The total elapsed time here (17 months) is given by the sum of stage times (23 months) minus overlap (6 months).

Thus, we have the following identities: If E_j is the expenditure on stage j and M represents the cost of marketing start-up, the total expenditure (E) on an innovation is

$$(6.1) \qquad E \equiv \sum_{j=1}^{5} E_j + M.$$

If T_j is the length of stage j and L_j is the overlap between stage j and stage $(j + 1)$, the total elapsed time (T) of the innovation process is

FIGURE 6.2

The Timing of the Stages of an Innovation Project

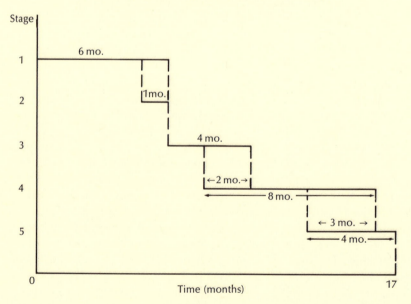

$$T = \sum_j T_j - \sum_j L_j = 23 \text{ mo.} - 6 \text{ mo.} = 17 \text{ mo.}$$

(6.2)
$$T \equiv \sum_{j=1}^{5} T_j - \sum_{j=1}^{4} L_j.$$

For the purpose of examining the distribution of expenditure and time among stages, we shall work with percentage figures: The cost of each stage will be computed as a percentage of total expenditure (E), and the duration of each stage will be computed as a percentage of total elapsed time (T). The resulting percentages are called "relative stage costs" and "relative stage times."[6]

Data were collected for product innovations in three product groups: chemicals, machinery, and electronics. Each firm provided data on one or more innovations. The samples for time and for cost information are largely identical, but in a few cases a product has been included only in the cost sample or only in the time sample because reliable data were available only for cost or only for time. The chemical group consists mostly of polymers developed for industrial use, such as synthetic elastomers and synthetic fibers, but also includes a few organic chemicals, such as starches. The machinery sample is composed almost entirely of materials-handling equipment. The electronics sample includes communications equipment, computers, and control systems. Table 6.1 shows the number of innovations in each subset of the sample and the number of firms included. It should be noted that all of the innovations in the sample were commercialized. Our data, like those of the studies cited above, pertain only to innovations that reached the market.

TABLE 6.1

Number of Firms and Product Innovations
for Which Data Regarding Cost and Time
Were Obtained

PRODUCT GROUP	NUMBER OF INNOVATIONS	NUMBER OF FIRMS
Chemicals		
Cost data	17	6
Time data	16	6
Machinery		
Cost data	9	3
Time data	10	4
Electronics		
Cost data	12	5
Time data	12	5

6. Note that marketing start-up cost is included in E, while marketing start-up time is not included in T. In part, this is because marketing start-up activities can fairly readily be carried out while other parts of the innovation process are going on. Note too that marketing start-up costs are excluded when we examine time-cost trade-offs, since we are concerned only with the effect of time on R and D, tooling, construction, and manufacturing costs.

4. The Distribution of Costs

Table 6.2 shows, for each product group, the average percentage of total innovation expenditure arising in each of the five stages and in marketing start-up. The largest percentage of total costs generally occurs in stage 4, during which tooling occurs and the manufacturing facilities are designed

TABLE 6.2

*Average Percent of Total Cost Arising
in Each Stage of Innovative Activity*

STAGE	CHEMICALS	MACHINERY	ELECTRONICS	WHOLE SAMPLE	PANEL ESTIMATES
			(percent)		
1. Applied research					
Mean	16.9	3.0	3.9	9.5	
Standard deviation	17	5	6		
2. Specifications					5–10
Mean	13.1	3.5	2.9	7.6	
Standard deviation	17	6	3		
3. Prototype or pilot plant					
Mean	12.6	40.9	44.0	29.1	10–20
Standard deviation	8	17	17		
4. Tooling and manufacturing facilities					
Mean	41.4	37.1	30.4	36.9	40–60
Standard deviation	29	10	18		
5. Manufacturing start-up					
Mean	8.3	4.5	13.6	9.1	5–15
Standard deviation	8	6	9		
Marketing start-up					
Mean	7.4	11.0	5.5	7.7	10–25
Standard deviation	12	12	5		

and constructed. For the sample as a whole, this stage accounts, on the average, for almost 40 percent of total costs. The next-largest percentage of total costs generally occurs in stage 3, during which the prototype or pilot plant is constructed. For the sample as a whole, this stage accounts, on the average, for almost 30 percent of total costs. For the sample as a whole, each of the other stages (1, 2, 5, as well as marketing start-up) accounts for a much smaller percentage of total cost—about 7–10 percent, according to Table 6.2.

It is interesting to compare these results with the estimates made by the Panel on Invention and Innovation in its report to the Commerce Department. Its figures are simply "educated guesses" based on the Panel members' experience. As the report explains:

> In order to arrive at a reasonable indication of the distribution of costs in successful product innovations and, particularly, to examine the role of research and development in the total process of bringing a new product to market, we pooled the knowledge of experienced members of the Panel. On this basis we tried to discern a representative pattern in the distribution of costs in successful product innovation. There was sufficient similarity in the experiences we covered to convince us that it would be desirable to present the following "rule of thumb" figures as the basis for our discussion.[7]

The Panel's figures are presented in the last column of Table 6.2. In general, these estimates show substantial agreement with our data: In both sets of figures—their estimates and our averages for the entire sample—stages 3 and 4 together account for more than one-half of the total expenditure on innovative activity, and the two initial and two final stages are less costly relative to total expenditure than stages 3 and 4. However, despite this overall agreement, there are a number of differences in the two sets of figures. Comparing our overall averages (fourth column) with the Panel's estimates (fifth column), we see that our data suggest that stages 1–3 are more costly than the Panel estimated, while stage 4 and marketing start-up are less costly. For all of these stages, our averages fall outside their estimated range. These differences may be due in part to differences in the nature and range of industries covered by the figures.

While estimates of the cost of a "typical" innovation such as those made by the Panel and averages such as we have computed are useful for getting a general view of the nature of the innovation process, the great variability around the means should be emphasized. Any particular innovation may show a substantially different pattern than the average. For example, as our data show, there are differences *among product groups* in the way costs are distributed among the stages of innovative activity.[8] In particular, there seem to be two quite different patterns for stages 1, 2, and 3, the electronics and machinery figures being quite similar and the chemicals figures being different from the other two.[9] But this is only part of the story. *Within each product group,* there is wide variation in the distribution of costs, as indicated by the large standard deviations in Table 6.2. In stages 1, 2, and 5 (as well as in marketing start-up), the standard deviations are often larger than the means; and in stages 3 and 4, they are often about half as large as the means.

7. U.S. Department of Commerce, *op. cit.*, p. 9.

8. Specifically, stages 1 (applied research) and 2 (preparation of product specifications) account for a much larger percentage of total costs in chemicals than in machinery and electronics; on the other hand, stage 3 accounts for a larger percentage of total cost in machinery and electronics than in chemicals. It is possible that the chemical sample's proportion of costs in stage 3 is lower than would be the case in a larger sample.

9. However, in stages 4 and 5, as well as in marketing start-up, there is no tendency for the figures for the chemical innovations to be quite different from those for the other two product groups.

TABLE 6.3
Average Percent of Total Elapsed Time in Each Stage of Innovative Activity

STAGE	CHEMICALS	MACHINERY	ELECTRONICS	WHOLE SAMPLE	MILITARY PRODUCTS	MINING MACHINERY
			(percent)			
1. Applied research						
Mean	62.0	10.6	13.4	28.7	—	—
Standard deviation	28	18	19		—	
2. Specifications						
Mean	34.6	9.2	12.7	18.8	12.6	11.1
Standard deviation	28	14	9			
3. Prototype or pilot plant						
Mean	35.0	57.0	58.9	50.3	42.8	44.5
Standard deviation	22	21	12			
4. Tooling and manufacturing facilities						
Mean	21.9	41.3	29.8	31.0	18.2	22.8
Standard deviation	18	17	16			
5. Manufacturing start-up						
Mean	7.8	7.8	19.4	11.7	26.4	22.2
Standard deviation	6	13	7			
Time overlap[a]						
Mean	59.1	26.0	27.5	37.5	—	—
Standard deviation	49	3i	26		—	

[a] The overlap measure here is $\dfrac{\sum_{j=1}^{4} L_j}{T} \times 100$, where L_j is the overlap in months between stages j and $j + 1$ and T is total elapsed time of the project.

5. The Distribution of Time

Table 6.3 shows, for each product group, the average percentage of the total duration of the innovation process during which each stage was going on. The stage that generally went on for the longest time was stage 3, during which the prototype or pilot-plant work was carried out. For the sample as a whole, this stage accounts, on the average, for about 50 percent of the total duration of the innovation process. Stage 1 (applied research) and stage 4 (tooling and construction of manufacturing facilities) also went on for large proportions of the total elapsed time: For the sample as a whole, each of these stages accounts for about 30 percent of the total elapsed time, on the average.

It is interesting to compare these results with those of the few other studies of this sort that have been made. In his study of the mining-machinery industry, cited above,[10] Saville presents some data similar to ours. He breaks down the total elapsed time into four stages, identical to our stages 2, 3, 4, and 5. (In his data, the possibility of time overlap is not recognized specifically, and as noted above, applied research is not included in his study as a part of the innovation process.) Saville's data are given in the last two columns of Table 6.3. Besides his own data for mining machinery, he provides a summary of data for military products. The data for "military products" are averages of nine U.S. defense products, ranging from a service uniform to an airplane. The "mining machinery" data are based on sixteen mining-machinery products for which Saville obtained information. He concludes that "the period taken to design, build, and test a prototype is the biggest single factor in the whole development programme."[11] Our data support this conclusion. Prototype or pilot-plant work (stage 3) clearly takes longer than any of the other stages of innovative activity, averaging more than half of the total elapsed time for the sample as a whole.

Table 6.3 also indicates some intergroup differences in the distribution of time. For the first three stages, these differences are similar to the intergroup differences in expenditure: The machinery and electronics group averages are similar, while chemicals show a different pattern from the others. As with expenditure, the relative time spent on research (stage 1) and preparation of specifications (stage 2) seems much larger for chemicals than for the other groups. The intergroup differences in the relative duration of prototype or pilot-plant work are also similar to the cost differences: Machinery and electronics innovation projects spent a greater proportion of the total time in stage 3 than did chemicals. The size of the intergroup

10. Saville, *op. cit.*
11. *Ibid.*

difference in the duration of stage 3 is not as great as the cost difference, however.

The role of overlap and the data on this aspect of the innovation process will be considered in greater detail in Chapter 7. At this point, the figures in Table 6.3 should merely be noted. The pattern of intergroup differences observed previously again appears here. Electronics and machinery are quite similar to each other, with overlap totaling about one-quarter of the total elapsed time. The average overlap in the chemicals group, on the other hand, is much greater—about 60 percent of the total lead time. Again, electronics and machinery are quite similar, while chemicals differs considerably from them both.

6. Research and Development in the Product-Innovation Process

Much previous work on the economics of technological change—and relevant aspects of government policy—has been concerned with a firm's research and development expenditures. What proportion of the total costs incurred during the innovation process are spent for research and development? This is an important question because there is a tendency in some quarters to emphasize the importance of R and D expenditures and to neglect the other expenses involved in the innovation process. Definitions of research and development vary somewhat, depending on the use for which they have been formulated. The economist studying a firm's annual investment in the production of technology, the policy-maker attempting to formulate policy to encourage technological progress, and the manager trying to determine the most efficient organizational structure may all, with good reason, use slightly different definitions. Probably the most widely accepted definition is the one used by the National Science Foundation to obtain data from firms on their total annual R and D expenditure.

In trying to compare the National Science Foundation definition with our stages of innovative activity, a key question is: Where does R and D end? The following three parts of the NSF definition indicate its guidelines to answering this question. The NSF includes in R and D (italics ours):

Engineering activity required to advance the design of a product or process to the point where it meets specific functional and economic requirements and can be turned over to manufacturing units. The *design, construction and testing of preproduction prototypes* and models and *"engineering follow-through"* in the early production phase is included.

If your company's research and development frequently involves the development of a "process" as in chemicals and petroleum, such development activity would include operations beyond the bench scale, primarily the *design and operation of pilot plants* or semi works.

The development of *designs for special manufacturing equipment and tools is* included but *tool making* and tool tryout are *not* included.[12]

Thus, to the extent that our stage 4 may include "engineering follow-through" or development of designs for "special" manufacturing equipment and tools, the sum of the costs of our first three stages will understate research and development costs, as defined by the NSF. To find out the percentage of the total innovation costs accounted for by R and D, as defined by the NSF, we showed each of the managers the NSF definitions. In the majority of cases, the managers felt that our first three stages were equivalent to R and D as defined by the NSF. In a few cases, mainly in the machinery group, they felt that the sum of the costs of the first three stages understated R and D costs as defined by the NSF. In these cases we asked the managers to make estimates of R and D costs according to the NSF definition.

The results, shown in Table 6.4, indicate that the product groups were fairly similar with regard to the percentages of total costs incurred in the innovation process which were spent on R and D. On the average, for all product groups, R and D accounted for just about one-half of the total

TABLE 6.4

R and D as a Percentage
of the Total Cost of the Innovation Process,
Average Percentage in Each Product Group

Chemicals group	42.7
Machinery group	51.6
Electronics group	50.7

cost of the innovation process. To prevent misunderstanding, note once again that these data pertain only to commercialized product innovations. The results for process innovations may be different. Also, a great deal of R and D does not have a commercialized outcome. The ratio of all R and D expenditures—whether or not they have a commercialized outcome—to all innovation costs is obviously higher than the ratio of R and D expenditures that do have commercialized results to the corresponding innovation costs.

Economists sometimes have assumed that research and development expenditures could be treated as synonymous—or nearly so—with the costs of product innovation. Judging from our data, this assumption is a poor one, since an amount approximately equal to the R and D expenditures must be spent on non-R and D innovative activity in the case of the

---

12. *Funds for Research and Development in Industry,* NSF 67–12 (National Science Foundation, 1965), pp. 121–122.

typical commercialized product.[13] This finding is important in at least three respects. First, it shows that the quantity of resources devoted to innovative activity in the United States—and other countries—is considerably greater than is indicated by the statistics on R and D expenditures. Second, to the extent that the ratio of R and D expenditures to the total costs of innovation varies among industries, countries, or periods of time, it shows that differences among industries, countries, or periods of time in R and D expenditures may be an inadequate measure of differences in the costs of innovation.[14] Third, it shows that when a firm innovates, it must be willing to risk a great deal more than its R and D expenditures alone, the result being that the difficulties and risks involved, particularly for smaller firms, are that much greater.

7. Relative and Absolute Rates of Expenditure

In this section, we begin by considering each stage's relative rate of expenditure—the percentage of the total cost (of the five stages) that occurs in each stage divided by the percentage of the total elapsed time in that stage. If its relative rate of expenditure is 1, a stage is equally important in terms of cost and time. If this rate is greater (less) than 1, the stage's portion of total cost is greater (smaller) than its portion of elapsed time. The relative rate of expenditure was computed for each stage for each innovation; the averages are presented in Table 6.5. Where a stage was not performed at all—i.e., where both cost and time equal 0—the innovation was not included in computing the group average for the stage.

Table 6.5 shows the same general pattern for each product group. It indicates that the relative rate of expenditure tends to increase as the project proceeds. The initial two stages account for a much smaller proportion of total cost than of total elapsed time. Stage 3 has a somewhat larger, and stage 4 shows the greatest, relative rate of expenditure. Stage 5 has a lower relative rate of expenditure than stage 4. Turning to differences among product groups, we find that the differences in stages 1 and 2 are small and do not seem to show any particular pattern. In stages 3, 4, and 5, however, a familiar pattern appears: The relative rates of expenditure in machinery

13. We also computed the average percentage of the total duration of a project during which R and D takes place, the results being 95 percent (chemicals), 67 percent (electronics), and 78 percent (machinery). The proportion of total elapsed time during which R and D takes place is apparently considerably greater than the proportion of total innovation costs which is spent on R and D. In part, of course, this is due to the fact that R and D involves lower expenditure rates than subsequent stages of the innovation process.

14. According to our data, R and D tends to be a smaller percentage of total innovation costs for projects costing over $500,000 than for projects costing less than $500,000, and for projects carried out by small firms than for projects carried out by big firms; but the differences are not statistically significant.

TABLE 6.5

Ratio of Each Stage's Percentage of the Total Cost
(of the Five Stages) to Its Percentage of the Total
Elapsed Time, Averages for Each Product Group[a]

STAGE	CHEMICALS	MACHINERY	ELECTRONICS
1. Applied research	0.33	0.28	0.43
2. Specifications	0.58	0.45	0.41
3. Prototype or pilot plant	0.59	0.95	0.81
4. Tooling and manufacturing facilities	2.25	1.30	1.13
5. Manufacturing start-up	1.30	0.82	0.82

[a] Where a stage was not performed at all, i.e., both the stage's percentage of the total cost and its percentage of the total elapsed time equal 0, the innovation was not included in computing the average for that stage.

and electronics are similar, but they differ significantly from the rate observed in chemicals.

Next, let's look at the absolute rate of expenditure in each stage. For many purposes the absolute rate of expenditure is more important than the relative rate. For example, a firm must know how much investment a project is likely to require at various stages as it progresses. For the innovations in our sample, we computed absolute expenditure rates for each quarter of the total duration of the innovation process. Since our data specified only the expenditure in each stage, and the time schedule, the computation here involved the assumption that within a stage, the expenditure was evenly distributed over the elapsed time. The results indicate that for most of the innovations the expenditure rate increased consistently from one quarter to the next. However, there is some tendency for the rate to peak in the third quarter or earlier, especially in the electronics group, where about two-thirds of the projects show this pattern. This may be related to the duration of the innovation process, since most of the electronics innovations had short durations, relative to the total sample. These relationships are summarized in Tables 6.6 and 6.7, which clearly show that it is the shorter, non-chemical projects which tend to have expenditure rates that peak relatively early in the project.[15]

15. Nelson, Peck, and Kalachek present data for the development of nylon showing a continually rising expenditure rate through the entire project. Norden investigated the distribution of man-hours required in electromechanical innovations. He considered R and D work only and found that *cumulative* man-hours were well approximated by a logistic curve. Of course, his results are not inconsistent with our results for an entire innovation project. As the R and D rate fell, non-R and D expenditures may have increased to more than offset the drop. This in fact is the picture Nelson *et al.* give for nylon. See Richard Nelson, Merton Peck, and Edward Kalachek, *Technology, Economic Growth, and Public Policy* (Washington, D.C.: The Brookings Institution, 1967) and P. Norden, "Curve Fitting for a Model of Applied Research and Development Scheduling," *IBM Journal of Research and Development* (July 1958).

TABLE **6.6**

*Number of Projects with Peak Expenditure Rate
in Each Quarter of Total Elapsed Time,
by Product Group*

	CHEMICALS	ELECTRONICS	MACHINERY	TOTAL
Peak in 1st quarter	0	0	0	0
Peak in 2nd quarter	1	3	1	5
Peak in 3rd quarter	3	5	3	11
Peak in 4th quarter	13	4	4	20

TABLE **6.7**

*Number of Projects with Peak Expenditure Rate
in Each Quarter of Total Elapsed Time,
by Total Elapsed Time*

TOTAL ELAPSED TIME (MONTHS)	PEAK IN 1ST QUARTER	PEAK IN 2ND QUARTER	PEAK IN 3RD QUARTER	PEAK IN 4TH QUARTER
0–40	0	4	8	6
41–80	0	1	3	4
81–120	0	0	0	6
121 and above	0	0	0	4
Total	*0*	*5*	*11*	*20*

8. The Time-Cost Trade-off

A product often can be developed and brought to market more quickly if more money is spent during the course of the innovation process. Recognizing the great importance of this time-cost trade-off, economists have studied it in various ways. For example, Scherer[16] has discussed theoretical aspects of the time-cost trade-off in uncertain work such as research and development; Peck and Scherer[17] have considered the role of the time-cost trade-off in military development projects; and lead time in specific types of development has been studied empirically by Novick in the case of weapons and by Saville in the case of mining machinery.[18] Our work modifies and extends these efforts in several ways. First, we focus on innovation rather than just research and development. The achievement

16. F. M. Scherer, "Government Research and Development Programs," in *Measuring Benefits of Government Expenditures,* ed. by R. Dorfman (Washington, D.C.: The Brookings Institution, 1965).
17. Merton Peck and F. M. Scherer, *The Weapons Acquisition Process* (Cambridge: Harvard University Press, 1962).
18. D. Novick, *Lead Time in Modern Weapons,* RAND Corporation, P–1240 (December 1957); and Saville, *op. cit.*

which is most important from the standpoint of the firm is the availability of a marketable product. Not until a product is actually available for sale will the investment in innovation begin to pay off. Attaining this availability involves more than just research and development, as we saw in section 6. Second, our study deals with industrial product innovations. The context is the modern corporation producing for industrial use, whereas (with the exception of Saville) the work noted above is concerned with large-scale military weapons development. Finally, while the above works deal with either the theoretical basis of the time-cost trade-off or the actually realized lead-time result, little or no attempt has been made to *estimate the time-cost trade-off function for particular innovations.* We make such an attempt in this study.

To begin with, we must discuss in more detail the concept of the time-cost trade-off function. Since product innovation involves uncertainty, cost and time should be treated probabilistically. (Of course, the outcome of innovation projects is generally uncertain too.) Actual times and costs which differ substantially from predictions are the rule rather than the exception, as we saw in Chapter 5. For a particular project, there exists a joint probability density over the project outcome (P), the time (t), and the cost of innovative activity (c). Let this density be $f(t,c,P)$. The trade-off we are concerned with is based on the conditional density, $f(t,c|P)$. By considering the joint density of time and cost conditional on a specific outcome we concentrate on alternative ways of obtaining the same result. The fact that P is fixed means that we are dealing with a specific new product. In what follows we will use the simpler two-variable density, $f(t,c)$, with the understanding that it is in fact conditional on a specific outcome.

A completed innovation project represents an observation drawn from a density, $f(t,c)$. The trade-off concept refers to the relation between expected cost and expected elapsed time. A *strategy* is a particular approach to the project which is characterized by a time-cost density and thus time and cost expectations. Expected time and expected cost depend on the strategy under consideration. For any given value of t, say t_0, there will be a set of strategies which have t_0 as the expected time in the marginal density, i.e., $E(t) = t_0$. Of this set of strategies there will be one for which the expected value of cost in the marginal density is a minimum. Call this $F_{t_0}(t,c)$. Thus, F_{t_0} characterizes the strategy with expected time of t_0 and expected cost a minimum. This is the strategy which will be relevant for the trade-off function.

The trade-off function is the locus of expected times and expected costs relating to the strategies characterized by capital-F densities. In Figure 6.3, points A and B are on the trade-off function while C and D are not. The latter will never be relevant since the same expected times could be achieved with lower expected cost. The function, then, is a representation

FIGURE **6.3**

Time-Cost Trade-off Function

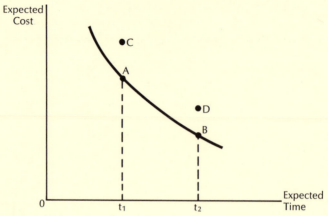

of strategies with a minimum expected cost for a given expected time. The densities are, of course, subjective probability distributions. Since an innovation is unique, the time and cost distribution for a particular strategy cannot be derived from frequency data on past projects, although past experience may be an important factor in determining the magnitude of the estimates for the project at hand.

One further aspect of the trade-off function must be specified. As Marschak[19] and others have noted, R and D decisions are often sequential in nature. A strategy is not chosen at the start of the project and rigidly pursued to its conclusion. Reevaluation often takes place. One reason is that learning which takes place in the course of the work changes management's view of the probable result of a given approach. Similarly, learning will affect the decision-maker's subjective probability distribution regarding time and cost. At any point in time he will see certain alternative expected-time–expected-cost possibilities for project completion. At a later time he may have a different idea of what expected-time–expected-cost points are possible. Thus, a different time-cost trade-off function exists at each point in time because of the difference over time in the firm's subjective probability distribution regarding time and cost.

Two specific trade-off functions, which we call *ex ante* and *ex post* trade-off functions, are of special interest. The *ex ante* trade-off function is based on expected values from the subjective probability distribution which exists before any work has begun. The *ex post* trade-off function is based

19. See Marschak's portions of Thomas Marschak, Thomas Glennan, and Robert Summers, *Strategy for R and D* (New York: Springer-Verlag, 1967).

on expected values from the subjective probability distribution which exists after the actual innovation has been completed. Both types are hypothetical in the sense that only one time-cost point is ever realized, a point which may in fact, because of random variation, not even be on the trade-off function. Both types of trade-off function are composed of points derived as answers to the question, If you were to use a strategy with expected completion time of t_0, what would be the (minimum) expected cost? The difference is that in the *ex ante* case the question is posed before the project is begun, while in the *ex post* case it is posed after the project has been completed. In other words, in the *ex post* case, the question really is: Looking back on the project, how much do you think it would have cost to have completed it in various alternative lengths of time?

9. The Sample and the Data

Data pertaining to the time-cost trade-off were obtained through a series of interviews with the men who managed the project or who were members of the group responsible for the project. At the time of the interviews, the innovations were in most cases completed, so the trade-off functions estimated are *ex post* functions.[20] The innovation process was considered to begin with the start of applied research and to end with the termination of manufacturing start-up. Using the actual time and cost results for the work as a reference point, the respondent was requested to estimate various points on the trade-off function. The interviewer suggested various values of expected time, and the respondent was asked to give the expected cost which would have been required to finish the project in that expected time. Also he was asked to estimate the minimum possible elapsed time for the project, i.e., that time which would have resulted from a top-priority effort where the work was completed as fast as possible regardless of cost. In most cases two or more interviews were conducted at different times. This procedure provided a check on the consistency of the response. The same suggested times usually elicited very similar expected-cost estimates at the different interviews. Estimated trade-off functions were obtained in this manner for twenty-nine product innovations. Usually from six to ten estimated points were obtained for each product innovation. Products included chemical, machinery, and electronics innovations and were drawn from eleven firms.

Scherer has suggested an approach like the one we used, but has pointed out a potential problem.

20. In those cases where the work was not completed at the time of the interview (about 15 percent of the sample), it was very near completion, and the respondents indicated with considerable confidence that the estimates would not change before completion.

One approach involves nothing more than Gedankenexperimente—asking the engineer in charge of an individual activity what the most likely time span would be if he had diverse levels of resources at his command. . . . To obtain useful time-cost trade-off estimates through Gedankenexperimente it seems essential to divorce the estimators from the consequences of their estimates. This condition is seldom met within the information systems presently applied by the government, but could be met in an experimental study whose direct data were kept out of the hands of the company and government program monitors.[21]

Our study certainly meets this condition, its sponsorship being academic and independent of any of the firms involved. Also, it was agreed to keep the material obtained confidential and to present only statistical results which did not identify the firms or product innovations. Thus, the problem cited by Scherer seems to be avoided. Another factor which is critical in this type of study is the choice of a person to make the estimates. Scherer suggests "the engineer in charge of an individual activity." This choice would certainly assure that the individual would be very familiar with the technical nature of the problem involved, a most important consideration. But there is a further element to be considered here. Different scheduling or phasing of activities will be used in different strategies. Variation in time and cost can arise both from variation in the time and cost of individual activities and from differences in the way in which various activities combine. Thus, in addition to being technically knowledgeable, the person interviewed should have an area of involvement in the project broad enough to give him an overall view of the entire process, including the possible methods of combining different activities into a complete time schedule. Our respondents generally were in a position which enabled them to get such an overall feel for the project. Occasionally, where he was unsure of a specific technical aspect of the program, the respondent called on other individuals in the firm for help in estimating.

Still another important point must be made about the nature of these data. As we have noted, the trade-off function is a hypothetical concept. An innovation is carried out only once. Only one time-cost point is ever realized, and that may not even be on the function. For this reason, as well as others, there may be considerable errors in the estimates of the time-cost trade-off function. Put bluntly, the managers may be wrong. But it is important to note that, from many points of view, this possibility really is irrelevant, since it is their opinions, right or wrong, that determine firm behavior. If they think that the time-cost trade-off function has certain characteristics, it is important that we know this fact. Whether it really has these characteristics is a more difficult question that neither we nor the managers are likely to answer soon.

At the same time, it should be recognized that these estimates, although

21. Scherer, *op. cit.*, p. 46.

imperfect, do not contain the large biases and errors found in Chapter 5. Recall that the estimates in Chapter 5 were made before the projects were begun, and were made in an institutional setting where certain kinds of bias could pay off for the estimator. In contrast, the estimates described in this section were made after the projects were completed and in an institutional setting where there was no possible incentive to bias. Although these estimates are obviously subject to error, there can be little doubt that they are honest and accurate reflections of the managers' judgments concerning the time-cost trade-offs, these judgments having been purged of considerable overoptimism by the managers' experience with the projects.

10. The Shape of the Trade-off Function

Economists generally assume that, within the relevant range, the trade-off function is negatively sloped. But little or nothing is really known about the shape of the trade-off function—although a number of previous writers have commented on the importance of obtaining a better understanding of its shape. For example, Marschak has noted: "It would be a valuable result . . . if analysis . . . were to reveal certain broad and reasonable conditions to imply a diminishing returns property: successive increases in a task's budget decrease its expected completion time, but by a successively decreasing amount."[22] To what extent do the data confirm the hypothesis that the trade-off function has a negative slope? To what extent do they confirm the diminishing-returns property? We plotted the raw data to examine each hypothesis. A sample plot is shown in Figure 6.4. Each point represents the respondent's estimate of expected cost corresponding to the expected time shown on the horizontal axis. In these plots—and later in our regression analysis of the trade-off function—we omitted end points such as A as being out of the relevant range for our discussion. A point like A would never be chosen by a firm which was interested in keeping expected time and expected cost both to a minimum. Needless to say, the omission of such end points does not bias our tests in favor of the hypotheses we are testing. There is widespread agreement that the time-cost trade-off function is likely to be negatively sloped and convex *only over a particular range.* (See Figure 4.1.) It therefore is quite legitimate for us to ask whether, *within a range indicated by the data,* the time-cost trade-off function has these properties.

As a rough test of the negative-slope and diminishing-returns hypotheses, we simply drew in the line segments between adjacent points. The plotted data are summarized in Table 6.8. The results strongly suggest that the negative-slope hypothesis is valid—within the ranges indicated by the

22. Marschak, *op. cit.,* p. 6.

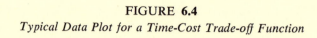

FIGURE **6.4**

Typical Data Plot for a Time-Cost Trade-off Function

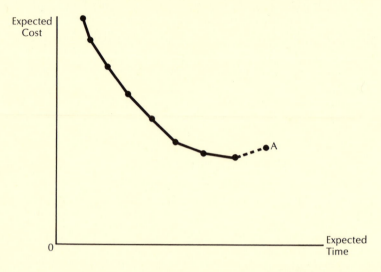

data (which includes most of the points). In all but one project, there was a negative slope throughout, i.e., every line segment was downward-sloping. In the remaining project, a single line segment was upward-sloping. The support for the diminishing-returns hypothesis is less conclusive although still substantial. We designated projects as having "diminishing returns throughout" if every line segment had a smaller slope or the same slope as the one to its left. Where this property did not hold for the entire set of points we counted the number of points "out of line," like point *B* in Figure 6.5. Table 6.8 indicates that about one-third of the projects showed

TABLE **6.8**

*Number of Trade-off Functions with a
Negative Slope and Diminishing Returns*

Negative Slope	
Throughout	28
Except for 1 data point	1
	29
Diminishing Returns	
Throughout	10
Except for 1 data point	13
Except for 2 data points	6
	29

FIGURE **6.5**

Data Plot for a Time-Cost Trade-off Function,
Showing "Diminishing Returns"
Except for One Point Out of Line

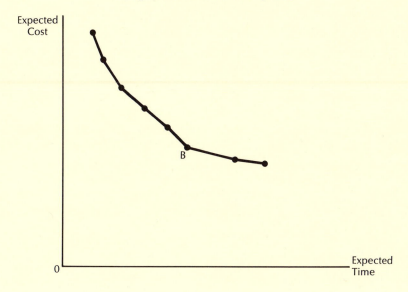

diminishing returns throughout; and if we include those with just one in-consistent point, more than three-quarters of the functions had the dimin-ishing-returns property. A further investigation of the diminishing-returns property was carried out by running the following regression for each innovation:

$$(6.3) \qquad C_i = a_0 + a_1 T_i + a_2 T_i^2,$$

where C_i is the expected cost of the ith innovation, T_i is the expected time for the ith innovation, and the a's vary from one innovation to another. Out of the 29 regressions, the estimate of a_2 was positive in 25 cases, 18 of which produced an estimate of a_2 which was statistically significant at the 0.05 level. In the 4 cases where the regression estimate of a_2 was negative, only 1 estimate was significantly different from 0.

Thus an examination of the data suggests that, in the relevant range, a downward-sloping, convex function will usually be a reasonable approxi-mation to the trade-off function. The support for the negative-slope assump-tion is very strong. There is somewhat more question about the diminishing-returns (convexity) hypothesis, but in our sample at least, a convex shape is strongly suggested in a large proportion of the cases.

11. Summary

The principal findings of this chapter are as follows: First, the largest percentage of the total cost of innovation generally occurs in the stage of the innovation process during which tooling occurs and the manufacturing facilities are designed and constructed. For our sample of thirty-eight product innovations in chemicals, electronics, and machinery, this stage accounted, on the average, for almost 40 percent of the total costs. The next largest percentage of the total costs occurs in the stage during which the prototype or pilot plant is built. This stage accounted, on the average, for almost 30 percent of the total costs.

Second, the average percentage of total cost accounted for by each stage of the innovation process—applied research, preparation of product specifications, prototype or pilot-plant construction, tooling and construction of manufacturing facilities, and manufacturing start-up—is not very different from the estimates made by the Panel on Invention and Innovation. However, there are considerable differences among product groups. Moreover, there are very large differences among innovations in the same product group. In view of the tremendous variation, one must be very careful about the use of these average percentages. They are merely rough guides.

Third, the stage of the innovation process that generally goes on for the longest period of time is the stage during which the prototype or pilot-plant work is carried out. For the sample as a whole, this stage went on for about 50 percent, on the average, of the total duration of the innovation process. Applied research and tooling and construction of manufacturing facilities also go on for large proportions of the total elapsed time, each of these stages continuing for about 30 percent of the duration of the project, on the average. Data for military products and mining machinery indicate that the prototype work is the longest stage of the innovation process in these areas too. Again, there are very large differences among innovations in these percentages.

Fourth, although there is sometimes a tendency to emphasize the importance of research and development and to neglect the other expenses involved in the innovation process, it turns out that only about half the cost of the innovation process for these products was accounted for by research and development, as defined by the National Science Foundation. Although economists sometimes have acted as if R and D expenditures could be treated as synonymous—or nearly so—with the costs of product innovation, the non-R and D costs seem to be substantial. Neither, of course, is it true that R and D absorbed only a very small percentage of the total innovation costs in these product groups.

Fifth, both the relative and absolute rates of expenditure tend to increase as a project moves from one stage to the next. The first two stages of the innovation process account for a much smaller proportion of total cost than of total time, whereas the opposite is true in later stages. For most of the innovations, the absolute rate of expenditure increased consistently from one quarter of the project to the next. However, there was some tendency for the expenditure rate to peak in the third quarter for some innovations, particularly in electronics.

Sixth, a product often can be developed and brought to market more quickly if more money is spent during the course of the innovation process. Although economists have recognized the importance of this time-cost trade-off, no attempt had been made to estimate the time-cost trade-off functions for particular innovations. We estimated the time-cost trade-off functions for twenty-nine innovations, on the basis of a series of interviews with managers who had the principal responsibility for these innovations. An examination of the data suggests that a downward-sloping, convex function will usually be a reasonable approximation to the time-cost trade-off function, at least within a substantial range. The empirical support for the hypothesis that the slope is negative is very strong. There is somewhat more question about the hypothesis of convexity, but in our sample at least, a convex shape is strongly suggested in a large proportion of the cases.

7 THE TIME-COST TRADE-OFF FUNCTION, OVERLAPPING STAGES, AND THE TIMING DECISION

1. Introduction

The previous chapter described the concept of the time-cost trade-off function and presented data concerning the shape of this function for twenty-nine product innovations. In this chapter, we explore this topic more fully. We analyze the determinants of the shape of the time-cost trade-off function, particular attention being given to the determinants of the elasticity of cost with respect to time. Also, we describe the extent to which various stages of the innovation process are carried out in parallel, and the relationship between such overlap and a project's cost structure. Finally, we see how rapidly these projects should have been carried out, if the object was to maximize expected profits (and if the managers' estimates of the relevant variables were correct); and we compare these durations with the actual durations. Our results shed new light on the nature, determinants, and application of the time-cost trade-off function.

2. The Time-Cost Trade-off Function: A General Representation

To begin with, it is convenient to assume that the time-cost trade-off function—or that portion of it that is downward-sloping—can be represented by a relatively simple equation, the parameters of which vary from innovation to innovation. In particular, we assume that the trade-off function can be represented by

$$(7.1) \qquad\qquad C = v e^{\frac{\phi}{t/\alpha - 1}},$$

where C is the expected cost of innovation, t is the expected time, and v, α, and ϕ are parameters that vary from innovation to innovation. Figure 7.1 shows the nature of this function, which has a number of properties that are desirable. It is convex and has both time and cost asymptotes. Since C

FIGURE 7.1

Graphical Representation of Equation (7.1),
for $\phi = 1$ and $\phi = 2$

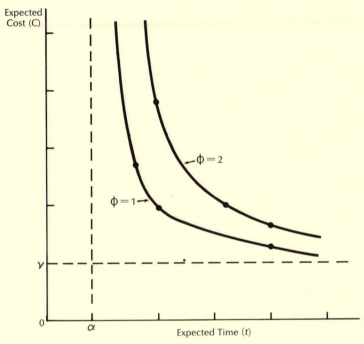

approaches v as t gets larger and larger, v can be considered the minimum expected cost of the innovation. Since t approaches α as C gets larger and larger, α can be considered the minimum expected time to complete the innovation. The elasticity of cost with respect to time, $-\dfrac{dC}{dt}\dfrac{t}{C}$, is equal to

(7.2) $$\frac{\phi(t/\alpha)}{(t/\alpha - 1)^2}.$$

Thus, for a given value of t/α, the elasticity of cost with respect to time is determined by ϕ.

If equation (7.1) holds,

(7.3) $$\ln C = \ln v + \phi \left(\frac{t}{\alpha} - 1 \right)^{-1}$$

For each innovation, values of C at various values of t were obtained from the respondents, as indicated in the previous chapter.[1] Also, an estimate of α for each innovation was obtained directly from the respondents. Thus, estimates of ν and ϕ could be obtained by regressing $\ln C$ on $1/(t/\alpha - 1)$. The results are summarized in Table 7.1. In general, the fit is fairly good although the number of observations is small. The values of R^2 (adjusted for degrees of freedom) are reasonably high. The range over which most

TABLE 7.1

Estimates of ν, α, ϕ and $\bar{R}^2$,
for Twenty-nine Innovations[a]

INNOVATION	ν	α	ϕ	$\bar{R}^2$
1	225	32	0.00523	0.61
2	84	24	0.09188	0.88
3	22	8	0.04184	0.74
4	274	15	0.00530	0.80
5	133	12	0.13246	0.83
6	163	9	0.38620	0.77
7	52	6	0.19958	0.87
8	2610	18	0.93982	0.94
9	15	5	0.04986	0.98
10	209	24	0.02741	0.80
11	276	18	0.25889	0.92
12	32	18	0.04442	0.88
13	354	20	0.13626	0.84
14	437	24	2.02550	0.84
15	292	20	0.06892	0.86
16	544	24	0.14806	0.78
17	185	15	0.10696	0.71
18	201	12	0.12630	0.65
19	9155	60	0.01395	0.75
20	5220	21	0.02361	0.81
21	2100	120	0.01539	0.92
22	1982	48	0.00880	0.93
23	1140	60	0.08006	0.73
24	620	48	0.83010	0.79
25	160	24	0.21138	0.69
26	1082	60	0.27708	0.95
27	1403	60	0.21411	0.98
28	595	34	0.02980	0.88
29	753	23	0.08056	0.92

[a] ν is the antilog of the least squares estimate of $\ln \nu$. It is expressed in thousands of dollars. α is expressed in months.

1. t is measured in months.

of the functions were estimated was $t/\alpha = 1$ to $t/\alpha = 2.5$, although in a few cases observations were included for points with t/α values as high as 5. Usually, though, t/α values over 2.5 were too hypothetical to be estimated well by the respondent, and in any case they seem less relevant for decision-making since most projects were actually completed with t/α equaling less than 2.5.

3. The Elasticity of Cost with Respect to Time

The elasticity of cost with respect to time is important in several ways. Although, as Marschak points out, the optimal decision process for innovation is generally sequential, long-run plans must be made, if only tentatively. Even if firm resource commitments are made for only a short time period, these commitments must be conditional on some knowledge or prediction about the set of longer-run possibilities. Thus, both for long-range planning and as a setting for short-run decision-making, estimates of the effect of changes in the total duration of the project on the expected total cost of the project are important. The elasticity of cost with respect to time is the relative expected extra cost of reducing the expected duration of the project by 1 percent. If equation (7.1) holds, this elasticity varies with t/α. When the strategy considered has a time expectation very near the minimum possible time, an alternative which will shorten time still further will increase costs considerably. On the other hand, when the expected time is much greater than the minimum, time-saving alternatives will increase costs less markedly. Table 7.2 shows the distribution of

TABLE 7.2

*Number of Innovations with Indicated Values
of Elasticity of Cost with Respect to Time,
Given Various Values of t/α,
for Twenty-nine Innovations*

VALUE OF ELASTICITY	VALUE OF t/α		
	1.00–1.29	1.30–1.79	1.80–2.49
	(number of innovations)		
0–0.25	0	3	7
0.25–0.49	1	8	2
0.50–0.99	2	5	1
1.00–1.99	6	5	2
2.00 and over	5	1	1
Total[a]	*14*	*22*	*13*

[a] The totals are less than 29 (the total number of innovations) because not every innovation had two or more points in each specified t/α range. Where an innovation had more than two points in a particular t/α range, the average of the arc elasticities in the range is given.

elasticity values for the innovations in the sample at selected t/α values. These elasticities do not depend in any way on the assumption that equation (7.1) holds. They are arc elasticities computed directly from the data provided by the respondents.

Table 7.2 shows clearly the great cost of time reduction when t/α is less than 1.3. In over one-third of the cases, if expected time is to be reduced by 1 percent, expected cost has to be increased by 2 percent or more in this range of values of t/α. The median value of the elasticity in this range of values of t/α is about 1.6. When t/α is between 1.3 and 1.8, the elasticity tends to be smaller, the median elasticity being 0.5. Moreover, in almost three-quarters of the cases, a 1-percent time saving can be "bought" for a cost increase of less than 1 percent. Finally, when t/α is between 1.8 and 2.5, the median value of the elasticity is less than 0.25, which indicates that in this range a 1-percent time decrease is available in the majority of cases at a cost increase of less than 0.25 percent. Of course, we must be careful in the interpretation of such results. They do not imply that after work has been started, cost can be increased continuously until the desired time is achieved. The time-cost points are expected values resulting from (possibly) very different approaches. These strategies encompass the entire scope of innovative activity and changes may not be feasible after work has begun.

The elasticities of cost with respect to time *at the actually realized t/α points* are given in Table 7.3. These figures give us an indication of the cost of saving time at approximately the times which actually resulted from the strategies used. As the table shows, over half of the elasticities are less than

TABLE 7.3

Number of Innovations with Indicated Values of Elasticity of Cost with Respect to Time, at Actually Realized Values of t/α, for Twenty-nine Innovations

VALUE OF ELASTICITY[a]	ACTUALLY REALIZED VALUE OF t/α			
	1.00–1.50	1.51–2.00	Over 2.00	Total
	(*numbers of innovations*)			
0	0	0	1	1
0.01–0.49	1	2	7	10
0.50–0.99	2	3	0	5
1.00–2.00	1	3	2	6
Over 2.00	5	1	1	7
Total	9	9	11	29

[a] Arc elasticities were computed between the point at the actually realized value of t and the point at the next lower value of t given by the respondent. The difference in t/α is often quite large.

1 at these points. Thus, if strategies were to be chosen for the projects which would reduce expected time 1 percent below that which was actually realized, the expected cost increase in most cases would be less than 1 percent.

4. Determinants of the Elasticity of Cost with Respect to Time (at a Given t/α)

The previous section showed that if we hold t/α constant, projects vary considerably with respect to the elasticity of cost with respect to time. Why is this so? What factors influence the value of this elasticity? Since the elasticity of cost with respect to time (at a given t/α) is directly related to ϕ (if equation (7.1) holds), another way to phrase the same question is: What factors influence the value of ϕ? The following hypotheses may be of use in answering this question.

First, the extent to which the innovation advances the state of the art may affect the value of ϕ. Other things being equal, we would expect that ϕ would be higher for a project representing a large state-of-the-art advance than for a project representing a smaller advance. That is, it should cost more to speed up a high-state-of-the-art-advance innovation. In a project attempting a considerable advance in the state of the art, there obviously is greater initial uncertainty and more learning to be done than in less ambitious projects. Later stages of the project depend more on what has been learned in earlier stages than they do in less ambitious projects. Thus, it tends to be more expensive to speed up more ambitious projects. Second, the size of the firm may also affect the value of ϕ. It has been noted that larger firms often tend to spend more to achieve given objectives. The cost of speeding up an innovation may also be positively related to firm size. Insofar as time reduction requires a certain flexibility of approach, a larger organization may be handicapped by inertia and by more difficult administrative problems. Even reaching agreement on how to proceed will take longer if more people and a longer chain of command are involved.[2]

Third, the extent of the firm's previous experience in the field of the innovation may be a determinant of ϕ. The nature of the influence of this factor is difficult to predict, however. It may be that people working in a

2. For example, see Jacob Schmookler, *Testimony before Antitrust Subcommittee of Senate Judiciary Committee* (May 27, 1965); A. Cooper, "R and D Is More Efficient in Small Companies," *Harvard Business Review*, May 1964; and Edwin Mansfield, *Industrial Research and Technological Innovation* (New York: W. W. Norton for the Cowles Foundation for Research in Economics at Yale University, 1968), Chap. 2. On the other hand, it could be argued that it is less expensive for a large firm to speed up a project because it is able to do many stages of a project simultaneously whereas this is beyond the capacities of a small firm. Clearly, the advantages of firms of various sizes depend on the nature of the project.

particular area are more aware of alternative approaches and thus better able to cut the cost of time reduction. On the other hand, it may be that a fresh viewpoint is necessary to reduce time and that people who have had experience in the area may be tied to traditional approaches and unable to find ingenious cheap ways to speed up the project. Fourth, the relative importance of labor cost may influence ϕ. In many cases, additional hours are worked at no increase in pay. This is the case where the workers involved are primarily salaried professionals whose motivation is partly derived from nonpecuniary incentives. Since many of the workers in innovative activity are often of this type, it may be that the increases in total labor cost accompanying a reduction in time are relatively moderate compared to other cost increases. Thus, a labor-intensive project—i.e., one whose costs are mostly labor costs—might be expected to have a low elasticity of cost with respect to time. Finally, ϕ may be influenced by the total project cost. If large projects require more coordination and integration of different tasks, they may be relatively more complicated and costly to speed up.

5. Empirical Results

To test these hypotheses, we ascertain the extent to which these factors can explain the observed variation in ϕ among the twenty-nine innovations. How can each of these factors be measured? Let's begin with the extent to which an innovation advances the state of the art. The measurement of this variable is a difficult problem for researchers in this area. Most measures have been derived from some type of questioning of experts in the field involved, examples being the measures used by Peck and Scherer[3] and by Summers.[4] Following much the same kind of procedure, we simply asked the respondents to evaluate each of their own innovations with respect to the extent to which it advanced the state of the art. If the advance in the state of the art was regarded as "large," a dummy variable (A) was set equal to 1; otherwise it was set equal to 0.[5] Laboratory experience was also represented by a dummy variable derived from the interviews. Respondents were asked to rate their innovations on a four-point scale ranging from "routine" to "mostly new to the lab." These data were summarized in a dummy variable set equal to 1 if the innovation work was "routine" or

3. Merton Peck and F. M. Scherer, *The Weapons Acquisition Process* (Cambridge: Harvard University Press, 1962).

4. Thomas Marschak, Thomas Glennan, and Robert Summers, *Strategy for R and D* (New York: Springer-Verlag, 1967).

5. Of course, there may have been some tendency to exaggerate the technical ambition of some projects. But this should make little differences so long as their relative position is not changed much. All that is of consequence is that the "large" advances tend to be greater than the others.

"closely related to previous capability," and 0 otherwise. Firm size was measured by annual sales for the most recent year available.

The regression results are summarized in Table 7.4. They seem consistent with most of our hypotheses. The extent of the advance in the state of the art has a significant effect on ϕ in all specifications of the equation. The sign is positive, confirming that projects that advance the state of the art substantially are relatively more expensive to speed up. Firm size also has the hypothesized effect: Innovations developed in large firms tend to be more expensive to speed up. (The regression coefficient of firm size is not significant in equations 2 and 3 in Table 7.4, but is significant in the

TABLE 7.4

Regression Coefficients[a] of Various Independent Variables in Four Regression Equations to Explain ϕ

INDEPENDENT VARIABLE	EQUATION 1	EQUATION 2[b]	EQUATION 3[c]	EQUATION 4[d]
Constant	0.03(.14)	0.17(.7)	—	—
Chemical-industry dummy variable	−0.36(2.1)	−0.32(1.9)	−0.29(1.7)	−0.32(1.9)
Firm size (millions of dollars of sales)	0.0005(1.9)	0.0002(1.4)	0.0002(1.4)	0.0003(2.2)
State-of-the-art advance	0.45(2.5)	0.31(1.9)	0.24(1.9)	0.28(2.6)
Laboratory experience	0.27(1.7)	0.26(1.6)	0.13(1.0)	—
Percentage of total cost of innovation going to labor	−0.48(1.4)	−0.61(1.8)	—	—
Total cost of innovation (thousands of dollars)	0.0001(1.5)	—	—	—
$\bar{R}^2$	0.21	0.17	0.12	0.12

a The *t* values are shown in parentheses.
b Equation 2 is the same as equation 1 except that the total cost of the innovation is excluded.
c Equation 3 is the same as equation 1 except that the total cost of the innovation and the percentage of the total cost of the innovation going to labor are omitted (and the constant is suppressed).
d Equation 4 is the same as equation 1 except that the total cost of the innovation, the percentage of the total cost of the innovation going to labor, and the laboratory-experience variable are omitted (and the constant is suppressed).

other formulations.[6]) A chemical-industry dummy variable (that is, 1 for chemical innovations and 0 otherwise) appears with a significant coefficient and is negatively related to ϕ; this indicates a tendency for chemical innovations to be less costly to speed up than the others.

The other independent variables—laboratory experience, total cost of

6. Note that the effect of firm size is not due to the fact that big firms carry out big projects and big projects are more costly to speed up. When the total cost of the project is included as an independent variable, the effect of firm size remains significant.

the innovation, and the percentage of the cost of the innovation that is labor cost—are not statistically significant, although in many instances they are close to being significant. Their regression coefficients have the expected signs in all cases.[7] Thus, while there is some indication that the influence of these factors is as we suggest, we cannot on the basis of our data rule out the possibility of a zero effect or an effect in the opposite direction.[8]

6. Factors Associated with ν and α

The value of ν represents the lowest expected cost of the innovation, regardless of time. It is the expected cost of the strategy with the lowest expected cost. Regression analysis indicates that ν is related to the firm's size and the extent to which the innovation advances the state of the art, the regression equation being

$$(7.4) \qquad \nu_i = -1344 + 2.63\, S_i + 881\, A_i, \qquad (\bar{R}^2 = 0.69)$$
$$ (0.33) \qquad (429)$$

where S_i is the amount of sales of the firm responsible for the ith innovation and A_i is the dummy variable representing the extent to which the ith innovation advances the state of the art. More than half the variation in ν in our sample is explained by firm size alone. Of course, this does not necessarily mean that it costs large firms more to innovate a *given* product. On the contrary, it may mean only that large firms tend to take on more costly projects. In order to avert risk, small firms may be less willing to accept them. (Standard errors are shown in parentheses.)

The value of α represents the expected duration of the project if it were carried out on a top-priority, "regardless of cost" basis. The managers we interviewed were asked to estimate this lead time directly. Regression analysis indicates that there is some association between α and the size of the firm and the extent of the state-of-the-art advance. Also, a significant intergroup difference was noted between chemical innovations and those in other industry groups. With C_i a dummy variable that is 1 if the ith innovation is in the chemical industry and 0 otherwise, the resulting regression is

$$(7.5) \qquad \alpha_i = 2.5 + 14.2\, A_i + 0.011\, S_i + 23.4\, C_i. \qquad (\bar{R}^2 = 0.48)$$
$$ (7.3) \qquad (0.006) \qquad (7.6)$$

The relationship between α and the size of the firm may be due to the same factors mentioned in connection with minimum cost. Bigger firms select larger-scale projects which both cost more and take longer. We would expect α to be greater for projects attempting large advances in the state of the art. The coefficient of the last term on the right in equation (7.5) seems to indicate that when the other factors are held constant, chemical innovations have higher values of α than other innovations.

7. Overlapping Stages

Table 7.5 shows the frequency with which various stages overlapped. More precisely, it records the number of innovations in which the duration of the stage in the left-hand column extended beyond the beginning of the stage specified at the top of each of the other columns. Thus it shows overlap not only between adjacent stages but also between any two stages of the innovation process. While overlap between adjacent stages was most prevalent (as might be expected), there were some cases of overlap between other stages. For example, applied research (stage 1) continued through the beginning of manufacturing start-up in three cases, thus overlapping all of the other stages of innovative activity.

TABLE 7.5

Frequency of Occurrence of Overlap Between Various Stages of the Innovation Process, for Twenty-nine Innovations

| | LATER STAGE | | | |
EARLIER STAGE	2. SPECI-FICATIONS	3. PROTOTYPE OR PILOT PLANT	4. TOOLING AND MANUFACTURING FACILITIES	5. MANUFACTURING START-UP
	(number of innovations)			
1. Applied research	11	10	7	3
2. Specifications	—	12	5	2
3. Prototype or pilot plant	—	—	18	4
4. Tooling and manufacturing facilities	—	—	—	16

The extent of overlap is not shown in Table 7.5. Two stages were counted as overlapping for this table if any part of one was performed simultaneously with any part of the other. What sorts of generalizations can be made about the extent of overlap in our sample? An examination of the data indicates that two patterns of overlap between adjacent stages—*j* and

$(j + 1)$—are especially common. The first pattern (pattern 1) is characterized by the simultaneous ending of the two stages. In most cases where this pattern was observed, stage $(j + 1)$ was shorter than stage j, and they ended at the same point. In a few of the cases we classified as pattern 1, stages j and $(j + 1)$ took the same length of time and ended simultaneously. The second common pattern (pattern 2) is characterized by stage j ending about halfway through stage $(j + 1)$. We classified any case as pattern 2 if stage j was going on during 30 to 70 percent of the duration of stage $(j + 1)$. Figure 7.2 illustrates these overlap patterns.

FIGURE 7.2

Two Common Patterns of Overlap Between
Stages of the Innovation Process

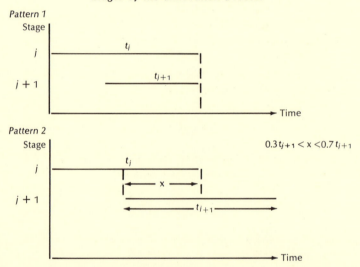

Table 7.6 shows the frequency with which these overlap patterns occurred in our sample. Pattern 1 was the predominant form of overlap between stages 1 and 2 and between stages 4 and 5. For each of these pairs of stages more than three-quarters of the occurrences of overlap were of the pattern-1 type. Pattern 2 was the most common form of overlap between stages 3 and 4. About two-thirds of the observed instances of overlap between these stages were classified as pattern 2. Neither pattern 1 nor pattern 2 seemed to occur frequently in the cases of overlap between stages 2 and 3. The relationships noted above did not seem to vary between product groups. Both the chemical subsample and the nonchemicals showed the same general characteristics. In each case, pattern 1 was most common among overlaps between stages 1 and 2 and between stages 4 and 5, while pattern 2 characterized most of the overlaps between stages 3 and 4.

TABLE 7.6

Frequency of Occurrence of Various Patterns of
Overlap Between Stages of the Innovation Process,
for Twenty-nine Innovations

	OVERLAP BETWEEN			
TYPE OF INNOVATION AND PATTERN OF OVERLAP	STAGES 1 AND 2	STAGES 2 AND 3	STAGES 3 AND 4	STAGES 4 AND 5
	(number of innovations)			
Chemical innovations				
Total number with overlap	6	10	8	6
Number with pattern 1	5	0	1	6
Number with pattern 2	0	4	4	0
Other	1	6	3	0
Nonchemical innovations				
Total number with overlap	5	2	10	10
Number with pattern 1	3	0	0	7
Number with pattern 2	0	0	7	2
Other	2	2	3	1

8. Overlap Structure

In order to compare the extent and type of overlap occurring in various projects, we use the concept of *overlap structure,* which is based on percentage measures that are comparable among projects with different absolute time dimensions. The overlap structure is a four-element vector (V_1, V_2, V_3, V_4) of the four overlaps between adjacent stages of innovative activity,[9] the measure of overlap between the jth and $(j + 1)$th stages being the ratio of the length of time the two stages go on simultaneously to the sum of the durations of the two stages.[10] That is,

$$(7.6) \qquad V_j = \frac{l_j}{t_j + t_{j+1}},$$

where l_j is the length of time the jth and $(j + 1)$th stages go on simultaneously, t_j is the duration of the jth stage, and t_{j+1} is the duration of the $(j + 1)$th stage.

What determines the value of V_j for a particular project? First, V_j

---

9. We do not consider explicitly the overlap between nonadjacent stages. As Table 7.5 shows, these types of overlap were much less frequent.

10. Another possible measure is $\left(\dfrac{l_j}{t_j} + \dfrac{l_j}{t_{j+1}} \right)$. This measure is closely related to V_j.

Whereas $V_j = \dfrac{l_j}{t_j} \left(1 + \dfrac{t_{j+1}}{t_j} \right)^{-1}$, this measure equals $\dfrac{l_j}{t_j} \left(1 + \dfrac{t_j}{t_{j+1}} \right)$.

clearly depends on how rapidly the project is carried out. Although projects differ with regard to actual duration and minimum expected duration, one can use a project's value of t/α as a rough measure of how rapidly—relative to the minimum time—it is carried out. In other words, t/α is a measure of how close the project comes to being carried out on a crash basis. Clearly, we would expect that, as t/α decreases, the amount of overlap will increase.[11] Second, we would expect V_j to be related to the size of the firm in which the innovative activity is carried out. A large firm may have enough personnel and other resources to carry out several activities at once. Indeed, in big firms different stages of innovative activity are often done in completely separate units or divisions of the firm. A smaller organization, on the other hand, has fewer specialized workers, and the same individuals may have to perform different functions. This may to some extent reduce the degree to which the firm can utilize strategies involving overlap. Thus we would expect to find a positive relationship between firm size and the extent of overlap.

To test these hypotheses, we assume that

$$(7.7) \qquad V_{ji} = \phi_{j0} + \phi_{j1}(t_i/\alpha_i) + \phi_{j2}(t_i/\alpha_i)^2 + \phi_{j3}S_i + U_i,$$

where V_{ji} is the value of V_j for the ith innovation, t_i/α_i is the value of t/α for the ith innovation, S_i are the sales of the firm carrying out the ith innovation, and U_i is a random error term. The results for V_1, V_2, and V_3 are as follows:

$$(7.8) \qquad V_{1i} = 57.6 - 35.2\, t_i/\alpha_i + 6.0\,(t_i/\alpha_i)^2 \qquad (\bar{R}^2 = 0.04)$$
$$(19.6) \qquad (3.3)$$

$$(7.9) \qquad V_{2i} = 24.7 - 10.5\, t_i/\alpha_i + 0.019\, S_i \qquad (\bar{R}^2 = 0.33)$$
$$(3.3) \qquad (0.005)$$

$$(7.10) \qquad V_{3i} = 12.9 - 1.1\,(t_i/\alpha_i)^2 + 0.011\, S_i \qquad (\bar{R}^2 = 0.14)$$
$$(0.5) \qquad (0.005)$$

In each of these equations, we have deleted statistically nonsignificant independent variables. The equation for V_4 is not presented because none of the regression coefficients was statistically significant in the regression.

The results—except for V_4—are quite in line with our hypotheses, t/α being inversely related to V_1, V_2, and V_3, and S being directly related to V_2 and V_3.[12] Figures 7.3, 7.4, and 7.5 show the relationships in equations

11. This is, of course, not *necessarily* the case. It would be possible for the individual times of stages to decrease to such an extent that t/α was reduced with a reduction in overlap. This possibility was discussed with the respondents. They were asked whether a project with a lead time of α—i.e., an all-out "crash program" effort—would contain more or less overlap than the actually completed project. In more than 75 percent of the cases in the sample, the estimate was that overlap would increase with reduced t/α. In the rest, respondents felt that there would be little change or a slight reduction in overlap with reduced t/α. It is perhaps surprising that so large a proportion fell into the latter category.

12. In the case of V_1, increases in t/α beyond $t/\alpha = 2.95$ are associated with higher values of

(7.8), (7.9), and (7.10). These figures indicate the way in which the extent of overlap is used by firms to speed up projects. They also provide valuable information concerning the extent to which large firms overlap stages more than small firms do. Heretofore, no information was available on either of these counts.

FIGURE 7.3

Relationship Between V_{1i} and t_i/α_i, in Twenty-nine Innovations

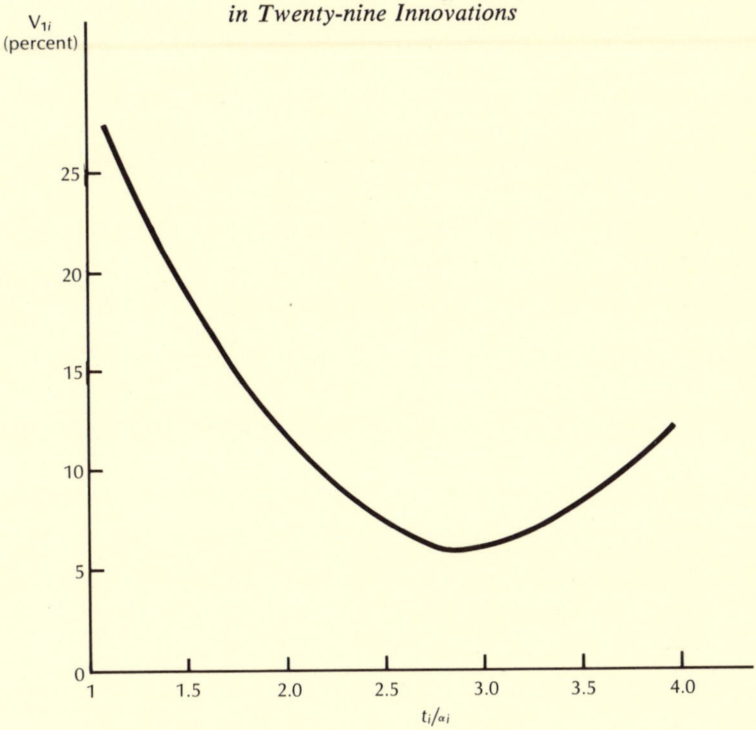

Source: Equation (7.8).

9. Cost Structure, Time, and Overlap

This section investigates the relationship between a project's overlap structure and the relative costliness of a certain stage of innovative activity. The managers we interviewed felt that increased overlap was an important source of the expected rise in cost associated with a decrease in expected time. In general it was felt that greater overlap between two adjacent stages

---

V_1. But only a small proportion of the cases have values of t/α exceeding 2.95, and this tendency for V_1 to increase in this range with t/α may not be statistically significant.

FIGURE 7.4

Relationship Between V_{2i} and t_i/α_i, for Various Values of S_i, in Twenty-nine Innovations[a]

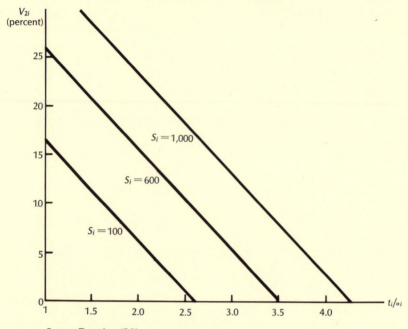

Source: Equation (7.9).

[a] S_i is measured in millions of dollars per year.

would lead to added cost in the later stage. The most commonly mentioned reason for this was characterized by one manager as the increased likelihood of "engineering-change notices." The problem arises when work in the later stage is critically dependent on information or results obtained in the earlier stage. When overlap is introduced, the later stage must be started before the results of the earlier-stage work are known. Estimates or tentative results must be used as the basis of the later work. If these are proved incorrect by information obtained through subsequent activity in the earlier stage, the expense of correcting mistakes and redoing work is considerable. This effect is most often noted in regard to overlap between stage 3 (prototype) and stage 4 (tooling and construction of manufacturing facilities), i.e., in cases where tooling and preparation of the production facilities are begun before all prototype engineering problems have been solved. When the prototype stage is finally completed, tooling may have to be modified or even discarded.[13]

13. Another effect of overlap on cost is simply the increased expense of the administration and coordination of simultaneous activities. On the other hand, there may be economies of scale in some of the relevant activities.

FIGURE 7.5

Relationship Between V_{3i} and t_i/α_i, for Various Values of S_i, in Twenty-nine Innovations[a]

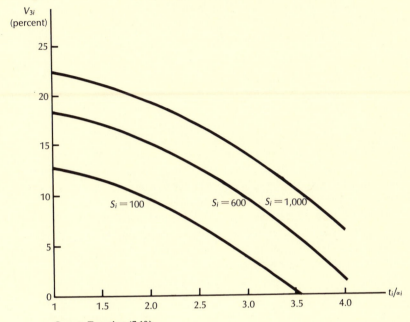

Source: Equation (7.10).

[a] S_t is measured in millions of dollars per year.

As a partial test of this hypothesis, we regressed C_{4i}, the relative costliness of stage 4 (tooling and manufacturing facilities), on V_{3i} (the overlap between stages 3 and 4) and V_{4i} (the overlap between stages 4 and 5). Specifically,

$$(7.11) \qquad c_{4i} = E_{4i} \Big/ \sum_{j=1}^{5} E_{ji},$$

where E_{ji} is the expenditure during the jth stage on the ith innovation. That is, C_{4i} is the proportion of (nonmarketing) costs for the ith innovation occurring in stage 4. The reason why V_{4i} is included in the regression is that when considerable overlap occurs between stages 4 and 5, some of the costs of stage 5 are likely to be charged to stage 4. The resulting regression is

$$(7.12) \qquad C_{4i} = 18.4 + 0.67\ V_{3i} + 0.91\ V_{4i},$$
$$\qquad\qquad\qquad (0.23) \qquad (0.25)$$

where $\overline{R}^2 = 0.44$. The results are quite in line with our hypotheses, the regression coefficients of V_{3i} and V_{4i} both having the expected sign and being highly significant from a statistical point of view. Moreover, it appears that about half the variation among projects in the relative cost of stage 4 can be explained by these two independent variables. These results are interesting, since they represent the first statistical evidence concerning the effect of overlap on costs.[14] Note, however, that these findings do not show that overlap increases the total cost of the project. All they show is that as overlap between stages 4 and adjacent stages is increased, the proportion of total costs incurred in stage 4 also increases. This is an interesting result, but only a beginning.

10. The Time-Cost Combination That Maximizes Expected Profits

What point on the time-cost trade-off function would have maximized the firm's expected discounted profits in the case of each of the innovations in our sample? To answer this question, one requires a great deal of detailed information regarding each innovation. To find out the managers' appraisals of some of the relevant variables, we asked them to make rough estimates, for various changes in the expected duration of the project, of the changes in the discounted value of the expected profits (gross of innovation costs) from the innovation. Let the resulting relation between expected discounted gross profits and the duration of the project be $R(t)$, where t is the length of the project. Figure 7.6 shows a case where $R(t)$ is linear, $C(t)$ being the time-cost trade-off function discussed in the previous chapter. Expected discounted profit is

$$(7.13) \qquad P(t) = R(t) - C(t),$$

and the first-order condition for the maximization of $P(t)$ is

$$\frac{dC}{dt} = \frac{dR}{dt}.$$

Substituting the trade-off function used in equation (7.1) for $C(t)$, we have

$$(7.14) \qquad \frac{-v e^{\frac{\phi}{t/\alpha - 1}} \alpha \phi}{(t - \alpha)^2} = \frac{dR}{dt}.$$

The value of t that satisfies equation (7.14) is the "optimal" duration of the project under the assumption of a linear utility function under uncertainty. It is the duration that *would have* maximized expected profit, *if the managers' estimates of $C(t)$ and $R(t)$ are correct.* Thus, a comparison of this "optimal" result with the time-cost combination that actually oc-

14. For some discussions of overlap from the point of view of military development, see Marschak, Glennan, and Summers, *op. cit.*; and B. Klein, "The Decision Making Problem in Development," in *The Rate and Direction of Inventive Activity* (National Bureau of Economic Research, 1962).

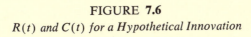

FIGURE 7.6

R(t) and C(t) for a Hypothetical Innovation

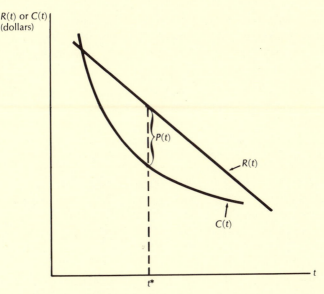

curred provides some indication of the way in which the actual time-cost combination differed from the expected time-cost combination that, after the project was over, appeared under this assumption to have been "optimal." (Needless to say, since the firm may not have wanted to maximize expected profit, the "optimal" result may not have been truly optimal.[15]) Inserting estimates of α, ϕ, ν, and dR/dt into equation (7.14), we determine the value of t that satisfies the condition for maximizing expected discounted profits. To do this, we require (in addition to the estimates of α, ϕ, and ν in Table 7.1) estimates of dR/dt for each innovation. As noted above, we asked the managers to estimate what the difference in expected discounted gross profits would have been if the project had been completed six months later or one year later or six months earlier or one year earlier than actually turned out to be the case. Such data could be obtained for sixteen innovations. From an examination of these estimates, it appears that, in the neighborhood of the actually realized time, $R(t)$ could generally be approximated linearly, in this sample of cases.[16] The expected loss in gross profit due to a one-month delay in completing the project was taken as an approximation to dR/dt. Using this value and the

15. Moreover, the "optimal" combination may not have been the combination that the firm aimed for. Thus, the difference between actual and "optimal" time and cost does not measure how far the firm "missed" its targets. Nonetheless, it is of interest to see what the differences look like.

16. $R(t)$ shifts over time with the expectations of the firm. Our estimates of $R(t)$ are *ex post*: They are the estimates made at the end of the project. In this sense, they are fully comparable with our estimates of $C(t)$.

estimates of α, ϕ, and ν, we solved equation (7.14) for t^*, the value of t that would have maximized expected profits.

Table 7.7 presents the value of t^*, as well as the minimum time (α) and the actually realized time (t), for each innovation. Also given is the difference, absolute and relative, between actual and "optimal" times. In every case in the sample, the project took longer than the "optimal" time, the value of ($t - t^*$) always being positive.[17] In other words, the expected

TABLE 7.7

*Comparison of t^*, t, and α,
for Sixteen Innovations*

INNOVATION	α	t	t^*	$t - t^*$	$(t - t^*)/t$
	(IN MONTHS)				(PERCENT)
Chemical 1	32	40	34.8	5.2	15
Chemical 2	120	144	125.2	18.8	15
Chemical 3	48	60	59.7	.3	1
Chemical 4	24	36	27.0	9.0	33
Chemical 5	34	46	44.8	1.2	3
Chemical 6	23	35	31.8	3.2	10
Machine 1	15	25	24.8	.2	1
Machine 2	20	40	29.0	11.0	38
Machine 3	24	73	66.0	7.0	11
Machine 4	24	94	40.0	54.0	135
Machine 5	18	77	29.5	47.5	161
Electronics 1	6	12	8.7	3.3	38
Electronics 2	9	25	15.0	10.0	67
Electronics 3	12	30	21.1	8.9	42
Electronics 4	18	41	28.0	13.0	46
Electronics 5	24	35	27.3	7.7	28

time that seemingly would have maximized expected discounted profits—according to the managers' own estimates of $C(t)$ and $R(t)$—was always exceeded. Why is this the case? In part, of course, this result may be due to the tendency, studied in Chapter 5, for projects characteristically to overrun time estimates. In addition, it could be due to the fact that the functions, $C(t)$ and $R(t)$, on which decisions were actually based were not *ex post* functions. Shifts over time in $C(t)$ and $R(t)$ could account for the result, if the "optimal" lead time when a strategy was chosen was greater than the

17. The difference between t_i and t^*_i is correlated significantly with the total cost of the project and the size of the firm carrying it out. In particular,

$$t_i - t^*_i = 3.01 + 0.03 S_i - 0.007 C_i,$$
$$(0.01) \qquad (0.003)$$

where S_i is the firm's sales and C_i is the total cost of the project.

ex post "optimal" time. However, the managers, when queried on this point, did not seem to feel that such shifts were as systematic or regular as the consistency of our result would imply, although they may have been a factor.

Another possibility is that our analyses fails to recognize a constraint that the firm must consider in choosing its strategies. It is obvious that the shorter the firm attempts to make a project, the more management time is required to monitor and oversee it. For example, a crash project to develop and produce a new product will require far more management time than a leisurely project aimed at the same goal. If management time is limited, this could also help to explain our empirical results. Still further, another possibility is that these firms are averse to risk and that the variance of profits is smaller when the duration of the project is greater. This too might help to explain the observed results.[18]

11. Summary

The major conclusions of this chapter are as follows. First, it is possible to represent the time-cost trade-off function—or that part of it that is downward-sloping—by a simple equation, the parameters of which vary from innovation to innovation. This equation has three parameters, one being the minimum expected cost of the project, another being the minimum expected duration of the project, and the third determining the elasticity of cost with respect to time. In general, this equation fits the data for the twenty-nine innovations quite well, the coefficient of correlation usually being 0.9 or more. The elasticity of cost with respect to time is the expected percentage increase in cost due to an expected reduction of the duration of the project by 1 percent. This elasticity becomes greater as the duration of the project is pushed closer and closer to its minimum value. When the duration of the project is less than 30 percent above its minimum value, this elasticity averages about 1.6 in our sample of innovations. When the duration of the project is about 30–80 percent above its minimum value, this elasticity averages about 0.5.

Second, with t/α held constant, the elasticity of cost with respect to time is directly related to a project's value of ϕ, if our simple equation holds. According to our data, a project's value of ϕ depends, in turn, on the extent to which the project advances the state of the art and on the size of the firm carrying out the project. Thus, projects that attempt greater advances in the state of the art and that are carried out by larger firms tend to be more costly than others to speed up. In our sample of projects, the

---

18. It might be added that one obvious limitation of the time-cost trade-off function is that it provides no information concerning risk. It is based entirely on the minimization of expected cost, given expected time. The importance of this limitation should be clear enough.

minimum expected cost of a project is directly related to the size of the technical advance and the size of the firm carrying out the project. The minimum expected duration of a project is also directly related to these variables. In large part, the relationship between firm size and a project's minimum expected cost or minimum expected duration reflects the fact that bigger firms carry out bigger projects.

Third, an important aspect of a project is the extent to which various stages are overlapped. There are two common patterns of overlap, one generally occurring between stages 1 and 2 and stages 4 and 5, the other generally occurring between stages 3 and 4. In our sample of projects, there is a statistically significant relationship between the extent to which various stages are overlapped and the speed at which the project is carried out and the size of the firm carrying out the project. The managers we interviewed felt that increased overlap was an important source of the expected cost increase associated with a decrease in expected duration. This effect was most often noted in connection with the overlap between the prototype stage and the stage entailing the construction of manufacturing facilities. The data indicate that the proportion of total costs occurring in stage 4 is directly related to the extent of overlap.

Finally, using the managers' estimates of the time-cost trade-off function and $R(t)$, we can determine the time-cost combination that would have maximized expected profit. It turns out that the actual duration exceeded this "optimal" duration in every case. In part, this may be due to the fact that the "optimal" duration does not take account of the fact that quicker completion of projects generally entails a greater demand on management time and attention. Also, the firms may have been averse to risk, and the variance of profits may have been smaller for strategies with longer expected duration.

8 INNOVATION AND DISCOVERY

IN THE ETHICAL

PHARMACEUTICAL INDUSTRY

1. Introduction

In this chapter, we focus attention on the process of innovation and discovery in one of the most dynamic and research-intensive industries in the American economy—the ethical drug industry. A pharmaceutical innovation is the first application of a pharmaceutical discovery. The distinction between an innovation and a discovery is important in the ethical pharmaceutical industry because the medical benefits of a pharmaceutical discovery cannot be fully realized until the drug is actually produced and distributed to the medical profession.[1] Fortunately, it is not too difficult to identify the innovator—the firm that was first to introduce a certain new drug to the market. What is more difficult is to trace an innovation back to its sources.

To begin with, we study the characteristics of the innovators—the firms which are first to convert pharmaceutical discoveries into commercialized products. To what extent have the largest firms been the innovators in this industry? What have been the relative contributions of large and small firms to pharmaceutical innovation? Do smaller firms now do less innovating, relative to larger firms, than in the past? Next, we look at the sources of the discoveries which lead to pharmaceutical innovations. How frequently is the same firm discoverer and innovator? To what extent do other

1. The history of penicillin is ample proof that a major medical advance has little medical or economic significance until it is actually applied. The benefits of Fleming's 1929 discovery were not realized until the widespread use of penicillin during World War II. The history of penicillin has been recorded in considerable detail in several sources. For a condensed description, see J. Jewkes, D. Sawers, and R. Stillerman, *The Sources of Invention* (New York: W. W. Norton, 1970), pp. 23–25 and 338–339. More extensive accounts are provided in L. J. Ludovici, *Fleming—Discoverer of Penicillin* (London: Andrew Dates, Ltd., 1952); Ruth Fox, "A Science Milestone—Sir Alexander Fleming and the Story of Penicillin," *Science Digest* (September 1953); and Alexander Fleming, *Penicillin—Its Practical Application*, second ed. (London, 1946).

domestic firms, foreign firms, universities, and government research agencies provide the discoveries which lead to pharmaceutical innovations? How do the medical importance and commercial significance of innovations based on discoveries made by external sources compare with those of innovations based on discoveries made by the innovating firm? Finally, we examine the time lag between discovery and innovation for pharmaceutical products. We try to determine how the time lag varies among types of products and how the time lag has changed over time. We also try to find out whether the lag is shorter when the discoverer himself innovates, as has been suggested elsewhere.[2]

2. The Basic Data

In order to examine the relationship between innovation and the size of firm, the sources of innovation, and the lag between discovery and innovation, it is necessary to develop a list of relevant pharmaceutical innovations. The list of pharmaceutical innovations we use is based on a study of significant pharmaceutical advances conducted by the American Medical Association's Commission on the Cost of Medical Care.[3] This 1963 study of significant pharmaceutical advances was based on a survey of approximately four hundred physicians and pharmacologists.[4] Each participant in the survey was sent a list of eighty-nine important therapeutic agents in the United States introduced since 1934.[5] (The methods used to develop the list of eighty-nine innovations are described in footnote 5.) Each respondent was asked to indicate the items which he considered the most significant developments of the 1935–1962 period.[6] The list of pharmaceutical advances sent to each participant, and the survey results, are reproduced in Tables 8.1 and 8.2, respectively.

2. See J. Enos, "Invention and Innovation in the Petroleum Refining Industry," in *The Rate and Direction of Inventive Activity* (Princeton, N.J.: Princeton University Press, 1962).
3. The American Medical Association Commission on the Cost of Medical Care, *The Cost of Medical Care*, Vol. III, (Chicago: American Medical Association, 1964).
4. The survey results for the study of medical advances indicated that many breakthroughs were possible, in part, because of certain drug developments. As a result the Commission on the Cost of Medical Care decided to institute a systematic review of important pharmaceutical advances.
5. The list of eighty-nine innovations was developed in the following way. The staff of the Commission on the Cost of Medical Care abridged to 140 items the list of all drugs developed during 1935–1962, using prescription volumes reported in National Disease and Therapeutic Index surveys. The American Medical Association's Department of Drugs constructed a separate list of 120 therapeutic agents which it considered important. The commission staff and the AMA Department of Drugs jointly selected eighty-nine drugs from the two lists and prepared the summary list shown in Table 8.1.
The eighty-nine drugs were included in an August 2, 1963 questionnaire which was mailed to a sample of 397 physicians and pharmacologists selected from a list of 2,780 consultants to the American Medical Association Council on Drugs.
6. The explanatory letter which accompanied the questionnaire defined a "significant advance" as one which greatly benefited mankind and the medical profession. An alternative definition of "a single chemical entity or group of drugs, which physicians could least do without" was also suggested. The panel of participants was asked to consider only therapeutic agents introduced in the United States and not to use prescription volume or other economic bases in making a selection.

TABLE 8.1

*Important Therapeutic Agents Now in Use
in the United States and Introduced Since 1934*

Local anesthetics
    Lidocaine
    Mepivacaine

Antihistaminics
    Diphenhydramine and 30 others

Anti-infectives
    Antibacterial
        Chloramphenicol
        Erythromycin, salts and esters
        Nitrofurans
        Oleandomycin
        Penicillin: 10 basic penicillins, plus salts and esters
        Streptomycin
        Sulfonamides
        Tetracyclines, 4 derivatives, plus salts and esters
    Antitubercular
        Cycloserine
        Ethionamide
        Isoniazid
        P-aminosalicylic acid, salts and esters
        Pyrazinamide
        Viomycin
    Antifungal
        Amphotericin B
        Griseofulvin
        Hydroxystilbamidine
        Nystatin
    Antiviral
        Idoxuridine

Antineoplastics
    Busulfan
    Chlorambucil, including nitrogen mustards
    Dromostanolone
    Radiophosphate
    Sodium Aminopterin
    Thio-tepa
    Triethylenemelamine

    Vinblastine

Antiparasitics
    Antiamebic
        Arsthinol
        Glycobiarsol
        P-ureidobenzene arsonic acid
    Antimalarial
        Amodiaquine
        Chloroquin compounds
        Pyrimethamine
    Anti-trichomonal
        Metronidazole
    Anthelmintic
        Dithiazanine
        Piperazine derivatives
        Pyrvinium

Autonomics
    Bronchodilator
        Cyclopentamine
        Isoproterenol
    Cholinergic
        Bethanechol
        Ambenonium
    Anticholinergic
        Methantheline and others

Cardiovasculars
    Antihypertensive
        Ganglionic blocking agent
        Guanethidine
        Hydralazine
        Methyldopa
        Rauwolfia and Veratrum
        Sympatholytic agents
    Vasoconstrictor
        Mephentermine
        Phenylephrine
        Propylhexedrine

Central depressants
    Analgesic
        Phenylbutazone

(*Table continues on the next page*)

TABLE **8.1** (continued)

Propoxyphene	Estrogen-gestogen mixtures
Narcotic analgesic	Progesterones
Meperidine	Testosterone
Methadone	Levo-Thyroxin
General anesthetic	Antithyroid agents
Halogenated hydrocarbons	Antidiabetes agents
Anticonvulsant	*Immunologics*
Hydantoins	Immune globulins
Methadiones	Vaccines (poliomyelitis, measles,
Phenacemide	influenza, etc.)
Primidone	*Metabolics*
Succinimides	Vitamins
Hypnotic	Cyanocobalamin
Barbiturates	Menadione and derivatives
Non-barbiturates	*Relaxants*
Tranquilizer	Skeletal muscle relaxants
Chlorpromazine and others	(a) about 7 surgical, peripherally
Antiparkinsonism agent	acting preparations
Trihexyphenidyl and others	(b) about 8 centrally acting
Hematologics	preparations
Anticoagulants	*Diuretics*
Blood-plasma substitutes	Chlorthalidone
Hormones, synthetic substitutes, and	Oral organomercurials
antigonists	Quinethazone
Cortisone, salts and esters	Spironolactone
Estradiol, estrone, salts and esters	Thiazides

Source: The American Medical Association Commission on the Cost of Medical Care, *The Cost of Medical Care,* Vol. III (Chicago: American Medical Association, 1964), pp. 20–22.

The limitations of this list of pharmaceutical advances should be noted before we proceed further. One set of problems results from the Commission's decision to reduce the number of pharmaceutical advances listed by using one entry to represent an entire class of drugs. In some instances, such as tranquilizers and antihistaminics, this decision resulted in the omission of some distinct innovations.[7] In order to incorporate some of

7. The tranquilizer entry in the AMA list is chlorpromazine, a phenothiazine compound which revolutionized the treatment of mental illness at the time of its introduction in 1954. The majority of the other tranquilizers marketed by 1962 were phenothiazine compounds and hence they could legitimately be considered modifications of chlorpromazine. Between 1954 and 1962, however, two chemically distinct classes of tranquilizer drugs—the meprobamates and the benzo-diapans—were introduced. As new chemical classes, these drugs constitute separate innovations. Similarly, the one entry for antihistaminics, "diphenhydramine and 30 others," encompasses four distinct classes of drugs.

TABLE 8.2
Percent of Consultants Responding to AMA Survey
Who Chose the Thirty-one Most Often Mentioned Pharmaceuticals

	TOTAL ALL SPECIALTIES	INTERNAL MEDICINE	NEUROLOGY AND PSYCHIATRY	PHARMA-COLOGY	RADIOLOGY	SURGERY	ALL OTHER
Number of usable returns	304	125	41	23	22	20	73
Penicillin	93.8	93.6	100.0	91.3	86.4	90.0	94.5
Adrenocorticosteroids	91.8	91.2	97.6	87.0	86.4	100.0	90.4
Vaccines	88.8	90.4	90.2	78.3	86.4	95.0	87.7
Synthetic anticoagulants	87.8	89.6	82.9	87.0	81.8	95.0	87.7
Streptomycin	84.2	88.0	87.8	78.3	81.8	75.0	80.8
Isoniazid	83.9	86.4	80.5	87.0	86.4	85.0	79.5
Chlorpromazine and other tranquilizers	83.9	83.2	97.6	87.0	68.2	90.0	79.5
Hydantoins	81.3	86.4	100.0	87.0	59.1	80.0	67.1
Diphenhydramine and 30 other antihistaminics	80.6	77.6	90.2	82.6	81.8	80.0	79.5
Thiazides	79.6	83.2	73.2	91.3	54.5	85.0	79.5
Sulfonamides	76.6	78.4	73.2	78.3	72.7	65.0	79.5
Tetracycline derivatives	76.6	77.6	58.5	87.0	63.6	90.0	82.2
Rauwolfia and Veratrum alkaloids	74.3	74.4	75.6	65.2	68.2	80.0	76.7
Meperidine	71.7	73.6	65.9	69.6	59.1	75.0	75.3

(Table continues on the next page)

TABLE 8.2 (continued)

	TOTAL ALL SPECIALTIES	INTERNAL MEDICINE	NEUROLOGY AND PSYCHIATRY	PHARMA-COLOGY	RADIOLOGY	SURGERY	ALL OTHER
Chloramphenicol	69.4	70.4	56.1	60.9	77.3	75.0	74.0
Oral antidiabetes agents	68.4	73.6	68.3	73.9	63.6	75.0	57.5
Chloroquin compounds	65.1	73.6	58.5	87.0	54.5	35.0	58.9
Antithyroid agents	60.2	62.4	61.0	56.5	59.1	70.0	54.8
Immune globulins	59.2	58.4	56.1	30.4	50.0	70.0	71.2
Aminosalicylic acids	57.6	56.0	46.3	69.6	72.7	80.0	52.1
Isoproterenol	52.3	56.0	41.5	69.6	40.9	70.0	45.2
Anticholinergics	46.1	40.8	68.3	21.7	59.1	40.0	47.9
Ganglionic blocking agents	42.1	52.8	41.5	34.8	22.7	25.0	37.0
Phenylephrine	41.8	32.8	46.3	39.1	54.5	55.0	47.9
Halogenated hydrocarbon anesthetics	39.8	28.8	34.1	52.2	50.0	65.0	47.9
Surgical skeletal muscle relaxants, peripherally acting preparations	36.8	21.6	58.5	47.8	22.7	75.0	41.1
Organomercurial diuretics	36.5	43.2	19.5	60.9	45.5	25.0	27.4
Estrogen-progestogen contraceptives	35.9	32.8	46.3	34.8	31.8	35.0	37.0
Antiparkinsonism agents	35.5	32.0	80.5	34.8	9.1	35.0	24.7
Hypnotic barbiturates	33.9	33.6	34.1	26.1	45.5	35.0	32.9
Lidocaine and other local anesthetics	33.6	21.6	36.6	39.1	36.4	40.0	47.9

Source: The American Medical Association Commission on the Cost of Medical Care, *The Cost of Medical Care*, Vol. III, (Chicago: American Medical Association, 1964), pp. 16–17.

these omitted innovations, we expanded the AMA list of innovations (Table 8.1) to include what seem to be the major distinct innovations in a therapeutic area.[8] Another set of innovations which is omitted from the AMA list is composed of the various pharmaceutical improvements which can accumulate over a period of years to be very important in particular chemical families.[9] There is no satisfactory way to cope with the myriad of improvement innovations, and consequently, they are excluded entirely.

Data compiled by Paul de Haen were used to determine the identity of the firm that was first to introduce each innovation and the year when the innovation was introduced.[10] The expanded list of innovations is presented in Table 8.3. The innovations are listed by trademark name (as opposed to generic name in Table 8.1) with the name of the innovating firm and year of introduction shown.[11] The innovations are grouped into two time periods —1935–1949 and 1950–1962—for purposes of subsequent analysis. The important pharmaceutical advances between 1935 and 1962 produced a dramatic growth and restructuring of the ethical pharmaceutical industry. With the advent of the broad- and medium-spectrum antibiotics, tranquilizers, adrenocorticoids, diuretics, and so on, the dominance of the older full-line firms ended and industry leadership was diffused among the research-oriented specialty drug firms. The years 1949–1950 are generally

8. The distinct innovations which were omitted from the AMA list were identified by consulting standard pharmacological references, such as Goodman and Gilman, *The Pharmacologic Basis of Therapeutics,* third ed. (1965) and W. Modell, *Drugs of Choice,* fifth ed. (1968).

9. For example, the sulfonamide class of drugs has been marked by several improvements. Sulfanilamide was the first member of this class to be employed in the case of bacterial infections in man. It was supplanted in 1938 by sulfapyridine, which was replaced, in turn, by sulfathiazole in 1939. Sulfadiazine became the drug of choice in the early 1940's and has retained a prominent position among the sulfonamides ever since. Since 1940 nine other major derivatives have been synthesized and introduced for the treatment of various types of bacterial infections.

Similarly, cortisone, which was introduced commercially in 1950, was followed by hydrocortisone (1952), prednisone (1955), methylprednisolone (1957), and triamcinolone (1959). Each of these products represented an improvement in potency and safety.

10. Paul de Haen, *Non-Proprietary Name Index,* Vol. I, lists the trademark name, generic name, firm, and year of introduction for all new chemical entities introduced in U.S. ethical pharmaceutical markets since 1941. For the pre-1941 innovations, it was necessary to consult the literature on the industry. A principal reference was T. Mahoney, *The Merchants of Life* (New York: Harper, 1959).

Since the De Haen list only considers introductions in U.S. markets and not in world markets, we are really studying the relationship between size of firm and innovation in U.S. markets. Is it possible that some of the innovations in Table 8.3 were first introduced outside of the U.S. by a U.S. firm other than the one listed in Table 8.3? This is highly unlikely. In fact, the data in Table 8.3 concerning the identity of the innovator would not change if world markets were considered.

The inclusion of world markets is more likely to affect the date of innovation than the identity of the U.S. innovator. It is conceivable that in those cases where a U.S. firm both discovers and develops a new drug product, the firm may first introduce it in a foreign market rather than the U.S. market. The stricter regulations for the testing and marketing of new drug products in this country increase the possibility that this may occur.

The situation may be different when an external source, such as a university or foreign firm, discovers a new drug. In some cases, the discoverer may grant worldwide marketing rights to the U.S. innovator. Or on the other hand, marketing rights outside of the U.S. may be reserved by the discoverer, if the discoverer is a foreign pharmaceutical firm, or granted to a foreign drug firm. In either case, the identity of the American firm that was first to introduce the drug would remain the same.

11. In a few cases, two firms were credited with introducing the product simultaneously. For example, this occurred for sulfanilimide, streptomycin, isoniazid, Seromycin and Oxamycin (trademark names for cycloserine), and Fulvicin and Grifulvin (trademark names for griseofulvin).

TABLE 8.3
Pharmaceutical Innovations

PRODUCT	FIRM	YEAR	MEDICAL IMPORTANCE	ECONOMIC IMPORTANCE
	1935–1949			
Sulfanilimide	Lederle, Sharp & Dohme	1935	0.062	0.015
Neo-Synephrine	Winthrop	1935	.034	.007
Dilantin	Parke-Davis	1938	.066	.007
Estrone	Abbott, Parke-Davis	1939		.001
Nembutal	Abbott	1941	.028	.016
Heparin	Upjohn	1942	.071	.000
Premarin	Ayerst	1943		.009
Demerol	Winthrop	1944	.058	.015
Dicumarol	Abbott	1944		.000
Penicillin	Squibb	1945	.076	.283
Streptomycin	Merck, Squibb	1946	.069	.091
Tubocurarine	Squibb	1946	.030	.007
Thiouracil	Lilly	1946	.049	.004
Benadryl	Parke-Davis	1946	.066	.013
Aralen	Winthrop	1946	.052	.004
Tridione	Abbott	1946		.000
Pyribenzamine	CIBA	1946		.007
Dolophine	Lilly	1947		.000
Metandren	CIBA	1947		.003
Priscoline	CIBA	1948		.007
Aureomycin	Lederle	1948	.063	.210
Tolserol	Squibb	1948		.007
Isuprel	Winthrop	1948	.042	.004
Lidocaine	Astra	1949	.028	.009
Chloromycetin	Parke-Davis	1949	.057	.100
Mustargen	Merck	1949		.000
Milibis	Winthrop	1949		.001
Artane	Lederle	1949	.028	.004
Cortisone	Merck	1949	.074	.144
Rubramin	Squibb	1949		.012
Chlor-Trimeton	Schering	1949		.009
Pamisyl	Parke-Davis	1949	.047	.004
Urecholine Chloride	Merck	1949		.000
Benzedrex	Smith Kline & French	1949		.007
Clopane HCl	Lilly	1949		.000
Wyamine	Wyeth	1949		.000
Syncurine	Burroughs Wellcome	1949		.001

TABLE **8.3** (continued)

PRODUCT	FIRM	YEAR	MEDICAL IMPORTANCE	ECONOMIC IMPORTANCE
	1950–1962			
Banthine	Searle	1950	.068	.016
Camoquin	Parke-Davis	1950		.000
Bistrum Bromide	Squibb	1951	.062	.000
Phenurone	Abbott	1951		.000
Phenergan	Wyeth	1951		.002
Bentyl	Merrell	1951		.004
Expandex	Commerical Solvents	1951		.000
Faxedil Triethiodide	Lederle	1951		.000
Anectine	Burroughs Wellcome	1952		.000
Ilotycin	Lilly	1952		.026
Thiomerin	Lakeside	1952	.054	.005
Butazolidin	Geigy	1952		.008
Apresoline	CIBA	1952		.007
Hedulin	Walker	1952		.001
Isoniazid	Hoffmann-LaRoche, Squibb	1952	.123	.001
Balarsen	Endo	1952		.000
Raudixin	Squibb	1953	.109	.045
Milontin	Parke-Davis	1953		.000
Furadantin	Eaton	1953		.026
Diamox	Lederle	1953		.013
Daraprim	Burroughs Wellcome	1953		.000
Antepar	Burroughs Wellcome	1953		.003
Nystatin	Squibb	1954		.004
Viocin Sulfate	Pfizer	1953		.000
Hydroxystilbamidine Isethionate	Merrell	1954		.000
Triethylene Melamine	Lederle	1954		.000
Tyzine	Pfizer	1954		.003
Thorazine	Smith Kline & French	1954	.123	.192
Synthroid	Travenol	1955		.001
Salk Vaccine	Lilly, Parke-Davis	1955	.130	.080
Doriden	CIBA	1954		.011
Myleran	Burroughs Wellcome	1954		.002
Miltown	Wallace	1955		.122
Pyrazinamide	Merck	1955		.000
Cycloserine	Lilly, Merck	1956		.001
Vanquin	Parke-Davis	1956		.000

TABLE **8.3** (continued)

PRODUCT	FIRM	YEAR	MEDICAL IMPORTANCE	ECONOMIC IMPORTANCE
Matromycin	Pfizer	1956		.005
Flexin	McNeil	1956		.003
Robaxin	Robins	1957		.005
Orinase	Upjohn	1957	.100	.058
Diuril	Merck	1957	.117	.091
Halothane	Ayerst	1957	.060	.022
Darvon	Lilly	1957		.021
Enovid	Searle	1957	.054	.013
Leukeran	Burroughs Wellcome	1957		.001
Sinaxar	Armour	1958		.001
Fungizone	Squibb	1958		.000
Delvex	Lilly	1958		.000
Griseofulvin	Schering, McNeil	1959		.026
Thio-Tepa	Lederle	1959		.000
Norflex	Riker	1959		.001
Lucarthan	Burroughs Wellcome	1960		.000
Librium	Hoffmann-LaRoche	1960		.098
Aldactone	Searle	1960		.004
Ismelin	CIBA	1960		.001
Athrombin-K	Purdue-Frederick	1960		.000
Hygroton	Geigy	1960		.007
Carbocaine HCl	Winthrop	1960		.002
Velban	Lilly	1961		.000
Hydromox	Lederle	1962		.003
Aminopterin, Sodium	Lederle	1962		.000
Aldomet	Merck	1962		.037
Trecator	Ives-Cameron	1962		.000
Rubeovax	Merck	1962		.016
Herplex	Allergan	1962		.001
Flagyl	Searle	1963[a]		.011

[a] Although Flagyl was included in the study by the American Medical Association, it is given a 1963 introduction date by Paul de Haen.

regarded as the beginning of this leadership evolution, and we therefore might expect our results for the 1935–1949 and 1950–1962 periods to be different.

The list of innovations in Table 8.3 includes major medical advances, such as the sulfonamides, penicillin, and the broad- and medium-spectrum antibiotics, as well as some relatively minor advances. It therefore becomes necessary to weight each innovation by its relative importance. The first column of figures in Table 8.2 provides a measure of an innovation's medical importance.[12] Although tabulated survey results were only available for the thirty[13] most important innovations, we decided to use these data to provide some preliminary indication of the medical significance of the innovations. The weighting for each of these innovations was obtained by taking the percentage of all consultants who regarded a particular innovation as being among the most important (that is, the figure given in Table 8.2) and dividing it by the sum of these percentages. The column in Table 8.3 labeled "Medical Importance" shows the resulting weighted values for the innovations included among the thirty most important. An alternative weighting scheme was developed to reflect the economic impact of each drug innovation. Each innovation was weighted on the basis of its sales during the first five years following introduction (divided by the total of these sales).[14] The result obtained in this fashion for each innovation is shown in the column labeled "Economic Importance" in Table 8.3.[15]

3. Innovation and Size of Firm

The relationship between innovation and size of firm has been a much-debated issue among economists. On the one hand, Schumpeter has contended that very large firms have carried out most modern innovations.[16] He and his followers assert that innovation requires very large firms because of the huge costs involved, and that a firm must possess considerable market power if innovating is to be worthwhile.[17] On the other hand, the

12. This measure of medical importance, based on the definitions in note 6, is beset by many difficulties. We would like to have some measure of a drug's contribution to improved medical practice. But whether this measure is of much use is difficult to say. In any event, it seemed worthwhile to present results based on it.

13. Note that thirty, not all thirty-one of the innovations included in Table 8.2, are included in Table 8.3. For one of the drugs in Table 8.2, we could not obtain all of the required information.

We attempted to obtain tabulated results for all of the innovations in Table 8.1 from the American Medical Association. The AMA was unable to locate these data in its archives.

14. This approach of weighting innovations has been employed in other studies. In his study of innovation in the iron-and-steel, petroleum-refining, and bituminous-coal industries, Mansfield asked trade associations, engineering associations, and trade journals in these industries to rank innovations, using total savings from new processes and total sales volume of new products as indexes of importance. See Edwin Mansfield, *Industrial Research and Technological Innovation* (New York: W. W. Norton for the Cowles Foundation for Research in Economics at Yale University, 1968), Chap. 5. Mueller used weights to distinguish the economic importance of Du Pont's major product and process innovations during the 1920–1950 period. See W. Mueller, "The Origin of the Basic Inventions Underlying Du Pont's Major Product Innovations, 1920 to 1950," in *The Rate and Direction of Inventive Activity* (Princeton, N.J.: Princeton University Press, 1962). Also, in his study of technical change in the ethical drug industry, Comanor weighted all new products introduced between 1955 and 1960 by their sales during the first two years on the market. See William Comanor, "Research and Technical Change in the Pharmaceutical Industry" *Review of Economics and Statistics* (May 1965).

15. These economic weights are biased in favor of more recent innovations because of the expansion of the ethical pharmaceutical market. While the use of two time periods—1935–1949 and 1950–1962—eliminates extremely large differences in market size, the market growth within each time period introduces some bias of this sort.

16. For example, see Joseph Schumpeter, *Business Cycles* (New York: McGraw-Hill, 1939).

17. For further discussion of these views, see John Kenneth Galbraith, *American Capitalism* (Boston: Houghton Mifflin, 1952); A. Kaplan, *Big Enterprise in a Competitive System* (Washington, D.C.: The Brookings Institution, 1954); D. Lilienthal, *Big Business: A New Era* (New York:

need for very large firms to support innovation has been questioned by Mason and others.[18] In recent years some empirical evidence has been provided on this subject. Studies have been made by Mansfield of the relationship between innovation and size of firm in three industries: bituminous coal, petroleum refining, and iron and steel.[19]

In this section we shall examine the extent to which the largest firms performed the innovating in the ethical pharmaceutical industry. We shall use the list of innovations in Table 8.3 for the purposes of this analysis. In addition, we require data regarding the size of ethical drug firms for the two time periods. The sales data used to measure the size of firms were obtained from trade literature and past studies of the industry.[20] These sales data were used in conjunction with the list of innovations to determine the number of innovations introduced by the largest firms. We compare the share of the innovations carried out by the largest four firms with the share of industry output held by these four firms. The figure for the market share of the four largest firms for the 1935–1949 period was based on the 1939 market share. For the 1950–1962 period, the 1950 market share of the four largest firms was used.[21] The share of innovations contributed by these large firms was determined in three different ways. The unweighted shares of the innovations and shares of innovations weighted by the first five years of sales were calculated. In addition, we determined weighted shares of the thirty most important innovations in Table 8.3, using the survey responses to weight the medical importance of these innovations. We would expect the market share of the largest firms to equal their share of innovations under the following conditions: First, the largest firms devote the same proportion of their resources as do smaller firms to inventive activity and to the testing and development of other people's ideas. Second, they obtain applicable results as easily. Third, they are as efficient and as quick to apply the results.

The results of the analysis for the two time periods are shown in Table

Harper, 1953); H. Villard, "Competition, Oligopoly, and Research," *Journal of Political Economy* (December 1958); and Edwin Mansfield, *The Economics of Technological Change* (New York: W. W. Norton, 1968).

18. E. Mason, "Schumpeter on Monopoly and the Large Firm," *Review of Economics and Statistics* (May, 1951).

19. Mansfield, *Industrial Research and Technological Innovation, op. cit.*, Chapter 3. Also, some data were obtained for the railroad industry.

20. Primary sources of sales data were F-D-C Reports; J. F. Bohmfalk, "Markets for Pharmaceuticals," *Chemical and Engineering News* (November 30, 1963), p. 5012; and Arthur D. Little, Inc., "The Technology Behind Investment" (Cambridge, Mass., 1952). Sales data was also obtained from the following unpublished MBA theses written at the University of Pennsylvania: B. L. Brussock, "An Investment Analysis of the Ethical Drug Industry, 1946–1955" (1957); J. J. Hughes, Jr., "The Pharmaceutical Industry, 1953–1957" (1959), and P. Capen, "An Economic Analysis of the Pharmaceutical Industry" (1959).

These sales data pertain to drug sales in the U.S. In addition, we used as a measure of a firm's size its worldwide drug sales. Also, since some drug firms are subsidiaries, we used the sales of the parent company as a measure of size. Regardless of which measure is used, the results indicate that the largest firms did not contribute more innovations, relative to their size, than somewhat smaller ones. On the contrary, regardless of which measure of size is used, the ratio of number of innovations to firm size was a maximum at sales of about $10 million in 1935–1949 and at either $20 million or $1 million, depending on weighting, in 1950–1962.

21. We should note here that sales levels in the ethical drug industry increased considerably during both time periods. Since sales growth was influenced by innovative performance, we choose sales figures at the beginning of each period to preserve the independence of this variable.

TABLE **8.4**

Percent of Innovations and Industry Sales
Accounted for by Four Largest
Ethical Pharmaceutical Firms

ITEM	UNWEIGHTED	MEDICALLY WEIGHTED	ECONOMICALLY WEIGHTED
	(percent of industry total)		
1935–1949			
Innovations	37	45	50
Total sales	50	—	—
1950–1962			
Innovations	27	48	33
Total sales	33	—	—

8.4. What conclusions can be drawn from these data? To begin with, according to the unweighted data, the Schumpeterian hypothesis does not seem to hold in the ethical pharmaceutical industry. In both time periods the market share of the four largest firms exceeds their unweighted share of the industry's innovations. Although the largest four firms held 50 percent of the ethical pharmaceutical market in 1939, they only contributed 37 percent of the innovations from 1935 through 1949. Similarly, the 1950 market share of the four largest firms was 33 percent while their share of the 1950–1962 innovations was 27 percent. However, use of the two weighting systems alters somewhat the relationship between size of firm and innovation for both time periods. During 1935–1949, the four largest firms contributed a weighted 45 percent of the thirty most important innovations and an economically weighted 50 percent of all innovations, as compared to an unweighted 37 percent of all innovations. When weightings are used for the 1950–1962 period, we see that these firms accounted for 48 percent of the thirty most important innovations and 33 percent of all innovations on an economically weighted basis. Thus, it appears that in the earlier period, the largest firms did not carry out a disproportionately large share of the innovations, regardless of the weighting used. On the other hand, in the later period, this conclusion can be drawn when economic weightings are used but not when medical weightings are used.

On an unweighted basis, the innovative performance of the four largest firms, relative to their market share, has improved over time. The unweighted share of innovations (37 percent) contributed by the four largest firms during 1935–1949 was considerably below their market share (50 percent). The gap narrowed during the 1950–1962 period as the largest four firms held 33 percent of the market and contributed 27 percent of the unweighted innovations. This is also true when medical weightings are used. However, when economic weightings are used, the market share of the four largest firms is found to be exactly equal to their share of innovations in both time periods. Finally, a comparison of the results of Table 8.4 with those for other industries suggests that the innovative performance of the four largest ethical drug firms is somewhere between that of the four largest petroleum and coal firms, on the one hand, and the four largest steel firms, on the other. The largest ethical drug firms turned out fewer innovations, relative to their market share, than the largest petroleum and coal firms, but more, relative to their market share, than the largest steel firms.[22]

4. A More Complete Analysis

In this section we expand the analysis of section 3 and examine the innovative performance of the full range of firm sizes in the ethical pharmaceutical industry. We analyze the relative innovative performance of small, medium, and large ethical pharmaceutical firms within the 1935–1949 and 1950–1962 time periods. In the next section, we ask whether the innovative performance of small, medium, and large firms has changed over time. These results should be of considerable interest. At present, information of this sort is available only for the coal, petroleum, and steel industries. The results for the coal and petroleum industries indicate that when the innovative performance of firms relative to their size was considered, the large firms tended to be more innovative than the small firms, but that there was no evidence that the largest firms carried out any more innovations, relative to their size, than somewhat smaller firms. The results for the steel industry indicate that relative to their size, the small firms were more innovative than the large firms in the industry. In each of these three industries, the smallest firms did less innovating, relative to the largest firms, during 1939–1958 than they did during 1919–1938.[23]

In order to determine the average relationship between size of firm and the number of innovations carried out by a firm in the ethical pharmaceutical industry, we adopt the following model. We assume that

$$(8.1) \qquad n_j = a_0 + a_1 S_j + a_2 S_j{}^2 + Z_j'',$$

where n_j is the number of innovations carried out by the jth firm, S_j is the firm's size (measured in terms of sales), and Z''_j is a random error term.[24] We use equation (8.1) for both the 1935–1949 and 1950–1962 time

22. On an unweighted basis, the four largest petroleum firms held 33 percent of the industry capacity during 1919–1938 and contributed 54 percent of all innovations. These figures were 39 percent and 43 percent during 1939–1958. For the coal industry, capacity held by the largest firms was 11 percent in 1919–1938 as compared to an unweighted 18 percent of all innovations. Capacity increased to 13 percent of the industry total in 1939–1958, while the share of innovations rose to 27 percent. The results were opposite in the steel industry, where the largest firms accounted for 62 percent of the capacity in 1919–1938 but only contributed 32 percent of the innovations. For 1939–1958, capacity of 63 percent compared with 51 percent of all innovations. See Mansfield *op. cit.*

23. *Ibid.*

24. There are, of course, difficulties associated with this type of analysis. For a more complete discussion of these problems, see Mansfield, *op. cit.*, Chap. 6.

The firms included in the analysis are the 1939 and 1950 members of the American Drug

periods, letting the computed regression be $N(S_j)$ and ignoring the sampling errors. The ratio $N(S_j)/S_j$ is calculated and we then determine the level of sales for which this ratio is at a maximum.

When the unweighted number of innovations is used as n_j, the regression results for the 1935–1949 period are

$$(8.2) \qquad n_j = -0.24 + 0.23\ S_j - 0.0034\ S_j^2,$$
$$ (0.24) \quad (0.04) \qquad (0.0010)$$

and the estimated number of innovations divided by firm sales reaches a maximum at a sales level of $10 million. For the 1935–1949 period, this sales level corresponds to that of the tenth-largest firm. The results do not change when each firm's economically weighted number of innovations or medically weighted number of innovations is used as n_j. The ratio $N(S_j)/S_j$ still reaches a maximum at a sales level of $10 million.[25]

The results for the 1950–1962 period, unlike those for the earlier period, are affected by weighting. Taking n_j as the unweighted number of innovations, the 1950–1962 regression results are

$$(8.3) \qquad n_j = 0.31 + 0.07\ S_j - 0.0003\ S_j^2.$$
$$ (0.22) \quad (0.02) \qquad (0.0002)$$

On this basis, the maximum value of the ratio of the estimated number of innovations to firm sales is attained at a sales level corresponding to that of very small firms in this industry. However, for the 1950–1962 period, the maximum value of this ratio is found at a sales level of $20 million when the weighted numbers of innovations are substituted in equation (8.3). A sales level of $20 million corresponds to that of the twelfth-largest firm during this time period.[26]

Manufacturers Association. This association of ethical pharmaceutical manufacturers was in existence from 1912–1958 and was the predecessor of today's Pharmaceutical Manufacturers Association. There are fewer firms in the 1939 sample because several of the 1950 firms were not formed until after 1939.

25. Equation (8.2) is based on forty-one firms, and the correlation coefficient is 0.72. For 1935–1949, the results for the economically weighted innovations are

$$n_j = -0.81 + 0.39\ S_j - 0.0076\ S_j^2.$$
$$(0.53) \quad (0.10) \qquad (0.0023)$$

The regression for the medically weighted innovations is

$$n_j = -0.63 + 0.31\ S_j - 0.0047\ S_j^2.$$
$$(0.35) \quad (0.07) \qquad (0.0015)$$

For both of these equations, the ratio is at a maximum when $S_j = $10 million.

26. Equation (8.3) is based on fifty-eight firms, and the correlation coefficient is 0.66. For 1950–1962, the results for the economically weighted innovations are

$$n_j = -0.18 + 0.12\ S_j - 0.0007\ S_j^2.$$
$$(0.41) \quad (0.04) \qquad (0.0004)$$

The regression for the medically weighted innovations is

$$n_j = -0.17 + 0.097\ S_j - 0.0005\ S_j^2.$$
$$(0.34) \quad (0.031) \qquad (0.0003)$$

For both of these equations the ratio is at a maximum when $S_j = $20 million. This is the size of the twelfth-largest firm.

Needless to say, there is no contradiction between (1) our finding in section 3 that the largest four firms accounted in 1950–1962 for as large a proportion of the economically weighted innovations as of sales—and a larger proportion of the medically weighted innovations than of sales—and (2) our finding in this section that the ratio of economically weighted or medically weighted innovations to firm size in 1950–1962 was at a maximum at about the size of the twelfth-largest firm. The point is that because the smallest firms did very little innovating (as measured when these weightings are used), the largest four firms could do more than their share while still doing less, relative to their size, than somewhat smaller firms. To students of industrial organization, the important thing to note is that the firms that have contributed the most innovations, relative to their size, are not the largest firms, but somewhat smaller ones. It is also important to note that this is true in the other industries included in Mansfield's previous studies.

5. The Changing Role of Small and Large Firms

The regression coefficients in equations (8.2) and (8.3) are also used to determine whether the relative importance as innovators of small and large drug firms has changed over time. For each value of S_j, we compute the ratio of the average value of n_j in 1950–1962 to its average value in 1935–1949. If the ratio rises for increasing values of S_j, we conclude that small firms carried out fewer innovations, relative to large firms, in 1950–1962 than in 1935–1949. Because the values of the ratios are quite sensitive to the particular measure of innovative results (i.e., unweighted, economically weighted, medically weighted), findings obtained with each of the three measures are presented (Table 8.5).[27] On an unweighted basis, the value of the ratio is highest for the smallest pharmaceutical firms. The ratio declines with increases in size of firm, but increases again when we reach the size of the industry's larger firms. Thus, the number of innovations seems to have increased most among the smallest firms, but more among the larger firms than among the medium-sized firms. The results using medical weights are similar to those obtained with the unweighted number of innovations: The ratio is at a maximum for the smallest firms, declines to a minimum value at the $10-million sales level, and then increases with firm size. However, the results for the economically weighted innovations differ considerably: The value of the ratio generally increases with firm size, rising to a maximum at the size of the largest firms.

27. The difference in the range of firm sizes for the 1935–1949 and 1950–1962 periods creates some problems in this analysis. The largest firm in 1939 had sales of $50 million while the largest firm in 1950 had sales of $120 million. For obvious reasons, we cannot extrapolate beyond the range of firm sizes in either period. Consequently, our analysis contrasts larger firms with smaller firms but we cannot draw conclusions concerning the relative innovative performance of the industry's largest firms.

TABLE 8.5

*Average Number of Innovations Carried Out by
Firms of Given Size in 1950–1962 Divided by Average
Number Carried Out by Firms of the Same Size in 1935–1949*

SIZE OF FIRM (SALES, IN MILLIONS OF DOLLARS)	RATIO OF AVERAGE NUMBER OF INNOVATIONS IN 1950–1962 TO AVERAGE NUMBER IN 1935–1949		
	UNWEIGHTED	ECONOMICALLY WEIGHTED	MEDICALLY WEIGHTED
2	2.14	—[a]	∞[b]
5	0.79	0.44	0.41
10	.57	.41	.37
20	.63	.49	.43
30	.60	.69	.51
50	1.11	∞[b]	1.10

[a] According to the regressions in equations (8.2) and (8.3), the average number of innovations was negative in both 1935–1949 and 1950–1962. It seems reasonable in this context to substitute zero for such negative numbers. Thus, the ratio would have no meaning.

[b] According to the regression in equation (8.2), the average number of innovations in 1935–1949 was negative. The division of zero into a positive result for 1950–1962 yields infinity.

These results contrast with those obtained by Mansfield for the coal, petroleum, and steel industries: In each of these industries the relative importance of smaller firms as innovators has declined over time.[28] A major factor accounting for this characteristic of the drug industry is its changing market structure. The 1950's and 1960's witnessed the segmentation of the ethical pharmaceutical market into several new submarkets. Some of these smaller submarkets, such as ophthalmics and dermatologicals, have not provided the market potential required by larger firms, and consequently, they have been dominated by smaller firms. These smaller firms have developed the specialized research skills needed to carry out innovations in these new therapeutic markets. The fact that some of their 1950–1962 innovations have had considerable medical significance explains why both the unweighted and medically weighted innovations in Table 8.5 reach a maximum among the smallest firms. However, the small size of these submarkets limits the economic impact of these innovations and this accounts for the differences which result when the ratios are calculated on the basis of economic weighting.

6. Sources of Pharmaceutical Innovations

To what extent are institutions or individuals external to the innovating firm the source of the discoveries which lead to pharmaceutical innovations?

28. Mansfield, *op. cit.*, Chap. 6.

Previous studies have indicated that many of a firm's innovations are based to a considerable extent on inventions made outside the innovating firm.[29] For example, Mueller, in his study of the origins of the inventions underlying Du Pont's major innovations from 1920 to 1950, found that external sources contributed the bulk of these inventions.[30] Moreover, an Arthur D. Little study of the origins of major innovations in three mature industries—textiles, machine tools, and construction—concluded that external sources contributed a high proportion of the innovations.[31] In this section, we shall present and analyze data concerning the origin of sixty-eight pharmaceutical innovations.[32] The origin of major innovations has been a controversial issue in the ethical pharmaceutical industry. Comanor noted the lively and prolonged confrontations between the industry and the Senate Subcommittee on Antitrust and Monopoly (Kefauver Committee) concerning the medical value of industry research. The committee contended that nearly all of the important discoveries in recent years had been derived from research work performed outside the industry and that commercial laboratories were concerned primarily with molecular manipulations of new drugs therapeutically quite similar to drugs already on the market. The industry countered that most of the new drugs that were extensively utilized in 1962 originated in industry laboratories. These opposing views of the nature and significance of the pharmaceutical industry research effort collided in what Comanor termed the "battle of the lists," with each party's list reflecting a different view of what constitutes significant drug developments.[33]

The list of innovations in Table 8.3 provides a useful way of exploring this question in a more objective setting. Since the AMA list, of which Table 8.3 is an expansion, was generated for different uses and under different conditions than the lists produced at the Senate hearings, it is highly unlikely that the choice of innovations was made in a way that would bias findings concerning their sources. In addition, the availability of weightings will enable us to comment on the medical significance and economic importance of those innovations which originated within the industry. Before presenting the results, let us emphasize their roughness. Any attempt to trace an innovation back to a single source is a hazardous and often quite

29. It might be noted that about one-third of the innovations analyzed in Chapters 6 and 7 were based to some extent on technology of a specific sort derived from organizations other than the innovating firm.

30. Mueller, op. cit.

31. Arthur D. Little, Inc., "Patterns and Problems of Technical Innovation in American Industry," The Role and Effects of Technology in the Nation's Economy, Hearings before a Subcommittee of the Select Committee on Small Business, United States Senate, 88th Congress, First Session; see also D. Schon, "Innovation by Invasion," International Science and Technology (March, 1964).

32. We should note that these sixty-eight are not a random sample selected from the items in Table 8.3. They are the innovations for which data regarding the source could be obtained. While our findings are therefore biased in this respect, they are biased in the direction of the more important, rather than the less important, innovations. Table 8.6 includes 90 percent of the thirty-one most significant innovations listed in Table 8.3.

33. William Comanor, "The Drug Industry and Medical Research: The Economics of the Kefauver Committee Investigation," Journal of Business (January, 1966). Also see U.S. Senate, Administered Prices in the Drug Industry (Hearings Before the Subcommittee on Antitrust and Monopoly), Part XVIII.

arbitrary task. In some cases, the development of an innovation is contingent upon a series of separate inventions. In other instances, the innovation appears to involve a continuing accumulation of knowledge, with each piece of knowledge seemingly inseparable from the previously compiled stock. Moreover, the concept of a pharmaceutical discovery is a highly elusive one, as the development history of many drugs illustrates. A number of drugs were first synthesized with the objective of treating a particular disease, and hence, their biological activity was discovered immediately after they were synthesized. However, the relevant biological activity of several other drugs was not discovered until many years after the compounds were synthesized or isolated from their natural source.[34] In our analysis we define the discovery of a new drug as the first identification of the drug's biological activity. Therefore, the source of a pharmaceutical discovery represents the institution or individual(s) who first identified the drug's biological activity, and the date of discovery is the date of this identification.

The sources of the sixty-eight pharmaceutical innovations are listed in Table 8.6.[35] The sources were grouped into the following categories: innovator (i.e., the same firm discovered and introduced the drug); foreign firm; university, hospital, or research institute; and other external sources (government agencies, individual inventors, other domestic pharmaceutical firms, and so on).[36] The following analyses were then performed: First, the proportion of innovations attributable to each source was computed for

34. Librium, which was identified as a tranquilizer in 1957, was first synthesized in 1933. The muscle-relaxant properties of tubocurarine were discovered in 1932; yet curare, the active component of the drug was a substance known to the American Indians. Mustargen (nitrogen mustard) was synthesized in 1854 and was used as a chemical-warfare agent during World War I; its anticancer properties were observed in 1942. We should also note that an important finding concerning the nature of the underlying disease process often provides the impetus for the actual drug discovery. The discovery of anticoagulant drugs could only proceed after the identification of an anticoagulant substance in human blood. Similarly, the development of antihistaminic drugs stemmed from the finding that allergies are caused by the substance histamine. In these instances, the discovery of a drug's biological activity is the final step in a sequence of discoveries.
For a historical tracing of the key scientific events which led to the development of Enovid, the oral-contraceptive pill, see *Technology in Retrospect and Critical Events in Science* (TRACES), Vol. I, prepared for the National Science Foundation by the Illinois Institute of Technology (December 15, 1968).
35. The sources of two-thirds of the sixty-eight innovations were identified by tracing the history of the innovation in the relevant medical journals. The sources of the remaining innovations were obtained from published literature on the U.S. ethical pharmaceutical industry, in particular, Mahoney, *op. cit.*, and the lists of innovations in U.S. Senate, *Administered Prices in the Drug Industry, op. cit.*, pp. 10840–10854. We should note that the controversy surrounding these lists of innovations involved the question of what constitutes a significant innovation and not the identity of the sources cited. Since our list of innovations has been developed independently, the Senate data on sources is useful for our purposes.
36. In many respects, discoveries which originate in universities, hospitals, research institutes, and the like, may be the work of individual inventors. For example, Table 8.6 lists the University of Pittsburgh as the source of Salk vaccine, although the discovery is closely associated with one individual. Table 8.6 identifies the institutions or firms where the innovation was discovered. The individuals listed as sources under "Other External Sources" in Table 8.6 are those independent inventors without any institutional affiliation. For a more detailed discussion of what is meant by the individual inventor, see Jewkes, Sawers, and Stillerman, *op. cit.*, pp. 93–97.
Five of the innovations listed under "Innovator and Discoverer Same Firm" were introduced by the American operating company and discovered by the foreign operating company of the same firm. While the discovery was therefore made outside of the U.S., it still seemed appropriate to consider the innovator and discoverer one and the same. In no case in this category was the innovator a foreign firm which did not have an American operating company.

TABLE 8.6
Source of Pharmaceutical Innovations

INNOVATION	SOURCE	INNOVATOR	TIME INTERVAL (IN YEARS)
Innovator and Discoverer Same Firm			
Aureomycin	Lederle	Lederle	1
Furadantin	Eaton	Eaton	9
Enovid	Searle	Searle	3
Darvon	Lilly	Lilly	4
Diamox	Lederle	Lederle	3
Diuril	Merck	Merck	1
Benadryl	Parke-Davis	Parke-Davis	1
Chlor-Trimeton	Schering	Schering	1
Pyribenzamine	CIBA, U.S.A.	CIBA, U.S.A.	1
Bentyl	Merrell	Merrell	1
Banthine	Searle	Searle	1
Thio-Tepa	Lederle	Lederle	7
Isoniazid	Hoffmann-LaRoche, Squibb	Hoffmann-LaRoche, Squibb	7
Milontin	Parke-Davis	Parke-Davis	2
Daraprim	Burroughs Wellcome	Burroughs Wellcome	2
Milibis	Winthrop	Winthrop	1
Camoquin	Parke-Davis	Parke-Davis	4
Benzedrex[a]	Smith Kline & French	Smith Kline & French	3
Artane	Lederle	Lederle	1
Aldactone	Searle	Searle	3
Fungizone	Squibb	Squibb	3
Librium	Hoffmann-LaRoche	Hoffmann-LaRoche	3
Ismelin	CIBA, U.S.A.	CIBA, U.S.A.	1
Doriden	CIBA, Switzerland	CIBA, U.S.A.	3
Butazolidin	Geigy, Switzerland	Geigy, U.S.A.	3
Priscoline	CIBA, Switzerland	CIBA, U.S.A.	9
Lidocaine	Astra, Sweden	Astra, U.S.A.	2
Apresoline	CIBA, Switzerland	CIBA, U.S.A.	2
Tridione	Abbott	Abbott	2
Phenurone	Abbott	Abbott	3
Aldomet	Merck	Merck	9
Ilotycin	Lilly	Lilly	1
Foreign Firm			
Griseofulvin	ICI, England	Schering, McNeil	13
Orinase	Hoechst, Germany	Upjohn	15
Estrone[a]	Schering, Germany	Abbott, Parke-Davis	10
Thorazine	Rhone-Poulenc, France	Smith Kline & French	4
Nembutal	Bayer, Germany	Abbott	11
Demerol	I. G. Farben, Germany	Winthrop	4
Phenergan	Rhone-Poulenc, France	Wyeth	13

TABLE **8.6** (continued)

INNOVATION	SOURCE	INNOVATOR	TIME INTERVAL (IN YEARS)
Sulfanilimide	I. G. Farben, Germany	Lederle, Sharp & Dohme	7
Flagyl	Rhone-Poulenc, France	Searle	5

University, Hospital, or Research Institute

Penicillin	Oxford U., England	Squibb	17
Streptomycin	Rutgers U.	Merck, Squibb	5
Chloromycetin	Yale U.	Parke-Davis	2
Estrone[a]	St. Louis U.	Abbott, Parke-Davis	10
Dilantin	Kiel U., Germany,	Parke-Davis	2
Aminopterin, Sodium	Children's Hospital, Boston	Lederle	15
Cortisone	Mayo Clinic	Merck	1
Salk vaccine	U. of Pittsburgh	Lilly, Parke-Davis	2
Myleran	Chester Beatty Research Institute	Burroughs Wellcome	5
Leukeran	Chester Beatty Research Institute	Burroughs Wellcome	5
Vanquin	Western Reserve U.	Parke-Davis	4
Thiouracil	Harvard U.	Lilly	4
Antepar	Faculté de Médecine de Paris	Burroughs Wellcome	4
Neo-Synephrine	Stanford U.	Winthrop	3
Herplex	Massachusetts Eye and Ear Infirmary	Allergan	2
Tubocurarine	U. of Nebraska	Squibb	8

Other External Sources

Nystatin	N.Y. State Department of Health	Squibb	3
Miltown	Dr. F. Berger	Wallace	1
Aralen	Office of Scientific Research & Development	Winthrop	3
Benzedrex[a]	G. Alles	Smith Kline & French	3
Raudixin	Sen. G.	Squibb	22
Mustargen	U.S. Army National Research Council	Merck	7
Trecator	Hoffmann-LaRoche	Ives-Cameron	9
Halothane	British Medical Research Council	Ayerst	6
Clycoserine	Commercial Solvents	Lilly, Merck	2
Expandex	Cronwell & Ingelmar	C.S.C.	8
Dicumarol	Wisconsin Experimental Research Station	Abbott	10
Pyrazinamide	Lederle	Merck	4
Balarsen	Ernst Friedheim	Endo	4

[a] Discovery shared by more than one source.

all sixty-eight innovations on both a weighted and unweighted basis (Table 8.7). Next the innovations were grouped by time period to observe the variations in sources over time (Table 8.8). Finally, the innovations

TABLE 8.7

Sources of Sixty-eight Innovations

SOURCE	UNWEIGHTED	MEDICALLY WEIGHTED	ECONOMICALLY WEIGHTED
Innovator	0.46	0.34	0.29
Foreign Firm	.12	.18	.22
University, Hospital, or Research Institute	.23	.37	.38
Other	.19	.11	.11

TABLE 8.8

Sources of Innovations, by Time Period

TIME PERIOD	UNWEIGHTED		MEDICALLY WEIGHTED		ECONOMICALLY WEIGHTED	
	INNOVATOR	EXTERNAL SOURCE	INNOVATOR	EXTERNAL SOURCE	INNOVATOR	EXTERNAL SOURCE
1935–1949	0.38	0.62	0.22	0.78	0.28	0.72
1950–1962	.57	.43	.56	.44	.57	.43

were categorized by type of drug (using the SIC classifications) to determine the origins of innovations in different therapeutic areas (Table 8.9).[37]

Three major findings emerge from Tables 8.7–8.9. First, external sources—sources other than the innovating firm—have played a major role in the technological progress of the ethical pharmaceutical industry in the United States. These external sources provided 54 percent of the discoveries which produced pharmaceutical innovations during 1935–1962. The weighted figures reflecting medical and economic significance are even higher—66 percent and 71 percent, respectively. Foreign firms, and universities, hospitals, and research institutes, have all been important sources. of discoveries. In particular, the innovations contributed by universities, hospitals, and research institutes (23 percent of the unweighted total) had substantial medical (37 percent) and economic (38 percent) importance. Of course, the drug industry is not unique in this respect. It is important to recognize that external sources are very important in the case of firms in other industries as well. For example, as noted above, 60 percent of Du

37. See Chapter 4 for a discussion of these product classifications.

TABLE 8.9

Sources of Innovations, by Product Category

PRODUCT CATEGORY	NUMBER OF INNOVATIONS	UNWEIGHTED		MEDICALLY WEIGHTED		ECONOMICALLY WEIGHTED	
		INNOVATOR	EXTERNAL SOURCE	INNOVATOR	EXTERNAL SOURCE	INNOVATOR	EXTERNAL SOURCE
Central nervous system	17	0.53	0.47	0.17	0.83	0.28	0.72
Parasitic and infective diseases	22	.36	.64	.14	.86	.33	.67
Neoplasms, endocrine system	10	.15	.85	.14	.86	.05	.95
Cardiovascular	7	.57	.43	0	1.00	.56	.44
Digestive and genitourinary	5	1.00	0	1.00	0	1.00	0
Biologicals	1	0	1.00	0	1.00	0	1.00
Respiratory system	6	.58	.42	.66	.34	.73	.27

Pont's major innovations during 1920–1950 were invented by organizations other than Du Pont.

Second, the grouping of the innovations into two time periods indicates that external sources have declined in importance over time (Table 8.8). During the 1935–1949 period, external sources were dominant, contributing 62 percent of the discoveries on an unweighted basis, 78 percent of the discoveries as measured with medical weighting, and 72 percent of the discoveries with economic weighting. All three of these percentages declined considerably during the 1950–1962 period: the unweighted percentage was 43 percent, the medically weighted was 44 percent, and the economically weighted was 43 percent. The decline in importance of external sources during this period is due entirely to a drop in the percentage contributed by universities, hospitals, and research institutes. It is difficult to pin down the reasons for this drop, but one possible reason may have been that the drug industry increased its research and development spending—or its spending on the relevant kind of R and D—at a more rapid rate during this period than did universities, hospitals, and research institutes.

Third, there is considerable variation among product categories in the sources of discoveries (Table 8.9). In some categories, such as drugs for neoplasms and the endocrine system, and for parasitic and infective diseases, external sources have provided most of the discoveries. The reverse is true for digestive and genitourinary drugs and respiratory-system drugs. A major factor accounting for these differences among product categories is the existing state of the art within the categories. In those categories where there is reasonably high correlation between the results of animal tests and clinical trials, such as digestive and genitourinary drugs and respiratory-system drugs, biological test systems have greater potential for uncovering new and useful chemical structures. Pharmaceutical firms have devoted substantial resources to such test systems. The result has been a high proportion of internally discovered innovations (100 percent for digestive and genitourinary drugs and 58 percent for respiratory-system drugs). In product categories, such as drugs for neoplasms and the endocrine system, where the limited predictability of animal tests makes biological test systems less effective, the nonscreening approaches of external sources have been relatively more fruitful.[38]

Finally, it is worth noting that the probability that an innovation was based on a discovery made outside the innovating firm seems to have been related during 1935–1949 to the size of the innovating firm. In particular, if the innovator was a smaller firm, it was more likely to have discovered

---

38. Strictly speaking, our explanation for the variation in sources of innovation among product categories only holds for external sources which are not pharmaceutical firms. But this has little effect on our results.

the new drug than if it was a larger firm. Larger firms seemed to rely more heavily on external sources for the discoveries underlying their innovations than did smaller firms. Needless to say, the fact that bigger firms were much more likely to exploit and to push to commercial fruition the discoveries of other organizations is not to their discredit. It is important that firms be able and willing to exploit other people's inventions. But at the same time it is important to note that the four biggest firms accounted during 1935–1949 for a smaller share of the discoveries *made by the United States drug industry* than they did of the innovations. (Of course, their share of these discoveries was also less than their share of the market.) During 1950–1962, there was no statistically significant relationship between size of firm and the probability that an innovation was based on an external discovery. Also, during 1950–1962, the four largest firms accounted for about the same share of the discoveries as they did of the innovations.

7. *The Lag Between Discovery and Innovation*

In this section we consider the time interval between a pharmaceutical discovery and the introduction of the new drug which resulted from the discovery. The relatively limited data hitherto available on the time interval between invention and innovation have been provided by John Enos, who estimated this interval for eleven important products and processes in the petroleum industry and for thirty-five important products and processes in a variety of other industries. Enos found that the interval averaged eleven years in the petroleum industry and about fourteen years in the others.[39] We begin by looking at the distribution of the time intervals between discovery and innovation for sixty-eight pharmaceutical innovations.[40] If we assume that each of the various activities or events which together comprise an innovation is independent of the others; that the events follow one another in sequence; and that the amount of time required to accomplish each varies randomly, following some common but unspecified probability distribution, then we might expect the distribution of intervals to be normal.[41] In fact, the frequency distribution for the sixty-eight pharmaceutical innovations, as given by Table 8.10, is nonnormal, exhibiting a skewness which is similar to that found by Enos. However, the mean and standard deviation of the distribution (mean—5.0 years, standard deviation—4.1 years) indicate that the time interval is both shorter and less

---

39. Enos, *op. cit.*
40. As in the case of the data on sources, the time intervals for two-thirds of the innovations in Table 8.6 were obtained from the relevant medical literature. The time intervals for the remaining innovations were obtained from Goodman and Gilman, *op. cit.*
41. See Enos, *op. cit.*, p. 304, for a further discussion of these assumptions.

TABLE **8.10**

Frequency Distribution of the Lag Between
Discovery and Innovation

TIME LAG (YEARS)	NUMBER OF INNOVATIONS	TIME LAG (YEARS)	NUMBER OF INNOVATIONS
1	13	7	4
2	10	8	2
3	12	9	4
4	9	10	2
5	4	11–16	5
6	1	17–22	2

variable in the ethical drug industry than in the petroleum-refining industry or in industry as a whole.[42]

Was there a tendency for the time intervals to be different during 1935–1949 than during 1950–1962? The time lags for twenty-seven innovations in the 1935–1949 period averaged 5.2 years, while the forty-one innovations carried out during the 1950–1962 period had an average lag of 4.5 years. While these data suggest that the time lag may have decreased over time, the difference is not statistically significant at the 5-percent level. Does the time interval tend to be shorter in cases where the innovator is also the inventor? The answer—which supports Enos's findings—seems to be Yes (Table 8.11). The average lag when the innovator made the

TABLE **8.11**

Time Lag, by Source of Innovation

SOURCE	NUMBER OF INNOVATIONS[a]	AVERAGE TIME LAG (YEARS)
Innovator	31.5	3.1
Foreign Firm	8.5	9.7
University, Hospital, or Research Institute	15.5	5.7
Other External	12.5	6.6
Total	*68*	*5.0*

[a] When an innovation is shared by two sources, one-half is awarded to each source.

42. It is important to note the extreme differences between the time period for the sample of pharmaceutical innovations and the time period for Enos's sample. All of the drug innovations occurred between 1935 and 1962, with the earliest discovery dating back to 1930. Enos's sample included innovations and inventions dating back to the early eighteenth century. However, if we only include those innovations in Enos's sample that occurred in 1935–1962, the results are much the same as those given in the first paragraph of section 7. Also, it should be noted that "discovery" in the pharmaceutical industry may not really be comparable with "invention" in Enos's industries. The slipperiness of these terms need not be belabored.

pharmaceutical discovery was 3.1 years, while the average lag for externally discovered innovations was 6.9 years. The difference between these mean time intervals is statistically significant at the 5-percent level. (The time lag was longest for discoveries provided by foreign firms.)

What sorts of differences exist, among product categories, in the value of this time interval? The analysis of time lags by product category (Table 8.12) is based on the five-digit SIC classification.[43] It turns out that the

TABLE 8.12

Time Lag, by Product Category

PRODUCT CATEGORY	NUMBER	AVERAGE TIME LAG (YEARS)
Central nervous system	17	3.6
Parasitic and infective diseases	22	5.0
Neoplasms, endocrine system	10	7.2
Cardiovascular	6	8.8
Digestive and genitourinary	5	1.8
Biologicals	1	2.0
Respiratory system	7	4.3
Total	*68*	*5.0*

time lag was longest for cardiovascular drugs and neoplasm and endocrine-system drugs and shortest for digestive and genitourinary drugs and central-nervous-system drugs. (However, the sample sizes are so small that little statistical significance can be attached to some of these differences.) To study the joint effects on the time interval of calendar year, source of innovation, and product category, we regress the time interval on these independent variables, dummy variables being used to denote the source of the innovation and the product category. The results, after we eliminate several nonsignificant variables, are

$$(8.4) \quad L_j = 8.70 - 6.46\,S_{1j} - 4.30\,S_{2j} - 3.38\,S_{3j}$$
$$(1.29) \quad (1.44) \quad (1.65) \quad (1.67)$$
$$+ 5.16\,P_{1j} + 2.43\,P_{3j},$$
$$(1.51) \quad (1.34)$$

where L_j is the time interval between discovery and innovation for the jth innovation, S_{1j} is a dummy variable that is 1 if the discoverer and innovator of the jth innovation were the same firm (and 0 otherwise), S_{2j} is a dummy variable that is 1 if the discoverer of the jth innovation was a university, hospital, or research institute (and 0 otherwise), S_{3j} is a dummy variable

43. See Chapter 4 for a description of these SIC classifications.

that is 1 if the discoverer of the jth innovation was "other external sources" (and 0 otherwise), P_{1j} is a dummy variable that is 1 if the jth innovation is a cardiovascular drug (and 0 otherwise), and P_{3j} is a dummy variable that is 1 if the jth innovation is an endocrine-system drug (and 0 otherwise). Thus the average time lag varies significantly among product categories, as well as among sources. However, an interesting aspect of equation (8.4) is that calendar time is a nonsignificant variable. When the other variables in the equation are taken into account, the time lag does not seem to have decreased significantly over time.[44]

8. Summary

The principal conclusions of this chapter are as follows: First, we compare the market share of the four largest firms with their share of innovations, on both a weighted and an unweighted basis, for the 1935–1949 and 1950–1962 time periods. When unweighted data are used, the Schumpeterian hypothesis does not hold in either time period, the market share of the four largest firms exceeding their unweighted share of the innovations. When weighted data are used, the same conclusion holds for the earlier period: Regardless of whether economic or medical weightings are used, the results indicate that the largest firms did not carry out a disproportionately large share of the innovations. In the later period, this conclusion can be drawn if economic weightings—but not medical weightings—are used.

Second, a more complete analysis of the data indicates, however, that in both time periods and regardless of the weightings used, the firms that contributed the most innovations, relative to their size, were not the largest firms, but somewhat smaller ones. When we explicitly consider the innovative performance of drug firms of all sizes, we find that, relative to their size, the tenth- or twelfth-largest firms (depending on the time interval and weighting system employed) account for the largest number of innovations (except for the unweighted data, which indicate that the maximum ratio of

---

44. The regression results before the various nonsignificant dummy variables are excluded are

$$L_j = 9.13 - 0.01\,T_j - 6.39\,S_{1j} - 4.49\,S_{2j} - 3.43\,S_{3j} + 4.82\,P_{1j}$$
$$\quad\ (1.94)\ \ (0.11)\quad\ (1.53)\quad\ \ (1.76)\quad\ \ (1.73)\quad\ \ (1.66)$$

$$\qquad\ - 0.75\,P_{2j} + 2.23\,P_{3j} - 0.81\,P_{4j} - 0.13\,P_{5j}, \qquad (\bar{R}^2 = 0.28)$$
$$\qquad\quad (1.25)\qquad (1.45)\qquad (1.93)\qquad (1.86)$$

where T_j is the calendar year when the innovation was introduced, L_j is the time interval between discovery and innovation for the jth innovation introduced to the market, S_{1j} is a dummy variable indicating that the innovator and discoverer were the same firm, S_{2j} is a dummy variable representing a hospital, research institute, or university as the source, S_{3j} represents all other external sources, P_{1j} represents the cardiovascular product category, P_{2j} represents central-nervous-system drugs, P_{3j} represents endocrine-system drugs, P_{4j} represents digestive or genitourinary drugs, and P_{5j} represents respiratory drugs.

innovations to sales is attained among very small firms in the later period). Looking at the changes over time in the innovative output of firms of various sizes, we find that, in terms of the number of innovations and the medical significance of these innovations, the smallest pharmaceutical firms have become more innovative, relative to the larger firms. This situation is reversed, however, when we consider the economic impact of the innovations.

Third, external sources have provided discoveries for about one-half of the sixty-eight pharmaceutical innovations studied. If the medical and economic significance of the innovations is taken into account, this proportion increases to about 70 percent. Foreign firms and universities, hospitals, and research institutes have been the most important external sources. Although universities, hospitals, and research institutes have contributed only 23 percent of the innovations, these innovations represent 27 percent of the medically weighted innovations and 38 percent of the economically weighted innovations. The probability that an innovation was based on a discovery made outside the innovating firm seems to have been related during 1935–1949 to the size of the innovating firm. Large firms seem to have relied more heavily on external sources than did smaller firms. However, during 1950–1962, there was no statistically significant evidence of any such relationship.

Fourth, external sources have declined in importance over time. The share of discoveries contributed by external sources in 1950–1962 was 43 percent, compared with 62 percent for the 1935–1949 period. This has been due entirely to a drop in the percentage contributed by universities, hospitals, and research institutes. Substantial differences also exist among the sources of the discoveries in various product categories: For example, external sources have provided almost all of the discoveries for innovations in neoplasm and endocrine-system drugs, while all of the discoveries of drugs in the digestive and genitourinary class have been made by the eventual innovator. To some extent, these differences among product categories are due to differences in the effectiveness of various kinds of test systems in uncovering important new chemical structures.

Fifth, the average time interval between discovery and innovation for pharmaceutical innovations—5.0 years—appears to be shorter than the average in all other industries for which data are available. The time interval is almost four years shorter, on the average, when the innovator, rather than an external source, provides the discovery for the pharmaceutical innovation. When the effects of product category and source of discovery are held constant, there seems to be no statistically significant tendency for the time lag to decrease over time.

9 THE DIFFUSION OF A MAJOR

MANUFACTURING INNOVATION*

1. Introduction

Recent years have seen a burgeoning interest in the diffusion process, the process by which the use of an innovation spreads and grows. Studies have been made to determine the factors influencing the rate of diffusion and the characteristics of the firms that are relatively quick, or relatively slow, to adopt an innovation. These studies have helped to provide a clearer and more complete understanding of the diffusion process, but they are only a beginning. Much more work is required before a satisfactory understanding is achieved.[1]

This chapter studies the diffusion of numerical control in the tool-and-die industry. Numerically controlled machine tools are certainly one of the most important innovations in manufacturing in this century. According to one leading research institute, numerical control "is the most significant new development in manufacturing technology since Henry Ford introduced the concept of the assembly line."[2] One of the industries most affected by this innovation is the tool-and-die industry. The purpose of this chapter is to see how rapidly this innovation is spreading in the tool-and-die industry, the kinds of firms that are relatively quick to adopt it, the reasons given by firms for not using it, the opinions of firm owners concerning the impact of this innovation on the structure of the tool-and-die industry, and the usefulness of some simple models in describing the diffusion process.

Two important features of this study should be noted at the outset.

---

* An earlier version of this chapter appeared in *Technological Development and Economic Growth*, ed. by George Wilson, (Bureau of Economic and Business Research, Indiana University, 1971). We are indebted to the editor for allowing us to reprint this material.

1. For surveys of findings regarding the diffusion process, see Edwin Mansfield, *The Economics of Technological Change* (New York: W. W. Norton, 1968), Chapter 4, and E. Rogers, *The Diffusion of Innovations* (New York: Free Press, 1962).

2. Illinois Institute of Technology Research Institute, *Technological Change: Its Impact on Metropolitan Chicago* (1964), p. 1.

First, the study was made while the diffusion process was still going on. This situation was an advantage in that we could get better information of many kinds than if we had waited until the diffusion process was over, but it was a disadvantage in that only part of the story could yet be told. Second, the tool-and-die industry is composed of a very large number of small firms, which means that we had the opportunity to study the diffusion of an innovation in an industry where there is very little concentration and where the organization of decision-making in the firm is relatively simple. Other studies concerned with manufacturing have dealt chiefly with more concentrated industries in which the firms are larger.

2. Numerical Control

Numerical control of machine tools is a way of operating them by means of numerical instructions expressed in code. Prepared in advance and recorded on tapes or cards, these instructions control the sequence of machine operations. They determine the machine positions, the speed and direction of movement of the tool or workpiece, and the flow of coolant. The tapes are put on a control unit, which is an electronic system that drives the tool through the programmed operations. The role of the machine operator is confined largely to starting, loading, watching, and stopping the tool. The operator can alter the instructions after each job by simply replacing the roll of tape on the control unit with another, which contains a different program.[3]

Numerical control results in a great many economic advantages. First, there is the virtual elimination of templates, jigs, and fixtures. Simple, virtually universal work-holding devices can be used, the result being lower tooling costs, faster set-up time, shorter lead time, and decreased tooling storage space. Second, the flexibility of numerical control allows lot sizes to be tailored more closely to actual requirements. Together with the benefits noted above, this makes possible a reduction in inventories. Third, one numerically controlled machine can frequently do the work of two or more conventional machines, with the result that less capital and floor space may be needed. Fourth, machining time is usually reduced by the "self-confidence" of numerical control and its elimination of waste motion. Fifth, numerical control results in greater accuracy and uniformity—inspection is reduced, rejects are fewer, and scrap loss is decreased. Finally, otherwise

3. For further descriptions of numerical control, see F. Wilson, *Numerical Control in Manufacturing* (New York: McGraw-Hill, 1963); J. Macut, *Outlook for Numerical Control of Machine Tools*, Bureau of Labor Statistics, Bulletin 1437 (March 1965); E. Schwartz and T. Prenting, "Automation in the Metal Fabricating Industries," *Report to the President of the National Commission on Technology, Automation and Economic Progress* (February 1966); and *Proceedings of the Third Annual Meeting of the Numerical Control Society* (April 1966). The paragraph in the text follows Macut's excellent description very closely.

"impossible" part designs are often practical, and manufacturing scheduling is simplified.[4]

The research and development leading to numerical control seems to have gotten started in a serious way about 1947. It was stimulated by the need for new machining methods which would produce the many intricate parts of modern aircraft more quickly, cheaply, and accurately than conventional methods. John T. Parsons, who was the owner of a small firm in Michigan that produced rotor blades, won a study contract from the Air Force, after conceiving a jig borer that was coupled with automatic data-processing equipment. Parsons turned for assistance to the Servomechanism Laboratory of the Massachusetts Institute of Technology. Once the idea was shown to be feasible, MIT was given a direct contract for the development of an experimental milling machine. By the fall of 1952, MIT scientists and engineers had successfully developed the first such milling machine. Refinements were made at MIT and by numerous machine-tool builders and producers of control and computer equipment. In 1955, the first few commercial models were displayed at the National Machine Tool Show and placed in plants for operational use.

Since 1955, the use of numerical control by American industry has grown rapidly. In 1959, the first year for which annual figures are available, numerically controlled machine tools constituted 3.7 percent of the value of shipments of all metal-cutting machine tools. This percentage increased to about 12 percent in 1964 and about 20 percent in 1966. Among the major users of numerically controlled machine tools are the aircraft industry and the metal-working-machinery industry. In 1954–1963, these two industries accounted for shipments of about one-third of such tools.[5]

3. The Tool-and-Die Industry

"Tooling" has a number of meanings. It can refer to "punches, dies, molds, jigs or fixtures, all used singly or in combination in metal-cutting or metal-forming machine tools to produce consumer or industrial goods."[6] There is an enormous variation in the size, type, and complexity of the tools, dies, gages, molds, jigs, and fixtures that are manufactured by the tool-and-die industry. They range from enormous dies used in the aircraft industry to precision gages that can measure to millionths of an inch. Along with the

4. For example, see "NC—The Time to Act is Now," *Metalworking* (June 1964); L. Thayer's paper in Wilson, *op. cit.*; and the references in note 3.

5. See Schwartz and Prenting, *op. cit.*; "22% of Cutting Machine Sales Will Be NC," *American Machinist* (August 30, 1965); R. Hatschek, "NC Today," *American Machinist* (November 22, 1965); and "Numerical Control: The Second Decade," *American Machinist* (October 26, 1964).

6. National Tool, Die and Precision Machining Association, *Report to the National Commission on Technology, Automation, and Economic Progress* (November 8, 1965), p. 2. For the census definition of the industry, see *Census of Manufacturers, 1963.*

production of conventional tool-and-die products, another activity of the industry is precision machining, which involves the making of high-precision components, frequently models or prototypes. The work is performed according to specifications or designs provided by the customer who makes the product utilizing the component.

Industry gets its tooling from two sources: captive shops and contract shops. The captive shops are departments of large manufacturers which handle their company's routine needs for fitting and repairing tooling. The contract shops are independent tool-and-die firms. The industry—as defined by the *Census of Manufacturers* and the membership of the National Tool, Die and Precision Machining Association (NTDPMA)—consists of the contract shops. This chapter is concerned primarily with the independent contract shops, although some attention will obviously have to be focused on the captive shops as well.

In 1963, the tool-and-die industry consisted of close to six thousand independent shops, employing more than ninety thousand workers. A few of the largest firms may have employed several hundred or more persons, but the median shop employed about fifteen and median sales were about $275,000 per facility. The industry is composed almost entirely of small businesses; indeed, about 40 percent of the tool-and-die establishments included in the 1963 *Census of Manufacturers* employed less than five people. Concentration in the industry is relatively low; the largest four firms accounted for less than 10 percent of the industry's value of shipments in 1958. Many of the firms are started by men who have served an apprenticeship in the tool-and-die industry. These firms start out small and remain tied to one man. The tool-and-die industry is concentrated heavily in the East North Central and Middle Atlantic states, about 70 percent of all establishments being located in these two regions in 1963.[7]

The tool-and-die industry grew rapidly between 1958 and 1966, its value of shipments increasing by about 80 percent during that period. In the mid-sixties, the industry reported that it was operating at full—or more than full—capacity. Although adequate data are unavailable, it appears that the sixties were generally quite profitable for the industry, which is, of course, highly cyclical. According to a 1965 survey by NTDPMA, there has been a trend toward greater diversification of products and services provided by the industry. During 1956–1964, tooling became less important, while precision machining and other services became more important. Also, during the mid-sixties, the industry complained repeatedly of a shortage of skilled labor.[8]

7. See *Problems of the Tool and Die Industry and Associated Problems of Manufacturers and Distributors of Machine Tools,* House Select Committee on Small Business, 1966. For the concentration ratio in 1958, see *Concentration Ratios in Manufacturing Industry, 1958,* Senate Subcommittee on Antitrust and Monopoly, 1958, Part I, p. 34.

8. See National Tool, Die and Precision Machining Association, *op. cit.* The "other services" mentioned above are contract production and proprietary products.

4. The Rate of Diffusion, 1960–1968

The directories of the National Tool, Die and Precision Machining Association provide data concerning the percentage of tool-and-die firms using numerical control in 1967 and 1968. To estimate the pre-1967 growth in the percentage of firms using numerical control, we interviewed a carefully selected sample of forty firms in the Association, this sample being described in sections 5 and 10. Each firm was asked a variety of questions, including whether it was using numerical control, and if so, when it had begun using it. The results are shown in Table 9.1. The figures indicate that only about 1 percent of the firms had begun using numerical control at the beginning of 1961. By the beginning of 1966, the percentage had grown to 8 percent; and by the beginning of 1968, 20 percent of the firms were using numerical control.[9] Results of a mail survey described below bear out these findings.

Of course, the fact that a firm adopts numerical control does not mean that it does all of its work on numerically controlled equipment. To find out

TABLE **9.1**

Percent of Tool-and-Die Firms[a] *Using Numerical Control, 1960–1968*

YEAR (JANUARY 1)	PERCENT OF FIRMS
1961	1.1
1962	1.1
1963	2.3
1964	4.5
1965	5.7
1966	7.9
1967	13.6
1968	20.4

[a] Note that the results pertain only to members of the National Tool, Die and Precision Machining Association. See note 9.

9. The 1967 and 1968 directories provide exact information regarding the percentage of NTDPMA members using numerical control. To obtain the earlier figures in Table 9.1, we assume that the distribution of firms in the sample by the year when they began using numerical control is representative of the distribution of all NTDPMA members (with numerical control at the beginning of 1967) by the year when they began using numerical control. This assumption seems reasonable, since the sample of firms we interviewed was chosen in such a way that the sample percentages are unbiased estimates of the percentages for the entire NTDPMA membership. Results based on our mail survey are almost exactly the same as those in Table 9.1. This is an important confirmation of our results.

Note that all of our results pertain only to the approximately one thousand members of the NTDPMA, since the cost of extending the frame beyond the Association membership was out of the question. The Association members, which tend to be larger than the nonmembers, account for the bulk of the industry's output.

the extent to which users of numerical control are employing it—as well as to find out many other things—we carried out a mail survey of the membership of the Association. We received replies from 316 firms—about one-third of the Association membership. Table 9.2 shows, for the respondents

TABLE **9.2**

Frequency Distribution of Tool-and-Die Firms,
by Percent of Sales Accounted for by Numerically
Controlled Equipment, Ninety-seven Firms, 1967

| PERCENT OF SALES ACCOUNTED FOR BY NUMERICALLY CONTROLLED EQUIPMENT | TYPE OF SALES | | |
	TOTAL SALES	SALES OF CONVENTIONAL TOOL-AND-DIE PRODUCTS	SALES FROM PRECISION MACHINING
	(number of firms)		
0	0	46	23
1–9	46	29	17
10–19	26	8	19
20–29	14	2	13
30–39	1	1	1
40–49	1	0	3
50–59	2	1	3
60 or more	2	0	8
No answer	5	10	10
Total	*97*	*97*	*97*

to our mail survey that used numerical control, the percentage of all work done on numerically controlled equipment in 1967. According to the results, work performed on such equipment accounted in 1967 for less than 10 percent of total sales for about half the firms using numerical control. In only about 20 percent of the firms did it account for 20 percent or more of total sales. In interpreting those figures, one should recognize, of course, that many of these firms had been using numerical control for only a short period of time.[10]

The area where numerically controlled equipment tends to be used most often is precision machining. Of the firms who answered the question, about 75 percent of those with numerically controlled equipment used it for this purpose. In about one-third of the firms in Table 9.2, numerically controlled equipment was used to produce 20 percent or more of the sales in this area. Indeed, in about 15 percent of the firms, it was used to produce 50 percent or more of the firm's sales in this area. Turning to conventional tool-and-die

10. The ninety-seven firms in Table 9.2 comprise all the firms responding to our mail survey that said they were using numerical control. The survey was carried out about January 1, 1968. A copy of the precise wording of the questions that were asked is available on request.

products, we find that about half the firms in Table 9.2 did not use numerically controlled equipment at all on such work. In only about 5 percent of the firms did numerically controlled equipment produce 20 percent or more of sales in this area.

Finally, Table 9.3 shows that there is some variation among states in the percentage of firms using numerical control. In late 1966, this percentage tended to be higher in California, Indiana, Massachusetts, Minnesota,

TABLE **9.3**

*Percent of Tool-and-Die Firms Using Numerical Control,
January, 1967, by State*

STATE	PERCENT	STATE	PERCENT
Alabama	14	Minnesota	43
Arkansas	0	Missouri	14
California	28	Nebraska	0
Colorado	0	New Jersey	15
Connecticut	13	New York	13
Florida	0	North Carolina	0
Georgia	0	Ohio	15
Illinois	7	Oklahoma	0
Indiana	15	Pennsylvania	19
Iowa	14	Rhode Island	0
Kansas	0	South Carolina	0
Kentucky	0	Tennessee	5
Louisiana	0	Texas	8
Maine	100[a]	Virginia	33[b]
Maryland	20	Washington	0
Massachusetts	17	West Virginia	0
Michigan	13	Wisconsin	13

Source: National Tool, Die and Precision Machining Association, *Directory and Buying Guide*, (1967).
[a] There is only one firm in Maine.
[b] There are only three firms in Virginia.

New Jersey, and Ohio than in Connecticut, Illinois, Michigan, Missouri, New York, and Texas. In part, these regional differences may reflect the differences among regions in the type of work done by the tool-and-die industry. For example, California's tool-and-die firms are tied closely to the aircraft industry, whereas Michigan's tool-and-die firms are linked with the automobile industry. Obviously, they do somewhat different types of work.[11]

11. According to some observers, the aircraft industry and its suppliers have been somewhat quicker to utilize numerical control than the automobile industry and its suppliers. The states mentioned in the text were singled out because they account for the bulk of the tool-and-die firms.

5. Impact of Numerical Control on Costs and Profits

The mail survey and interviews also included questions regarding the profitability of numerical control. Practically all of the respondents using numerical control said that they were satisfied with its performance. A rough measure of the profitability of a firm's investment in numerically controlled equipment is the pay-out period—the length of time it takes for the cash earnings on the investment to return the original cost. Table 9.4 shows the frequency distribution of pay-out periods estimated by the respondents to the mail survey. The results indicate that the pay-out period was three years or less in about one-third of the cases, the median pay-out period being five years.

To determine in detail the impact of numerical control on various types of costs, we interviewed in late 1967 and early 1968 the managers of a carefully selected sample of twelve tool-and-die firms using numerical control. A two-stage sampling design was used to choose the firms, the primary sampling units being the areas in the NTDPMA directory. Six primary units were chosen with probability proportional to size of unit, and two firms were chosen at random in each primary unit.[12] The firms provided detailed estimates of the effect of numerical control on various types of costs.[13] The

TABLE 9.4

Frequency Distribution of Tool-and-Die Firms,
by the Pay-out Period
for Numerically Controlled Equipment

PAY-OUT PERIOD	NUMBER OF FIRMS	PERCENT OF FIRMS[a]
Less than 3 years	13	13
3 years	18	19
4 years	10	10
5 years	19	20
6 years	7	7
7 years	4	4
8 years	3	3
More than 8 years	14	14
No answer	9	9

[a] Because of rounding, the individual items do not sum to 100.

12. The appropriate size of primary unit here is the number of firms with numerical control in the unit. The primary sampling units that were chosen were Central Connecticut, Cincinnati, Detroit, Los Angeles, New York City, and Philadelphia. For a discussion of two-stage sampling designs of this sort, see W. Cochran, *Sampling Techniques* (Wiley, 1963).
13. More precisely, they were asked to estimate the annual saving (positive or negative) in various cost categories due to the use of numerical control rather than conventional equipment. In other words, they were asked to estimate the savings over what would have occurred if they had used conventional equipment to do the jobs they carried out in 1967.

median annual saving in direct labor hours due to the use of numerical control rather than a conventional machine tool was about two thousand hours per machine.[14] The median annual saving in jigs and fixtures was about $5,000 per machine. Savings in inspection costs, scrap costs, inventory, and the cost of materials handling varied a great deal and were difficult to measure, but they sometimes were substantial. Also, in most cases, there was a definite saving in floor space.

On the other hand, numerical control does not reduce all types of costs. In particular, numerical control can result in a substantial increase in annual maintenance costs. Although the median increase in annual maintenance costs was about $500 per machine, in several cases it was estimated to be over $10,000 (so far). Also, besides the relatively high first cost of numerically controlled equipment (median first cost—$46,000), there is a substantial investment in training operators, programmers, and maintenance men, the median lump-sum training cost being about $1200 per machine. Further, there are the considerable costs of programming, the median cost being about $4,000 per machine.

Relative to other potential investments and to the funds available for investment, how profitable has numerical control been to these firms? One very crude way to help answer this question is to compare the pay-out period from the investment in numerically controlled equipment with the maximum pay-out period that the firm would require before deciding to invest. The latter pay-out period is a measure of the profitability of the poorest investment that is still sufficiently attractive to be carried out. Estimates of this pay-out period were obtained for the twelve firms, the average being 7.7 years. Since this is considerably greater than the average pay-out period for the investment in numerically controlled equipment (4.8 years), the latter appears to have been considerably more profitable than the "marginal" investment.[15]

6. A Simple Model of the Imitation Process

To analyze the data in Table 9.1, we adopt a simple model proposed and used in previous work. The model assumes that for the jth innovation in the ith industry,

$$(9.1) \qquad \lambda_{ij}(t) = f_i(P_{ij}(t), \Pi_{ij}, S_{ij}, \ldots),$$

where $\lambda_{ij}(t)$ is the proportion of firms not using the innovation at time t

---

14. Since wage rates were about $4.00 per hour, this amounted to an annual saving of about $8,000 per machine. Note, however, that wage rates vary and that this is only a rough average.
15. Of course, it is difficult to make sure that the maximum pay-out period that is given pertains to investments with riskiness and other characteristics that are comparable with those of the investment in numerical control.

that introduce it by time $(t + 1)$, $P_{ij}(t)$ is the proportion of potential users of the innovation that have introduced it at time t, Π_{ij} is the profitability of installing this innovation relative to that of alternative investments, and S_{ij} is the investment required to install this innovation, as a percent of the average total assets of these firms. In other words, the model assumes that the probability that a nonuser will use the innovation between time t and $(t + 1)$ is dependent on the proportion of firms already using the innovation, the profitability of using the innovation, and the investment required to install the innovation. For simplicity, Π_{ij} and S_{ij} are assumed to remain constant for all relevant values of t.

Assuming that $\lambda_{ij}(t)$ can be approximated adequately by a Taylor's expansion that drops third- and higher-order terms, and assuming that the coefficient of $P_{ij}^2(t)$ in this expansion is 0, it can be shown that the growth over time in the number of firms having introduced the innovation should conform to a logistic function. Specifically,

$$(9.2) \qquad P_{ij}(t) = [1 + e^{-(\ell_{ij} + \phi_{ij}t)}]^{-1}.$$

It can also be shown that the rate of imitation depends only on ϕ_{ij}, and on the basis of our assumptions,

$$(9.3) \qquad \phi_{ij} = b_i + a_1\Pi_{ij} + a_2S_{ij} + z_{ij},$$

where the a's and b's are parameters and z_{ij} is a random error term.

This model has been tested against data for a dozen innovations in four industries, the results being quite favorable. In general, the growth in the number of users of an innovation can be approximated by a logistic curve. And there is definite evidence that more profitable innovations and those requiring smaller investments had higher rates of imitation, the empirical relationship being strikingly similar to the one predicted by equation (9.3).[16] Also, in Chapter 3, this model lay behind our use of the logistic function to represent the growth over time in the number of laboratories using quantitative project-selection techniques. It also lay behind our suggestion in Chapter 3 that the relatively slow rate of diffusion of these techniques, despite the smallness of the investment required to introduce them, may be due to their not being regarded as very profitable.

7. Estimates of ℓ and ϕ for Numerical Control

If this model holds in the case of numerical control in the tool-and-die industry, the growth in the proportion of tool-and-die firms using numerical

16. For a more detailed account of the material in this section, see Edwin Mansfield, *Industrial Research and Technological Innovation* (New York: W. W. Norton for the Cowles Foundation for Research in Economics at Yale University, 1968).

control should conform, at least approximately, to a logistic function. Allowing for the fact that some tool-and-die firms will not use numerical control, we have

$$(9.4) \qquad P(t) = \frac{K}{1 + e^{-(\ell + \phi t)}},$$

where K is the maximum proportion that will be reached, $P(t)$ is the proportion of tool-and-die firms using numerical control at time t, and ℓ and ϕ are the parameters of the logistic function. According to the estimates of the firms using numerical control in the sample of firms we interviewed, the percentage of users will eventually reach about 75 percent. According to a survey we conducted of machine-tool builders (and according to some experts outside the industry), it will reach about 85 percent. According to the estimates of the firms not using numerical control in the sample of firms we interviewed, it will eventually reach about 50 percent. Thus, we let $K = 0.80$ be the "optimistic assumption" and $K = 0.50$ be the "pessimistic assumption."[17]

Using the data in Table 9.1 regarding $P(t)$ in 1960–1968, we can estimate ℓ and ϕ under each assumption regarding K. Some simple manipulation of equation (9.4) results in

$$(9.5) \qquad \ln [P(t)/(K - P(t))] = \ell + \phi t$$

Thus, ℓ and ϕ can be estimated by straightforward regression techniques, the results being

$$(9.6) \qquad \ln [P(t)/(0.80 - P(t))] = -4.460 + 0.477t$$
$$(0.027)$$

and

$$(9.7) \qquad \ln [P(t)/(0.50 - P(t))] = -4.604 + 0.538t$$
$$(0.049)$$

The important parameter is ϕ, which measures the rate of imitation. A comparison of equations (9.6) and (9.7) shows that the estimate of ϕ does not vary greatly: In equation (9.6), it is 0.477; in equation (9.7), it is 0.538. Moreover, in both cases, the standard error (shown in parentheses) seems quite small.[18]

17. In the interviews with users and nonusers of numerical control, we asked each firm's owner what proportion of the NTDPMA membership would eventually use numerical control, in his judgment. (See notes 12 and 25 and the corresponding portions of the text for a description of the samples of users and nonusers.) The average percentage given by nonusers was 50.1, and the average percentage given by users was 74.7. It is quite understandable, of course, that the users' estimate would be higher than that of the nonusers. In addition, we asked a number of knowledgeable people in government, trade associations, and the machine-tool industry the same question, the average percentage they gave being 86.0. Fortunately, as we shall see, the value of K does not make much difference to our results, so long as it is somewhere in the suggested range. Note that t is measured in years from the beginning of 1961.

18. Note once again that these estimates are based only on data pertaining to the early part of the diffusion process, since this is all that has occurred as yet. It is possible, of course, that

8. A Comparison of Rates of Imitation

Is there any evidence that numerical control is spreading relatively slowly—or relatively rapidly—among NTDPMA firms? That is, is there any evidence that, if an innovation with characteristics similar to numerical control had been introduced in other industries (e.g., coal or steel), it would have spread more rapidly—or more slowly—than numerical control has among NTDPMA firms? A great deal of interest attaches to this question, since the tool-and-die industry is composed of a very large number of small firms. The results should provide some evidence bearing on the important issue of whether or not innovations tend to spread less, or more, rapidly in highly fragmented industries than in more concentrated ones.

According to previous work, an innovation's rate of imitation in the bituminous-coal, iron-and-steel, railroad, and brewing industries can be estimated by

$$(9.8) \qquad \phi_{ij} = \begin{Bmatrix} -0.29 \\ -0.57 \\ -0.52 \\ -0.59 \end{Bmatrix} + 0.530\,\Pi_{ij} - 0.027\,S_{ij},$$

where the symbols are as defined in section 6, and the first figure in braces pertains to the brewing industry, the second to coal, the third to steel, and the fourth to railroads.[19] Using equation (9.8), we can estimate how rapidly an innovation with values of Π_{ij} and S_{ij} equal to those of numerical control among NTDPMA firms would have spread in these other industries. Then we can compare the result with the observed rate of imitation.

In carrying out this procedure, the first step is to estimate Π_{ij} and S_{ij} for numerical control among the NTDPMA firms. The basic information on which these estimates are based is derived from the data described in section 5. The resulting estimates are $\Pi_{ij} = 1.62$ and $S_{ij} = 5.1$.[20] The next step is to estimate ϕ_{ij} for numerical control among the NTDPMA firms. Based on the data for 1960–1968, a reasonable estimate of ϕ_{ij} is 0.48–0.54,

---

these early data are misleading. All that we can say is that, based on experience to date, these seem to be the best estimates of ϕ.

19. For the derivation of equation (9.8), see Mansfield, *Industrial Research and Technological Innovation, op. cit.*, pp. 136–144.

20. These estimates are based on the experience of the twelve firms with numerical control included in the sample discussed in section 5. The figure for Π_{ij} comes from dividing the reciprocal of the average pay-out period for the investment in numerical control by the reciprocal of the average pay-out period for the "marginal" investment. The figure for S_{ij} is 100 times the ratio of average first cost of the numerically controlled equipment to the average total assets of the firms. The crudeness of these results should be obvious, although the sample was selected in such a way that no bias should result. Nonetheless it seems likely that the estimate of S_{ij}, although correct for the sample, is an underestimate for the industry as a whole. The effects of such an underestimate would be to strengthen the results of this section, since it would mean that the rate of imitation is even faster—relative to innovations in other industries—than indicated in this section. Note that the estimates of Π_{ij} and S_{ij} for the other innovations, underlying equation (9.8), were derived in a similar way. See *ibid.*

as we saw in section 7. Finally, one can compare this value—or range of values—of ϕ_{ij} with the value that would be predicted on the basis of equation (9.8) for each of the other industries, given that the innovation's Π_{ij} equals 1.62 and S_{ij} equals 5.1. Simple arithmetic shows that the latter is 0.43 for brewing, 0.15 for coal, 0.21 for steel, and 0.13 for railroads.

Thus, the results indicate that the rate of imitation in the case of numerical control among NTDPMA firms is greater than would be expected in any of the other industries for an innovation with equal Π_{ij} and S_{ij}. This finding —like the results of our previous studies—seems to suggest that, all other things being equal, innovations tend to spread more rapidly in less concentrated industries.[21] However, much more evidence will be required before we can be reasonably sure that this is—or is not—the case.

9. Characteristics of Early Users of Numerical Control

To determine whether—and if so, in what way—the characteristics of the firms using numerical control differ from those not using it, our mail surveys and interviews included questions which attempted to provide data regarding relevant characteristics of users and nonusers. On *a priori* grounds, there are a good many reasons for expecting the larger tool-and-die firms to be quicker, on the average, than the smaller ones to introduce numerical control. For example, the larger firms are more likely to have the financial resources to enable them to experiment, and they are more likely to have the technical know-how and the managerial qualities that are so important in determining a firm's speed of response to a new technique. This hypothesis is borne out by the results of our survey. The median number of employees of firms using numerical control at the beginning of 1968 was about 60, while that of nonusers was about 30. Moreover, among the users of numerical control, there is a significant inverse relationship between the size of the firm and the year when the firm began using numerical control (Table 9.5).[22]

Another variable that would be expected to influence whether or not a firm adopted numerical control before 1968 is the education of the firm's

21. This result is supported by previous findings which pertain to four other industries. They indicate that if the profitability of the innovation and the size of the investment are held constant, the rate of imitation tends to be higher in less concentrated industries. However, the relationship in this previous work was not statistically significant. See *ibid.*, p. 144.

22. These are the results from the sample of firms we interviewed. The results from the mail survey differ only in detail. For a description of the sample of nonusers that were interviewed, see section 10; for the sample of users, see section 5.

To some extent, the relationship between firm size in 1968 and the year that a firm first used numerical control is probably due to a difference between the growth rates of users and nonusers, users probably having had higher growth rates. But this can explain only part of the relationship, since the available evidence indicates that when they began using numerical control, the early users tended to be larger than the nonusers.

Of course, the fact that the larger firms tend to be quicker than the small ones to begin using an innovation does not contradict in any way the finding that the rate of imitation tends to be faster in less concentrated industries.

TABLE **9.5**

*Average Date of First Use of Numerical Control,
by Size of Firm, Eighty-nine Firms*[a]

NUMBER OF EMPLOYEES IN 1967	AVERAGE YEAR OF FIRST USE[b]
Less than 20 persons	1966
20–49 persons	1965
50–99 persons	1965
100–199 persons	1964
200 persons and over	1963

[a] Since eight firms did not provide information on number of employees or year of first use, not all respondents using numerical control could be included.
[b] The averages have been rounded to the nearest full year.

president. Better-educated entrepreneurs are likely to be in a better position to understand the issues regarding numerical control, to have the flexibility of mind to use it, and to be in contact with technical and university centers and the relevant literature. The data seem to bear out this hypothesis, most of the users (for which we have data) being college graduates, but most of the nonusers having finished high school or less. The difference is statistically significant.

Still another variable that would be expected to influence whether or not a firm adopted numerical control is the age of the firm's president. Younger entrepreneurs would be more likely to make the break with the past, their emotional attachment to old skills and old technology being weaker and their willingness to take risks probably being greater than those of their older rivals. The data available from the interviews are consistent with this hypothesis, the median age of the users being about 48 and the median age of the nonusers being about 55. However, age and education are themselves correlated, and when a multiple regression is run (age and education being independent variables, the dependent variable being a dummy variable showing whether or not a firm used numerical control before 1968), the effect of education is statistically significant, but the effect of age is not.[23]

To relate these findings to those regarding other innovations, note that the inverse relationship between firm size and the average date of first use of an innovation has been found to exist for a great many innovations. Moreover, there is evidence of a similar kind regarding the effects of age and education in the case of agricultural innovations. Thus, these results for numerical control in the tool-and-die industry are quite consistent with

23. The data regarding the age and education of the company presidents came from the interviews. Questions on this score were asked of half the firms in the sample.

the results of previous studies of other innovations.[24] It might also be noted that the observed relationship between a firm's speed of adoption of numerical control and the education of the firm's president is quite consistent with models that emphasize the interrelations between education and technological change in their effects on productivity change and economic growth. In part, the effect of education on economic growth depends on the rate of technological change, since an important effect of more education is to make managers and workers more adaptable to change and quicker to adopt innovations.

10. Reasons for Nonuse of Numerical Control

One of the advantages of carrying out a study while the diffusion process is still going on is that one can ask the nonusers why they have not adopted the innovation. To obtain such information, we interviewed in late 1967 and early 1968 the owners of a carefully selected sample of twenty-eight firms not using numerical control. A two-stage sampling design was used to choose the firms, the primary sampling units being the areas in the NTDPMA directory. Seven primary units were chosen with probability proportional to size, and four firms were chosen at random in each primary unit.[25] In response to the question, practically all of the owners said that numerical control would be unprofitable for them. When questioned in detail concerning the reasons why they felt that this was the case, they most frequently cited the fact that they did one-of-a-kind work. Many of them said that if they did work where lot sizes were somewhat larger, they would certainly use numerical control.[26]

24. See Mansfield, op. cit. Note that in Mansfield's study the effects of the age of the president are not significant. However, the firms included in this study were often very large and the president was probably not the relevant decision-maker in many cases.
25. The appropriate size of primary unit here is the number of firms without numerical control in the unit. The primary sampling units that were chosen were Chicago, Detroit, Los Angeles, Trenton (New Jersey), New York City, Chicago, and Southern Connecticut. Note that Chicago was chosen twice, the result being that eight firms were chosen at random in Chicago. This could occur because areas were chosen with replacement.
26. Judging from the literature and from interviews with both tool-and-die firms and machine-tool builders, one of the most important variables influencing the profitability of numerical control is batch size. According to many tool-and-die firms, numerical control is not profitable for extremely small batch sizes, notably one-of-a-kind work. To cast light on the minimum lot size for which numerical control is profitable, the Tool and Die Institute and IIT Research Institute conducted several experiments where the costs of production using numerical control were compared with those using conventional equipment. Three items—a punch, a female die, and a core insert—were produced both ways, and a cost comparison was made for each item. The results suggested that the minimum lot size that would make numerical control profitable was six pieces in the case of the punch, six pieces in the case of the die, and three pieces in the case of the core insert.
However, it is important to note, as the study itself does, that a different set of parts with different configurations could lead to a different conclusion. In particular, the results illustrate the fact that the number of pieces needed to realize economic advantages through numerical control decreases with the complexity of the part to be produced. For very complex parts, a number of tool-and-die firm owners agreed in the interviews that numerical control might be profitable even for one-of-a-kind work. But the evidence regarding the profitability of numerical control for one-of-a-kind work seems rather sketchy. See D. Smith, Technological Change in Michigan's Tool and Die Industry (University of Michigan, 1968).

However, another factor brought out in the interviews was the fact that a considerable number of the owners, by their own account, had important gaps in their knowledge and understanding of numerical control. About 30 percent of those interviewed said that, for one reason or another, they really knew relatively little about numerical control, and that this was a factor in their not using it. This result seems to accord with Warner's findings in northern Illinois. According to Warner, there "seems to be little doubt that lack of technical knowledge and active experience are major obstacles to much greater utilization of NC equipment."[27]

Still another reason that was stressed in a number of the interviews was that the owner was not very far from retirement and there was no one to take over the firm, either because the owner had no children or because they were not interested in continuing the business. Under these circumstances, the owner felt that it would be foolish to go to all the expense and trouble of installing numerical control. Instead, he had decided to stick with conventional methods until he wanted to quit—or until he was put out of business. Perhaps surprisingly, this attitude was expressed by a considerable proportion of the owners interviewed—about 10 percent. (In this connection, it should be noted that the average age of the owners of tool-and-die firms tends to be relatively high.)[28] Another factor—related to some we have already discussed—was resentment of the new equipment. None of the men we interviewed expressed this reaction directly, although some spoke wistfully of the old days. But many accused others of resenting the idea that a machine could be "endowed" with some of the skill and art of their very demanding craft. The owners that showed the most evidence of such resentment tended to be the older ones.

In conclusion, many of the nonusers felt that numerical control is not profitable for one-of-a-kind work. Also, there is evidence that lack of knowledge, the approaching retirement of shop owners, and resentment of change may be important drags on the rate of diffusion, there being considerable agreement among knowledgeable observers and members of the industry that this is the case.[29] However, two points should be noted. First, although lack of knowledge, approaching retirement, and resentment of change are important in explaining the behavior of some shops, they do not seem to be important in a great many others. Judging from the interviews, they may have been important in about 30 percent of the shops.[30] Second, there is no

27. J. Warner, *Introduction of Numerical Control Technology to Illinois Industry*, Northern Illinois University (September 1967).

28. For a discussion of the resistance to numerical control, see D. Smith, *op. cit.*, and his "Why Companies Balk at Technology Transfers," *Columbia Journal of World Business*, May–June, 1967. Note that many of the owners who said that their impending retirement was an important factor also said that they knew little about numerical control.

29. For a description of the importance of these factors in impeding the imitation process, see *ibid.*

30. Of course, this may be an underestimate since firm owners may not admit—or be entirely conscious of—the reasons for their behavior.

evidence that these factors are more of a drag on the rate of diffusion in the case of this innovation than in the case of most other innovations. Holding Π_{ij} and S_{ij} constant, this innovation seems to be spreading more rapidly than the others for which we have data.[31]

11. Expectations Regarding the Competitive Effects of Numerical Control

Few, if any, studies of the diffusion process have investigated the way in which the firms responding to a major innovation view its effects on the competitive structure of the industry. Is there considerable agreement among the firms as to the impact of numerical control? If not, how do the opinions of the users differ from those of the nonusers? To what extent are the firms' expectations consistent with their behavior and their plans? These questions are important, since firms' expectations play an important role in determining how they react to an innovation and how smoothly or how painfully the new technique is absorbed. Both in our mail survey and in the interviews, firms were asked to state their opinions concerning the extent to which firms without numerical control would be at a competitive disadvantage in the next few years, the effect in the next few years of numerical control on the total number of contract tool-and-die firms, the total amount of tool-and-die work, the share of the business going to the small (under ten employees) contract shops, and the share of the business going to the captive shops. Conventional tool-and-die work was separated from precision machining in these questions, since the effects of numerical control would be expected to be different in the two types of work. The opinions of the approximately three hundred firms that answered these questions in the mail survey are summarized in Table 9.6.[32]

The most frequent opinion was that in conventional tool-and-die work, firms without numerical control would be at a small competitive disadvantage, whereas in precision machining they would be at a great competitive disadvantage. With respect to conventional tool-and-die work, the most frequent opinion was that numerical control would have little or no effect on the total number of firms, the total amount of work, the share of the business going to the small firms, or the share of the business going to the captive shops. With respect to precision machining, the most frequent opinion was that numerical control would result in a decrease in the number of firms, a decrease in the small firms' share of the business, and an increase in the captive shops' share of the business. Although these were the most frequently held opinions, Table 9.6 shows that they were by no means unani-

31. Needless to say, this does not prove that these factors were less important in this case than in others. They may have been more important, but their effects may have been offset by other factors. All that can be said is that there is no evidence one way or the other.
32. The results of the interviews differ only in detail.

TABLE 9.6

Percentage Distribution of Tool-and-Die Firms, by Their Opinions Regarding
Short-Run Effects of Numerical Control on Firms Doing Conventional Tool-and-Die Work
and Precision Machining, Users and Nonusers of Numerical Control[a]

	CONVENTIONAL TOOL-AND-DIE WORK		PRECISION MACHINING	
	USERS OF NUMERICAL CONTROL	NONUSERS OF NUMERICAL CONTROL	USERS OF NUMERICAL CONTROL	NONUSERS OF NUMERICAL CONTROL
	(*percents*)			
Extent of competitive disadvantage of firms without numerical control				
Great	31	14	85	68
Small	48	49	14	27
Negligible	21	38	1	5
Effect on share of the business going to small contract shops				
Increase	24	11	24	47
Decrease	31	30	63	10
No difference	45	59	13	43
Effect on number of contract shops				
Increase	8	6	14	15
Decrease	40	30	58	49
No difference	52	64	27	36
Effect on share of business going to captive shops				
Increase	44	40	49	57
Decrease	10	18	20	23
No difference	46	42	31	20
Effect on total amount of conventional tool-and-die work				
Increase	19	15	—	—
Decrease	43	32	—	—
No difference	38	52	—	—

[a] Because of rounding, sums of individual items may not equal 100.

mous. On the contrary, there was only one case where 60 percent or more of the firms (both users and nonusers) were in agreement. In many cases, no opinion was shared by a majority of the firms. As would be expected, the opinions of the users of numerical control differed from those of the nonusers, the nonusers being more inclined to believe that the competitive effects of numerical control would be small and that it would make no difference in the number of firms, the total amount of work, and the share of the business going to the small firms.[33]

It is interesting to note that even when shop owners grant that the lack of numerical control will soon be a major competitive disadvantage, they do not necessarily intend to adopt it. On the contrary, if we look at the nonusers engaged in precision machining who felt that a firm in precision machining without numerical control would soon be at a great competitive disadvantage, we find that 60 percent of them did not plan to adopt numerical control in the next year or two. Judging from the interviews, the major reason was not that they felt that they were unable to obtain numerically controlled equipment. Instead, a large proportion insisted that although numerical control was profitable for many firms, it would not be profitable for them. Another large proportion admitted that it might be profitable to use it, but planned nonetheless to continue using the older, familiar methods.[34]

12. Summary

The principal conclusions of this chapter are as follows: First, numerically controlled machine tools are one of the most important innovations in manufacturing in this century. The research and development leading to numerical control seems to have started in a serious way about 1947. John T. Parsons, the owner of a small firm that produced rotor blades, won a study contract from the Air Force after conceiving a jig borer that was coupled with automatic data-processing equipment. Parsons turned for assistance to MIT. By the fall of 1952, MIT scientists had developed the first such milling machine. In 1955, the first commercial models were displayed.

Second, allowing for differences in profitability and size of investment, this innovation seems to be spreading more rapidly in the tool-and-die industry than innovations in other industries for which data are available. This finding is based on experience to date, and a final judgment cannot,

33. Note that the opinions pertain to the short-term effects of numerical control. We asked the firms to estimate the effects of numerical control in the period of two or three years after they responded (which was at the beginning of 1968). Perhaps there would have been more agreement concerning its long-term effects.

34. Of course, it must be pointed out that a substantial proportion of the firms *did* intend to use numerical control in the next few years. Judging by the sample of firms we interviewed, about 16 percent of those not using numerical control at the time of the interviews expected to begin using it within a year or two.

of course, be made until the diffusion process is completed. But experience to date with this innovation tends to support the hypothesis that innovations generally spread more rapidly in less concentrated industries. However, needless to say, much more evidence will be required before we can be reasonably sure that this is—or is not—the case.

Third, although this innovation seems to be spreading relatively rapidly, the diffusion process seems to be slowed perceptibly by lack of knowledge and resistance to change. About 30 percent of the nonusers that were interviewed said that they really knew little about numerical control. A considerable number of these nonusers were close to retirement and had decided to stick with conventional methods. Even when firm owners granted that the lack of numerical control would soon be a major competitive disadvantage, they did not necessarily intend to adopt it.

Fourth, practically all of the nonusers that were interviewed claimed that numerical control would be unprofitable for them, chiefly because they did one-of-a-kind work. Of course, this may well be true. However, in many of these cases, it appeared that the firms had not obtained much information concerning the innovation, despite all of the fanfare it aroused. Practically all of the users of numerical control said that they were satisfied with its performance, the median payout period for the investment in the innovation being five years. We obtained detailed estimates of the effect of numerical control on various types of costs from a carefully selected sample of firms throughout the United States.

Fifth, the early users of numerical control tend to be the larger tool-and-die firms. Whether or not a firm is using numerical control also seems to be related to the age and education of the owner. However, when both age and education are taken into account simultaneously, only the effect of education is significant. These results provide interesting new evidence concerning the characteristics of technical leaders and followers, and are quite consistent with models that emphasize the interrelations between education and technological change in their effects on productivity increase and economic growth.

Sixth, for the first time, we were able to obtain information concerning the opinions of firm owners concerning the effects of an innovation on the structure of their industry. The differences of opinion concerning the effects in the next few years of numerical control were very substantial. For example, there was a marked difference of opinion between users and nonusers of numerical control, as would be expected. However, there was fairly general agreement that numerical control would have more effect on firms engaged in precision machining than on firms producing conventional tool-and-die products. With regard to precision machining, the most frequent opinion was that numerical control would result in a decrease in the number of firms, a decrease in the small firms' share of the business, and an increase in the captive shops' share of the business.

10 CONCLUSIONS

1. Introduction

In this chapter, we bring together many of our results and discuss their implications for model-builders and policy-makers. As indicated below, these results have implications for economists interested in modeling the process of technological change, for economists and lawyers interested in formulating and carrying out public policy toward the giant corporation, for scientists and social scientists interested in various aspects of public policy-making concerning science and technology, and for managers, industrial scientists, and operations researchers interested in helping firms to utilize science and technology more effectively.

2. Technical Risks in Industrial Research and Development

The first point that should be made is that, judging by our data, the technical risks involved in the bulk of industrial research and development —outside military and other government-financed areas—seem quite modest. For example, among the 19 laboratories in the petroleum, chemical, electronics, and drug industries, the average probability of technical completion for a project was better than 50-50. This was true as well of the average estimated probability of technical success among our sample of 21 large chemical and petroleum firms. To a considerable extent, this seems to be due to the fact that the bulk of the R and D projects are aimed at fairly modest advances in the state of the art. For example, according to the directors of three laboratories in the sample, about 70 percent of the projects in their laboratories were aimed at only small advances in the state of the art.

This is an important point, both for analysis and for policy. Several recent studies of military research and development have indicated and dramatized the great advances in the state of the art achieved by research and development in the military sphere.[1] At the same time, case studies of major inventions in civilian fields have indicated the great technical risks often involved in work aimed at such major inventions.[2] Having read these studies, economists and others have sometimes been inclined to jump to the conclusion that most of the research and development carried out by industry for civilian purposes is not too different from military R and D or from work aimed at major inventions. Our previous discussion indicates that this clearly is not the case.

This conclusion has several implications, one being that some of the models that are used to characterize private research and development in the civilian sector—models that suppose that the bulk of this work is very risky, far-out work aimed at really major inventions—are misconceived and perhaps misleading. For example, models based on the presumption that there are large technical risks indicate that certain types of decision rules concerning R and D are optimal, whereas these decision rules may be quite inappropriate since the technical risks are in fact quite limited. Moreover, to the extent that policy-makers and others believe that the bulk of industry's investment in research and development is aimed at bigger advances than in fact is the case, they may be formulating policy concerning the nation's investment in research and development on the basis of a misconception. If, as some say,[3] it is important that the investment in more far-reaching R and D be increased, this misconception could be dangerous.

Of course, we are not saying that all industrial laboratories doing civilian work are concerned mainly with projects entailing relatively small technical risks. On the contrary, as our results show, there is a great deal of variation among laboratories in the extent of the technical risks that are taken. In general, as would be expected, the technical risks tend to be greater in those laboratories that devote a larger percentage of their resources to research rather than development. What we are saying is that the bulk of the R and D money spent by the firms in our sample—taken as a whole—seems to be devoted to projects that involve relatively small technical risks. In many respects, this is not surprising. From the point of view of the individual firm, it often seems wise to let others do the high-risk technological pioneering and to stick to less far-reaching research and development.

1. For example, see B. Klein, "The Decision Making Problem in Development," in *The Rate and Direction of Inventive Activity* (National Bureau of Economic Research, 1962), and Merton Peck and F. M. Scherer, *The Weapons Acquisition Process* (Cambridge: Harvard University Press, 1962).

2. J. Jewkes, D. Sawers, and R. Stillerman, *The Sources of Invention*, revised edition (New York: W. W. Norton, 1970).

3. Richard Nelson, Merton Peck, and Edward Kalachek, *Technology, Economic Growth, and Public Policy* (Washington, D.C.: The Brookings Institution, 1967). Also see Edwin Mansfield, *The Economics of Technological Change* (New York: W. W. Norton, 1968).

3. Causes of Technical Noncompletion of Projects

In the previous section, we stated that in the firms in our sample, the probability that a research and development project would achieve its technical objectives was generally greater than 50-50. By itself, this tells only part of the story. What is not evident from this statement is that many of the R and D projects that do not achieve their technical objectives are terminated before completion because new information concerning the market for the new product or process indicates that it would not be profitable to continue the project. In other words, poor commercial prospects rather than unanticipated or insoluble technical problems are responsible for their termination.

Specifically, in the three laboratories for which we have data on this score, about 60 percent of the projects that did not achieve their technical objectives were terminated before completion because of poor commercial prospects. Only about 40 percent were unsuccessful because of technical problems. Of course, the proportion of projects unsuccessful due to technical difficulties (rather than poor commercial prospects) was greater among those seeking larger advances in the state of the art. But even among projects that the laboratory administrators regarded as attempts at relatively large advances in the state of art, over 40 percent that did not achieve their technical objectives were terminated before completion because of poor commercial prospects, not technical difficulties.

These results are of importance for at least two reasons. First, they provide additional evidence that the projects carried out in the typical industrial laboratory involve relatively little risk from a technical viewpoint. After all, if most projects that do not achieve technical success are terminated before completion because of poor commercial prospects, the proportion that would have achieved technical success if they had not been stopped for this (good) reason must be considerably greater than the proportion actually achieving technical success. In fact, of the projects in the three laboratories that were not terminated for commercial reasons, about 75 percent achieved their technical objectives.

Second, these results suggest that some research and development projects may be begun with inadequate attention having been paid to the commercial prospects of the new product or process and the ability of the firm to exploit them. Of course, even with the best coordination between the marketing department (and other parts of the firm) and the R and D department, we would expect that many R and D projects would be dropped before completion for commercial reasons. After all, a new product that seems profitable today may have little appeal tomorrow because a competitor may have introduced a better product, prices may have changed, better information may have become available concerning the size of the potential market, and so on. But one cannot help wondering whether the seemingly large number of projects that were terminated before completion for commercial reasons could not have been reduced by better coordination between marketing and R and D.[4] According to some accounts, this co-ordination has sometimes been less than ideal in some of these firms.[5] For example, some R and D projects have been started because of their technical or scientific interest to the laboratory personnel, and with little professional attention to the potential market for the results.

4. Commercial versus Technical Risks

The risk of technical failure—discussed in the previous two sections—is not the only risk involved in industrial research and development. In addition, there is the risk of commercial failure, i.e., the risk that the new or improved product or process resulting from a technically successful R and D project will not seem sufficiently profitable to warrant its being commercially introduced or applied, or that, if it is introduced or applied, it will not be an economic success. Judging from the three laboratories for which we have data, the risk of commercial failure is considerable. Indeed, the probability of commercial failure generally seems much greater than the probability of technical failure.

In our three laboratories, about 40 percent of the R and D projects that were begun were not technically completed. Of those projects that were technically completed, 45 percent were not commercialized, presumably because commercialization did not seem profitable. Of those projects that were commercialized, about 60 percent did not earn an economic profit.[6] Thus, it is much more likely that a project will achieve its technical aims (this probability being about 0.60) than that, if it achieves these aims, it will earn an economic profit (this probability being about 0.20). In other words, it is much more likely that the laboratory can solve the technical problems involved in developing the new or improved product or process than that it will be economically worthwhile to solve these problems—in the sense that the new or improved product or process will turn out to be a commercial success.

These results, like those in the previous section, seem to imply that a

4. In all, about 53 percent of the R and D projects that were begun were stopped because of poor commercial prospects (27 percent being terminated prior to technical completion for non-technical reasons and 45 percent of the technically completed projects being terminated without being commercialized).
5. For some examples of this lack of coordination in other firms, see A. Gerstenfeld, *Effective Management of Research and Development* (Reading, Mass.: Addison Wesley, 1970).
6. Economic profit is defined as a return exceeding that available from alternative uses of the funds. See Chapter 3.

great deal of the risk involved in industrial research and development stems from potential difficulties faced by a new product or process in the marketplace, not from the purely technical uncertainties. Moreover, these results, like those in the previous section, make one wonder whether better coordination between marketing and R and D people could not reduce the large percentage of technically successful projects that are commercial failures. It is difficult, of course, to estimate the extent to which this large percentage is due to the laboratories' choosing projects without paying sufficient attention to their commercial prospects, or the extent to which it is caused by an inability of the marketing people to exploit the laboratories' results properly. But in either event, one wonders whether the percentage could not be reduced by better coordination—and incentives for pursuing policies benefiting the entire firm, not just particular departments. In this connection, it is worth noting that the commercial risks were considerably lower at laboratory X—*where marketing inputs were injected earlier into the decision-making process*—than at laboratories Y and Z.

It is also important to note that a trade-off seems to exist between technical risk and commercial risk. This trade-off, which appears to have been neglected in previous studies, should be recognized and incorporated into models of the decision-making process. The probability of technical success tends, of course, to be lower among projects aimed at larger advances in the state of the art. To compensate for the higher technical risks involved in such projects, firms apparently screen these projects carefully to make sure that the commercial risks involved are relatively low. In each of the laboratories for which we have data, the probability of commercial success (given technical completion) is higher for the projects attempting large or medium advances in the state of the art than for those attempting small advances in the state of the art. Indeed, the probability of commercial success (given technical completion) is so much greater for projects attempting large or medium advances in the state of the art that the probability that a project of this sort will be a commercial success (once a project is begun) is higher than for a project attempting a small advance in the state of the art.[7] It would be interesting to find out more about the extent to which firms take proper account of *both* types of risk. In some cases, one suspects that laboratories—more aware of, and responsive to, technical risks than commercial risks—tend to shy away from projects where lower commercial risks are attained by incurring higher technical risks, even though the acceptance of such projects might, on balance, result in an R and D portfolio better constituted to meet the firm's overall objectives. To a considerable extent, this problem, like others cited above, is due in considerable measure to difficulties in coordinating R and D with marketing. The importance of properly coupling R and D with marketing (and pro-

7. Of course, it should be noted once again that attrition rates are crude measures of risk.

duction) cannot be overemphasized: It lies at the heart of any successful system for product innovation.

5. Accuracy of Predictions of Technical Success

We have seen that a relatively large percentage of the research and development projects carried out by the industrial laboratories in our sample are technically successful. Does this mean that a laboratory's personnel can predict reasonably well whether a particular R and D project will be technically successful or not? Judging by the experience during the sixties of a major proprietary drug firm, it appears that a laboratory's estimates of the probability of technical success are of some use in predicting whether a particular project will be technically completed. There was a statistically significant relationship between the laboratory's estimates of a project's probability of technical success—this estimate being made before the project was begun—and whether or not the project in fact was technically completed.

However, these estimates do not seem to be of much use in predicting which projects will be technically completed and which ones will not. Even if they are employed in such a way that the probability of an incorrect prediction is minimized, they predict incorrectly in about 30 percent of the cases.[8] It is possible that the usefulness of the estimates may be increased by combining them with information concerning the extent of the technical advance sought by the project, there being some apparent tendency for the estimates to overstate the risk of failure for projects attempting small technical advances and to understate the risk of failure for projects attempting large technical advances. But further work is needed to test this possibility.

Used without some modification of this sort, it does not appear that the firm's estimates of the probability of technical success are very accurate predictors—although they are of some use. This finding is in accord with previous studies.[9] Apparently, despite the fact that the bulk of the firm's R and D projects will turn out to be technically successful, the firm is not able—or, at any rate, its formal estimates are not able—to predict with much accuracy which ones will not be technically successful. The situation

8. How poor this result is becomes apparent when we note that one could expect predictions made by chance to be incorrect in just about 36 percent of the cases. To see this, recall that the probability of a project's being technically successful was 0.76. Suppose that we choose at random 76 percent of the projects and predict that they will be successes. The expected number of projects that are predicted to be successes but that actually fail will be $0.76 \times 0.24\ N$, where N is the number of projects. Moreover, the expected number of projects that are predicted to be failures but that actually succeed will be $0.24 \times 0.76\ N$. Thus, the expected proportion of incorrect predictions is $2 \times 0.24 \times 0.76$, which equals 0.36.

9. Edwin Mansfield, *Industrial Research and Technological Innovation* (New York: W. W. Norton for the Cowles Foundation for Research in Economics at Yale University, 1968).

seems somewhat similar to the old story of the advertising manager who said that he knew that one-quarter of his expenditures would be a waste— but that he didn't know which quarter.

6. Cost and Time Overruns

Until the cost overruns on the Lockheed C-5A made the headlines, the subject of cost and time overruns seldom came up in polite conversation. Senator William Proxmire, in his investigations of the Lockheed C-5A, did for cost overruns what Nixon did for Agnew: He made them a household word. It became common knowledge that military R and D projects typically cost much more—and took longer—than estimated. This had long been clear to economists at the RAND Corporation, the Pentagon, and other places connected with military research and development.

In contrast to military research and development, practically nothing has been determined in previous studies about cost and time overruns in civilian R and D. Are the overruns as large in civilian R and D as in military R and D? What factors seem to influence the size of the overruns? Are these factors similar to those that seem to influence the size of overruns in military R and D? It is as important for us to understand the frequency, extent, and determinants of overruns in the civilian economy as in military work. Moreover, a comparison of the size of overruns in the military and civilian sectors may help us to determine whether the large overruns in military R and D are due to some deficiency in organization and planning that is unique to military work.

To help fill this gap, we studied the cost and time overruns in a major ethical drug firm and a major proprietary drug firm, the results being as follows: First, there are large cost and time overruns in these drug firms, the average ratio of actual to expected cost being 1.78 (in the ethical drug firm) and 2.11 (in the proprietary drug firm), and the average ratio of actual to expected time being 1.61 (in the ethical drug firm) and 2.95 (in the proprietary drug firm). Thus, if these firms are at all representative, large overruns are not confined to military work; they are typical of civilian research and development as well.

Second, a comparison of the overruns in these drug firms with the overruns in a dozen major military projects indicates that the cost overruns tend to be larger in military work than in the drug industry, while the time overruns tend to be smaller in military work than in the drug industry. The reasons for this are not difficult to find: In the military projects, more importance undoubtedly is attached to time, and less importance is attached to cost, than in the drug industry. It is well known that the military services have placed much greater emphasis on time and quality than on cost.

Third, it is somewhat unfair to compare the cost overruns for the military projects with the cost overruns for all drug projects, since the military projects generally attempt much greater advances in the state of the art than the drug projects. If we compare the cost overruns for the military projects with the cost overruns for the more ambitious drug projects—new chemical entities in the ethical drug firm and new products in the proprietary drug firm—we find that the cost overruns tend to be closer to the size of the military cost overruns. Specifically, they tend to be about 70 percent, on the average, of the size of the military overruns.[10] Thus, when civilian R and D projects are relatively ambitious, it appears that they begin to approximate weapons-system development in the extent of cost overruns.

Fourth, the factors that seem to influence the size of a project's cost overrun are much the same in the drug industry as in military work. In both cases, the extent of the attempted advance of the state of the art is important, more ambitious projects having greater overruns than less ambitious projects. Also, in both cases, the length of the project affects its cost overrun. However, in the drug industry—unlike military work—there is no evidence that cost overruns have tended to decrease over time. This is probably due in part to the fact that cost overruns in recent years have tended to increase in response to changes in drug-development procedures.

Fifth, although cost and time overruns are partly due to the uncertainty inherent in research and development, it is important that the reader recognize that they also stem from deliberate underestimations of time and cost. Low estimates are frequently used to marshal support for particular projects. This tendency toward downward adjustment of estimates seems to exist in the drug industry, and it has frequently been noted in military R and D. So long as there are incentives to shade estimates in this way—and little or no penalty for doing so—this tendency is bound to continue.

7. Quantitative Project-Selection Techniques: Uses and Limitations

In recent years, operations researchers and applied economists have spent a considerable amount of time and effort attempting to devise techniques to select research and development projects. Many articles have appeared in the professional and business journals describing methods that a firm might use to help determine which project proposals it should accept and which it should turn down. Most of these suggested techniques

10. To derive the figure of 70 percent, recall that the average increase of actual over estimated costs in the two drug firms was about 155 percent (130 percent for new chemical entities in the ethical drug firm and 180 percent for new products in the proprietary drug firm), while the average increase in actual over estimated costs for the sample of airplane and missile projects was 220 percent; 155 percent is about 70 percent of 220 percent.

are adaptations of capital-budgeting techniques, such as the use of pay-out periods and rates of return. Some of the more elaborate suggestions involve the use of linear and dynamic programming.

To what extent are firms making use of these quantitative project-selection techniques? Judging from our sample of nineteen industrial laboratories in the chemical, drug, petroleum, and electronics industries, about three-quarters of the laboratories use such techniques to allocate funds. However, it is important to note that many of these firms use these techniques in only a limited way: Intuition and hunch continue to play an important role. The probability of a quantitative technique being used is directly related to the size of the laboratory. Although a few laboratories began using these techniques in the early and middle fifties, the bulk of the laboratories have begun using them since 1960. The employment of these project-selection techniques is itself an innovation. It is interesting to compare the diffusion of this innovation with the diffusion of major innovations investigated in previous studies. Apparently, the percentage of laboratories using this innovation has conformed reasonably closely to the kind of S-shaped growth curve (the logistic curve) used in previous studies.[11] Compared with major innovations in the steel, railroad, brewing, and coal industries, quantitative project-selection techniques have spread relatively slowly, despite the relatively small investment required to introduce them. This may well have been due to skepticism concerning their usefulness.

Our own results do little to dispel such skepticism. In general, these quantitative project-selection techniques are based on estimates of the probability of technical success, the development time, and the development cost. As we stressed in the previous two sections, these estimates are subject to errors that are large and variable. In addition, these techniques usually are based on estimates of the probability of commercial success, the size of the market, and the capital-facility requirements of the project. According to laboratory administrators, these estimates are even less accurate than the ones discussed in the previous two sections.[12] Thus, if the laboratories in our sample are at all representative, these techniques rely heavily on estimates that, by practically any standard, are very poor.

Unfortunately, some laboratory administrators do not seem to realize how bad these estimates are. About one-half or more of the laboratory directors in our sample—and about one-third or more in Seiler's sample[13]—feel that estimates of a project's manpower requirements, its development cost, its capital requirements, its research cost, its probability of technical success, and its development time are good or excellent. Only about 10–20

11. Mansfield, *The Economics of Technological Change, op. cit.*
12. Of course, this may help to account for our finding, discussed in section 4, that the probability of commercial failure exceeds the probability of technical failure.
13. Robert Seiler, *Improving the Effectiveness of Research and Development* (New York: McGraw-Hill, 1965).

percent of the laboratory directors in our sample—and about 5–20 percent in Seiler's sample—regard these estimates as poor or untrustworthy. Given our findings concerning the size of the errors in estimates of development cost, time, and technical outcome, it appears that laboratory directors may be unduly optimistic about the accuracy of these estimates, unless, of course, they are able to make much better estimates than the firms for which we have data.

Needless to say, we are not condemning the use of quantitative project-selection techniques. The employment of such techniques does force people to think about the relevant factors. Moreover, it is useful for people to make their assumptions explicit. What we are saying is that these techniques should be viewed with more caution and applied with more flexibility than is sometimes the case. It is particularly important that sensitivity analyses be carried out to show the effects on the results of large errors in the estimates that are used. A great deal of harm can be done by an enthusiastic and well-meaning operations researcher who takes these techniques too seriously—or by a laboratory manager who takes the operations researcher too seriously.

8. Determinants of Development Cost

Although a great many studies have been made of the costs of production in various firms and industries, there is surprisingly little information concerning the costs of development. Even the most basic sorts of data are generally unavailable. For example, we do not have even crude estimates of how much it cost to develop the individual new products that have arisen in recent years in various sectors of the economy. Beyond this, little attempt has been made to test various hypotheses concerning the determinants of development costs. Economists have hypothesized that the cost of developing a new product depends on the size and complexity of the product being developed, the extent of the advance in performance that is sought, the development time, the available stock of knowledge, components, and materials, and the development strategy that is pursued. But there has been little or no attempt to test these hypotheses or to provide quantitative estimates of the effects of these or other factors.

To advance our understanding of this topic, we carried out what seems to be the first econometric investigation of the determinants of commercial development costs. Confining our attention to a single large ethical drug firm, we tried to explain a new drug's development cost by the nature of the new drug (product category, type and number of dosage forms, and spectrum of activity), the extent of the technological advance, the use of parallel development efforts, the priority attached to the project, and time.

These variables seem to explain the observed variation in development cost quite well. However, as might have been expected, this model is more successful for less ambitious development projects (compounded products and alternative dosage forms) than for the most ambitious ones (new chemical entities). Among the less ambitious projects, practically all of these variables have a statistically significant effect on a project's development cost; among the most ambitious development projects, only a couple of these variables have a statistically significant effect. In part, this is because variables that we cannot measure—as well as pure chance—probably play a more critical role in determining the cost of development in the most ambitious projects.

9. Predicting Development Costs and "De-biasing" Estimates

In our discussion of project-selection techniques, we noted the importance—from the point of view of the user of such techniques—of being able to predict the cost of developing a particular new product or process. We also described how poorly firms seem to predict these costs. Is there any possibility that econometric models of the sort discussed in the previous section can do better? Judging from the experience of the ethical drug firm, the answer seems to be Yes. When we compare the accuracy of "forecasts" generated by the models with the accuracy of estimates of development cost prepared at the outset of each project by the firm, we find that the model-generated "forecasts" are more accurate—particularly for new chemical entities—than the firm's forecasts (although this is not so for alternate dosage forms). We emphasize, however, that these models would require extensive refinement and testing before they could be used for forecasting purposes of this sort.

Another possibility would be to use the historical relationship between a project's cost overrun and the characteristics of the project to "de-bias" estimates of development costs. If, for example, this relationship indicated that the ratio of actual to estimated cost was 2.0 for a particular type of project, then cost estimates for this type of project would be multiplied by 2.0 to "de-bias" them. This "de-biasing" procedure has been suggested by some economists.[14] Our results in Chapter 5 could be used in this way if the various characteristics of a project could be determined in advance and if the relevant regression coefficients were reasonably stable. However, besides the other obvious qualifications, it is important to bear in mind that repeated use of this technique could lead to its downfall: Once estimators

14. See Summers' paper in Thomas Marschak, Thomas Glennan, and Robert Summers, *Strategy for R and D* (New York: Springer-Verlag, 1967).

knew that their estimates were being "de-biased" in this way, they might bias them more than in the past.[15]

10. The Role of Research and Development in the Innovation Process

Thus far in this chapter, we have focused almost entirely on research and development. Despite R and D's obvious importance, it must be recognized that R and D is only part of the process leading to the introduction of a new product or process. Some idea of the relative importance of R and D in the total set of activities leading to a new product is provided by our findings concerning the percentage of total innovation costs accounted for by R and D in three product groups—chemicals, electronics, and machinery: The results indicate that, in each of these areas, R and D accounted for about half of the total innovation costs for the new products in our sample.[16]

Besides research and development, what are the other major types of expenditures involved in product innovation? Our results indicate that the largest percentage of the total cost of product innovation generally occurs in the stage of the innovation process during which tooling occurs and the manufacturing facilities are designed and constructed. For our sample of innovations, this stage accounted, on the average, for almost 40 percent of the total costs. Also, costs associated with manufacturing start-up and marketing start-up accounted, on the average, for almost 15 percent of the total costs. The non-R and D stages of the innovation process also accounted for a large portion of the time involved. Tooling and construction of manufacturing facilities went on for about 30 percent, on the average, of the total elapsed time. Manufacturing start-up went on for about 10 percent of the total elapsed time.

These findings are important in at least three respects. First, they show that the amount of resources devoted to innovative activity in the United States—and other countries—is considerably greater than is indicated by the statistics on R and D expenditure. Second, to the extent that the ratio of R and D expenditures to the total costs of innovation varies among in-

15. For example, in the illustration in the text, if the estimator found out that his cost estimates were being multiplied by 2.0, he might shade them even further downward in an attempt to beat the system.

16. It is important to note that all of the product innovations in this sample reached the market. Obviously, large parts of a firm's—or a country's—R and D expenditures do not yield commercialized products. The ratio of all R and D expenditures—whether or not they lead to commercialization—to total innovation costs is obviously higher than the ratio of R and D expenditures which do result in commercialization to the corresponding innovation costs. Also, a substantial proportion of R and D is directed at new processes rather than new products.

Also, note that the guesstimate by the Panel on Invention and Innovation concerning the ratio of R and D costs to total innovation costs for successful innovations seems somewhat low for the firms included here. Although it is important to stress that R and D is only part of the innovation process, there also are obvious dangers in exaggerating the importance of the non-R and D costs.

dustries, firms of various sizes, countries, or periods of time, it shows that differences among industries, firms of various sizes, countries, or periods of time in R and D expenditure may be an inadequate measure of differences in the costs of innovation. Third, it shows that a firm, when it sets out to innovate, must be willing to risk a great deal more than its R and D expenditure alone, the result being that the difficulties and risks involved, particularly for smaller firms, are that much greater.

11. The Nature and Determinants of the Time-Cost Trade-off Function

A product often can be developed and brought to market more quickly if more money is spent during the course of the innovation process. Although economists have recognized the importance of this time-cost trade-off, no attempt has been made in previous studies to estimate the time-cost trade-off function for particular innovations. To help fill this gap, we estimated the time-cost trade-off functions for twenty-nine innovations in chemicals, electronics, and machinery, on the basis of a series of interviews with the managers who had the principal responsibility for the innovations. The data suggest that a downward-sloping convex function will usually be a reasonable approximation to the time-cost trade-off function (in the relevant range). The empirical support for the hypothesis that the slope is negative is very strong. There is somewhat more question about the hypothesis of convexity, but in our sample at least, a convex shape is strongly suggested in a large proportion of the cases.

Judging by our sample of innovations, it is possible to represent the time-cost trade-off function by a simple equation, the parameters of which vary from innovation to innovation. This equation has three parameters, one being the minimum expected cost of the project, another being the minimum expected duration of the project, and the third determining the elasticity of cost with respect to time. In general, this equation fits the data for the twenty-nine innovations quite well, the coefficient of correlation usually being 0.9 or more. In our sample of projects, the minimum expected cost of a project is directly related to the size of the technical advance and the size of the firm carrying out the project. The minimum expected duration of a project is also directly related to these variables. In large part, the relationship between firm size and a project's minimum expected cost or minimum expected duration reflects the fact that bigger firms carry out bigger projects.

The elasticity of cost with respect to time is the expected percentage increase in cost due to an expected 1-percent reduction in the duration of the project. The elasticity becomes greater as the duration of the project is pushed closer and closer to its minimum value. When the duration of the project is less than 30 percent above its minimum value, this elasticity averages about 1.6 in our sample of innovations. When the duration of the project is about 30–80 percent above its minimum value, this elasticity averages about 0.5. According to our data, a project's elasticity of cost with respect to time depends on the extent to which the project advances the state of the art and on the size of the firm carrying out the project: Projects that attempt greater advances in the state of the art and that are carried out by larger firms tend to be more costly than others to speed up.

These results cast new light on the trade-off in product innovation between time and cost. For the first time, some scraps of evidence are available concerning the way in which the shape of the time-cost trade-off depends on the nature of the product being developed, the nature of the organization carrying out the innovation, and the strategy used. Of course, these results are based on managers' opinions, and the managers may be wrong. But it is important to note that, from many points of view, this possibility really is irrelevant, since it is their opinion, right or wrong, that determines firm behavior. If they think that the time-cost trade-off function has certain characteristics, it is important that we know this fact.

12. The Important Role of Overlap

Our results emphasize that overlap—the beginning of one stage of the innovation process before a previous stage is completed—may be a major reason for the increased expected costs associated with a decrease in expected time. In our sample of innovations, the amount of overlap tended to increase as an innovation's time to completion was pushed closer and closer to the minimum time to completion. Moreover, there was a tendency for bigger firms to overlap stages to a greater extent than smaller ones. In general, it was felt by the managers we interviewed that increased overlap between two stages would tend to increase the cost of the later stage. The most commonly mentioned reason for this was characterized by one manager as the increased likelihood of "engineering-change notices." The problem arises when work in the later stage is critically dependent on information or results obtained in the earlier stage. When there is considerable overlap, the later stage must be started before the results of the work in the earlier stage are known. Estimates or tentative results must be used as the basis for the later work. If these estimates prove to be incorrect, the expense of correcting mistakes and redoing work may be considerable.

According to the managers, the effect of overlap on costs may be particularly great in the case of overlap between the prototype or pilot-plant stage and the tooling and construction stage. If tooling and the construction of the production facilities are begun before all prototype engineering problems are solved, the tooling may have to be modified or even scrapped when the prototype stage is finally completed. Our results are quite consistent with this hypothesis: The proportion of total costs incurred in the tooling and construction stage is directly related to the extent of the overlap between the prototype or pilot-plant stage and the tooling and construction stage. Note, however, that these findings are merely a beginning. Future work should investigate in more detail the determinants of the percentage distribution of cost and time in a particular project. Our results indicate that there is wide variation in the distribution of cost and time. Econometric models should be constructed to explain this variation more completely.

13. The Relevance of the Traditional Distinction Between Invention and Innovation

At this point, a word should be added about the traditional distinction between invention and innovation. This distinction was stressed repeatedly by Schumpeter, and since Schumpeter's death, it has been used in practically all discussions by economists of technological change. To what extent is this distinction as clear-cut and important today as it seemed to Schumpeter? One reason why economists make this distinction is that an invention has little or no impact on the economy until it is applied—and becomes an innovation. Certainly, this is as true today as in Schumpeter's time. Another reason why economists make this distinction is that the inventor and the innovator may be quite different people or organizations. In many cases, this is still the case, even in research-intensive industries. For example, Mueller found that 60 percent of Du Pont's most important innovations were based on inventions made outside of the innovating firm. And our findings indicated that about one-half of the major pharmaceutical innovations during 1935–1962 were based on discoveries made outside of the innovating firm.

Still another reason why economists make this distinction is that the size of the investment required for innovation is often assumed to be much greater than for invention. Whether or not this is true depends, of course, on the definition of an invention. If an invention is defined as being completed only when a prototype or pilot plant is completed, our results indicate that nearly as much money is often spent on invention as on the subsequent steps leading to the product's introduction to the market. On the other hand, if an invention is defined as being completed before a prototype or pilot plant is completed, our results indicate that much less money is generally spent on invention than on the subsequent steps.

However, having granted all of this, we must state that economists have too often tried to use a simple two-step model—invention and innovation—to characterize the entire process that, if successful, leads to a new product or process. As we have seen, this process contains a number of stages—applied research, preparation of product specifications, prototype or pilot-plant construction, tooling and construction of manufacturing facilities, and manufacturing start-up—and in many kinds of studies, it is important that these stages be sorted out and recognized. Although the two-step model is still serviceable for some purposes, it is high time that it be abandoned for a richer model in the many cases where it simply does not work.

For example, in those cases where a single firm does both the inventing and innovating, the traditional two-step model—invention and innovation—may not fit very well. Firms have tried hard to integrate the two stages, and it is difficult to know where one ends and the other begins. As we have seen, the firm is continually engaged in a learning process, the object being to achieve the project's technical and commercial goals. By the time the latter stages of development—for example, construction of a pilot plant or of test items—are completed, the firm is sometimes already beginning to probe the market for the new product.

14. The Importance of External Sources of Technology

In the previous section, we noted that even in research-intensive industries like chemicals and drugs, innovations are often based to a large extent on technology derived from organizations other than the innovating firm. Our results emphasize the importance of external sources of technology. With regard to the innovations studied in Chapter 6, about one-third were based to some extent on specific technology derived from outside the innovating firm. With regard to the pharmaceutical industry, about one-half of the major innovations during 1935–1962 were based on discoveries made outside of the innovating firm. With regard to numerical control, it is clear that the makers of the first commercial numerically controlled machine tools were heavily dependent for the basic technology on organizations and firms outside the machine-tool industry.

The apparent importance of outside sources of technology has implications both for economic theorists and for research managers. Unfortunately, its implications for the models of technological change constructed by economic theorists in recent years are somewhat negative—since these models seldom allow explicitly for the transfer of technology (except perhaps for allowing the firm's production function to shift with time, as well as with the firm's expenditure on R and D; and the crudeness of this procedure is obvious). Economists must begin to build the transfer of technology across firm and industry boundaries more adequately into their models of technological change. Without such an extension, these models are unlikely to be of much use in analyzing the returns from various kinds of R and D expenditures or in investigating the way in which technological change takes place.

The importance of outside sources of technology also has implications for research managers. If it is true that a large proportion of significant innovations are based on inventions made outside the innovating firm, it would seem to be extremely important for a firm to look outward for ideas and to avoid focusing too much attention exclusively on its own inventions. There is sometimes a tendency for R and D managers to devote too large a part of their resources to developments arising from their own laboratories and to neglect developments in other firms and industries. If something is "not invented here," it may be neglected or resisted.

15. The Research and Development Portfolios of the Giant Corporations

In recent years, economists and lawyers have shown a keen interest in finding out more about the role of the giant corporation in the process of technological change in the United States. Our findings break new ground in this area. To begin with, they provide evidence for the first time regarding the nature of the research and development portfolios of the giant firms in the chemical and petroleum industries. In particular, they indicate the extent to which the largest firms in our sample devote a larger proportion of their R and D expenditures to relatively basic research, to more risky projects, and to longer-term projects than do their somewhat smaller competitors.

Our results are quite consistent with the hypothesis that up to some point, increases in size of firm are associated with increases in the proportion of total R and D expenditures devoted to basic research, increases in the technical riskiness of the projects, and increases in the median expected time to completion. But the differences between the biggest firms in the sample and firms of one-half their size are seldom large, if they exist at all. That is, firms that are one-half as big as the largest firms in the sample invest about the same proportion of their R and D budget in more basic, risky, and long-term projects as do the largest firms in the sample.

This finding is of considerable interest. Previous studies have indicated that the largest firms in most industries spend no more, as a percentage of sales, on research and development than do somewhat smaller firms. However, these studies ignore the possibility that the largest firms may be doing a different kind of R and D than their somewhat smaller competitors, the result being that although total R and D expenditures might not be reduced, some types of R and D—the more basic, risky, and long-term R and D— might decrease substantially if the largest firms were broken up—or that these types might increase substantially if more firms were to grow to their size. Our results suggest that this is not the case in the industries for which we have data. Our results suggest that in these industries, firms as large as the largest firms in the sample are not required to ensure that the existing amount of R and D of a more basic, risky, and long-term nature is carried out. Similar studies need to be carried out in other industries. Such studies would be useful, although they alone would provide only a part of the data needed to guide public policy in this area.

16. The Inventive and Innovative Performance of the Largest Firms

Our findings provide three additional types of evidence concerning the inventive and innovative performance of the largest firms. Like the results discussed in the previous section, these findings generally indicate no significant advantages in this regard of the largest firms over firms that are somewhat smaller. First, the crude rankings by various experts of the effectiveness (output per dollar spent) of various firms' research and development programs in the petroleum and chemical industries reveal no tendency, when R and D expenditures are held constant, for a firm's ranking to increase with its size. (However, in chemicals, there is a tendency for a firm's ranking to increase with the amount it spends on R and D.) Of course, the rankings are extremely rough measures, but the striking similarity of these results to those of a previous study based on entirely different and independent data is impressive.[17]

Second, with regard to the trade-off between time and cost in product innovation, our results—based on data for chemicals, electronics, and machinery—suggest that large firms find it more costly than small firms to reduce the duration of a project. The cost of speeding up an innovation seems to be positively related to firm size. The reasons for this cost difference are difficult to pinpoint, and more work is required in this area. But certain factors seem fairly obvious. Insofar as time reduction requires a certain flexibility of approach, a larger organization may be handicapped by inertia and by more difficult administrative problems. Even reaching

17. E. Mansfield, *Industrial Research and Technological Innovation, op. cit.*

agreement on how to proceed will take longer if more people and a longer chain of command are involved.

Third, with regard to the size of innovating firms, our results for the ethical drug industry do not indicate that the largest firms carried out the largest number of innovations (unweighted or weighted) relative to their size. For 1935–1949, the estimated ratio of number of innovations to firm size reaches a maximum at the size of the tenth-largest firm. For 1950–1962, this ratio is highest among very small firms if unweighted data are used, and at the size of the twelfth-largest firm is weighted data are used. These results are quite similar to those of earlier studies of the petroleum, bituminous coal, and steel industries: In these industries too, the largest firms carried out no more innovations, relative to their size, than did somewhat smaller firms (considerably smaller ones in steel).[18]

17. Industrial Concentration and the Rate of Diffusion of New Techniques

Further, our findings provide new evidence concerning the effects of industrial concentration on the rate of diffusion of new techniques. Do innovations tend to spread more rapidly in industries with many small firms or in industries dominated by a few large firms? This is a very important question. Judging from our results concerning numerically controlled machine tools, the rate of diffusion tends to be more rapid in less concentrated industries. Allowing for differences in profitability and size of investment, this innovation seems to be spreading more rapidly in the tool-and-die industry than innovations in other, more concentrated, industries for which data are available. However, this finding is based on experience to date, and a final judgment cannot, of course, be made until the diffusion process is completed. Also, data are required for many more innovations before any definite conclusions can be reached. However, it might be added that this finding is quite consistent with the results of our previous studies.[19]

It should also be noted that large firms tend to be quicker, on the average, to begin using numerical control than small firms. A similar tendency was found in our previous studies of other innovations. In the case of the tool-and-die industry, where all of the firms are quite small, this tendency may be due to the fact that the larger firms are more progressive. But even if they are no more progressive than their smaller competitors, one would expect them to be quicker, on the average, than the smaller firms to

18. *Ibid.*
19. *Ibid.*

begin using an innovation. This point has been misunderstood by some economists in the past.[20]

18. *Small Business and Federal Research and Development Contracts*

Another question related to industrial organization that has received considerable attention, particularly in Congress, is whether or not small business is getting its proper share of federal research and development contracts. This is an extremely hard question to answer. It is difficult to formulate any operational criterion to indicate how many such contracts small business should receive. Nonetheless, some observers—including the House Select Committee on Small Business—believe that too few federal R and D contracts are being awarded to small business. To the extent that this is the case—and we have no data to confirm or deny it—what sorts of things might be done by government agencies to help small R and D firms? According to a sample of small R and D firms in the Philadelphia area, one of the most important things these agencies could do would be to provide earlier and more information concerning agency needs. Big firms can maintain liaison people who keep track of what is going on in various agencies, what the agency personnel are interested in, and what the agency needs are likely to be. Small firms are generally unable to do this. Whether or not the social benefits would exceed the costs of providing earlier and better information is difficult to say. But judging from our sample, this problem is more disturbing to very small firms than to somewhat larger ones. When a firm reaches an employment level of a hundred or more, it seems to be able to do much of the necessary liaison work itself.

What problems in this area seemed most important to the firms in the sample? About 70 percent of the small R and D firms in our sample felt that they were getting as many government R and D contracts as they reasonably could expect. The three problems in dealing with government agencies that the firms in the sample cited most frequently were bidding where it was felt that the agencies had chosen the source before requesting proposals, insufficient time, and excessive paper work. Needless to say, in interpreting these results, one should bear in mind that firms, like people, often find it hard to recognize and analyze their own problems. However, it is also relevant to add that Roberts, in his studies of military R and D procurement, concluded that in only a relatively few cases did companies not initially preferred by the government technical evaluators end up with the

20. W. Adams and J. Dirlam, "Big Steel, Invention, and Innovation," *Quarterly Journal of Economics* (May 1966), p. 168.

contracts. In his opinion, the social costs of the procurement process are unnecessarily high, due in part to the encouragement of many firms to bid even though they in fact have little or no chance of getting the contract.[21]

19. Implications for Technological Forecasting

Technological forecasting is presently a fashionable topic in industry and government. But even the most enthusiastic practitioners of technological forecasting admit that it is far from being a science: The sophistication of its methods and the reliability of its results seem low even when judged against the standards of the social sciences. However, despite the obvious difficulties in technological forecasting, it is a necessary part of decision-making by firms and government agencies. Just as there is no way to avoid forecasting the economic future—explicitly or implicitly—so there is no way to avoid forecasting the technological future.

Our findings seem to have at least two important implications for technological forecasting. First, it appears that major innovations generally take quite a long time to go from conceptualization to commercial introduction to widespread adoption. For example, the average time interval between the discovery of a new drug and its first commercial introduction seems to have been about five years—and this lag appears to be shorter than the lag in other industries. Moreover, in most cases for which we have data, it took a decade or more before the bulk of the firms in an industry began using a new technique. The implication for technological forecasting seems clear: If one is interested in forecasting the impact of major innovations at the point when they are widely diffused, the inventions that have already occurred—or are well along toward completion—are all that really matter in the short—and often the intermediate—run.

Second, the model of the diffusion process outlined in Chapter 9—and used extensively in our previous studies—seems to be of some help in forecasting the rate at which a new technique will displace an old one. This model was employed to make short-run forecasts for a government agency of the rate of diffusion of numerical control in the tool-and-die industry.[22] It has also been used by firms to forecast the rate of market penetration of innovations. In general, the results have seemed useful. Of course, this model cannot be employed indiscriminately to make such forecasts; the assumptions underlying it are discussed elsewhere in detail.[23] But where

21. E. Roberts, "Questioning the Cost-Effectiveness of the R and D Procurement Process," in *Research Program Effectiveness*, ed. by M. Yovits, D. Gilford, R. Wilcox, E. Staveley, and H. Lerner (New York: Gordon and Breach, 1966.)

22. See Edwin Mansfield, "Determinants of the Speed of Application of New Technology," paper presented at the 1971 Conference of the International Economic Association at St. Anton, Austria.

23. E. Mansfield, *op. cit.*

these assumptions hold reasonably well, it may be a valuable tool for technological forecasters.

20. *Limitations of the Studies*

Finally, it may be worthwhile to remind the reader of some of the limitations of the studies reported in previous chapters. For one thing, the basic information underlying our results pertains to only a small number of industries—chemicals, petroleum, drugs, electronics, machinery, and machine tools. For another, some of our models are relatively simple, and some of our data are rough. There would be little point in trying to indicate the specific limitations of each of our studies, since this has already been done in previous chapters. What is important for present purposes is that the reader recognize that many of our findings must be viewed as tentative.

At the same time, it is appropriate to add that although the data used at some points in previous chapters are not as precise or as plentiful as we would like, these data are a great deal better than anything heretofore available. Indeed, with regard to a great many of the questions taken up in previous chapters, practically no data at all existed in the past. (A remarkable characteristic of some of the work carried out in this area has been the frequency with which sample sizes of zero have been used.) The studies reported here are part of a continuing investigation of the economics of technological change. We hope to extend and build on these studies—as well as their predecessors—in the years ahead.

INDEX

INDEX